Reina Lewis is Artscom Centenary Prof~~~ ~~~~~~~ ~~~ ~~~~~~~~~~~ at the London College of Fashion, University of the Arts London. Her books include *Gendering Orientalism: Race, Femininity and Representation* (1996), *Rethinking Orientalism: Women, Travel and the Ottoman Harem* (I.B.Tauris, 2004) and *Re-Fashioning Orientalism: New Trends in Muslim Style* (forthcoming 2014). She is Editor, with Nancy Micklewright, of *Gender, Modernity and Liberty: Middle Eastern and Western Women's Writings: A Critical Sourcebook* (I.B.Tauris, 2006). She is also Series Editor, with Elizabeth Wilson, of the *Dress Cultures* series from I.B.Tauris and, with Teresa Heffernan, of the *Cultures in Dialogue* series.

'This intriguing collection offers a fresh perspective on modesty and fashion linkage, a topic that has become so important lately. By examining modest dressing across faiths and contexts, and detailing diverse ways religions, markets and the internet interact, shape and are shaped by lived experience, the chapters in this book vividly show why studying fashion and religion matters. The diversity of the book, with contributors from academia, business world and the media, and its focus on the interrelationships among fashion production and consumption practices of Christian, Jewish and Muslim faith groups make it a constant delight to read. Overall, a wonderful discussion of new configurations of "modest fashions" in the contemporary world.'

Özlem Sandıkçı, Bilkent University

Dress cultures

Series Editors: Reina Lewis & Elizabeth Wilson

Advisory Board: Christopher Breward, Hazel Clark, Joanne Entwistle, Caroline Evans, Susan Kaiser, Angela McRobbie, Hiroshi Narumi, Peter McNeil, Özlem Sandıkçı, Simona Segre Reinach

Across a digital world in which the same T-shirt can be designed in New York, manufactured in Hong Kong, boycotted in London and consumed by a global network of wearers, how do we locate individuality and cultural distinctiveness among the capitalist interplay of logo and subculture? As consumer citizens in a retail society, how does what we buy correlate with our age, gender, ethnicity and class, and how is uniqueness expressed among the proliferation of seemingly infinite choice?

Dress Cultures aims to foster innovative theoretical and methodological frameworks to understand how and why we dress, exploring the connections between clothing, commerce and creativity in global contexts.

Published and forthcoming in the *Dress Culture* series:

Modest Fashion: Styling Bodies, Mediating Faith
edited by Reina Lewis

Dressing for Austerity: Aspiration, Leisure and Fashion in Post-War Britain
by Geraldine Biddle-Perry

Sinophilia: Fashion, Western Modernity and Things Chinese after 1900
by Sarah Cheang

Thinking Through Fashion: Fashion, Dress & Cultural Theory
edited by Agnès Rocamora and Anneke Smelik

Queries, ideas and submissions to:

Reina Lewis: reina.lewis@fashion.arts.ac.uk
Elizabeth Wilson: mail@elizabethwilson.net
At the publisher, Philippa Brewster: philippabrewster@gmail.com

MODEST FASHION

Styling Bodies, Mediating Faith

edited by Reina Lewis

I.B.TAURIS

LONDON · NEW YORK

Published in 2013 by I.B.Tauris & Co Ltd
6 Salem Road, London W2 4BU
175 Fifth Avenue, New York NY 10010
www.ibtauris.com

Distributed in the United States and Canada Exclusively by Palgrave Macmillan
175 Fifth Avenue, New York NY 10010

ISBN: 978 1 78076 382 8 (HB)
        978 1 78076 383 5 (PB)

A full CIP record for this book is available from the British Library
A full CIP record is available from the Library of Congress

Library of Congress Catalog Card Number: available

Printed and bound in Great Britain by T.J. International, Padstow, Cornwall

CONTENTS

ILLUSTRATIONS

ACKNOWLEDGEMENTS

Much of the thinking behind this book arose from a research project called *Modest Dressing: Faith-based Fashion and Internet Retail* funded by the AHRC/ESRC Religion and Society Programme, 2010–11. Being part of the programme[1] was a remarkable experience and I have benefited enormously from the generous guidance of programme director Professor Linda Woodhead. Among the programme team I am grateful especially to Dr Rebecca Catto and Peta Ainsworth. The project received further funding in 2011–12 from the London College of Fashion (LCF) under the kind auspices of Professor Frances Corner whose willingness to see modesty debates as part of the creative and intellectual work of the college helped to provide the stimulating environment for a series of events that fed into the work of this book.

The project would not have been possible without the collaboration of my co-investigator Emma Tarlo with whom it is always a pleasure to share ideas.

Many of the ideas that led to this book were developed during conversations and interviews undertaken by the *Modest Dressing* project with designers, entrepreneurs, bloggers and individuals who generously shared information and ideas. Not all of these participants are referenced by name on these pages (sometimes by their request), but I hope that everyone who spoke with us will find a trace of their contribution in the richness of material that resulted. I am especially grateful to several people for answering questions, sharing contacts and acting as the most generous of interlocutors over the period of this project: Bim Adewunmi, Heather Akou, Gillian Appleby, David Bradwell, Sarah Cheang, Joanne Entwistle, Jonathan Evens, Ena Greengarten, Niloofar Haeri, Chris Jones, David Levene, Cyndy Lessing, Clare Lomas, Paul McDermott, Jacqueline Nicholls, David Purchase, Agnès Rocamora, Frances Ross, Özlem Sandıkçı, Iain Scobie, Jan Shure, Helen Thomas, Sean Tonkin, James Welch, and the many groups and individuals whose responses to conference papers and public talks helped define my thinking. Most of all I thank the contributors to this volume whose invigorating engagement with the topic of modesty and fashion has enriched my thinking more than I can say.

Many of the chapters included in this book appeared initially at two events at the London College of Fashion in 2011, support for which was provided by members of the University of Arts London research office and LCF press office. I owe an especial debt to Rachel Jillions, Melissa Langlands and Rebecca Munro. Also at LCF, Alastair Mucklow and David Hardy provided indispensible assistance in compiling the visuals for this book. Above all, I must thank Jane Cameron, the *Modest Dressing* project researcher, who worked tirelessly to pull this volume together.

Every effort has been made to trace the copyright holders of illustrations and text reprinted in this book. The publishers would be glad to hear from any copyright holders they have not been able to contact and to print due acknowledgement in the next edition.

NOTES

1   The AHRC/ESRC Religion and Society Programme is funded by the Arts and Humanities Research Council and Economic and Social Research Council.

CONTRIBUTORS

Jane Cameron is a researcher at the London College of Fashion. She has research interests in visual anthropology and the role of material culture in the study of religion. Her recent doctoral work at the University of Edinburgh has been on visual constructions and articulations of Buddhist identity within Dalit communities in India.

Barbara Goldman Carrel is Adjunct Associate Professor at the City University of New York. She received her BA in Anthropology from the University of Pennsylvania, an MA in Anthropology from New York University, and an MLS in Library Science from Drexel University. Her research on Hasidic women's dress focuses on how women of the Hasidic community negotiate between fashion and modesty, revealing how Hasidic women's clothing practices – modes of selecting, consuming and appropriating mass-produced fashion – and their distinctive dress code promote culturally specific notions of Hasidic identity, religiosity and womanhood in addition to marking significant distinctions within their community.

Liz Hoggard is an arts journalist based in London. She writes on film, fashion and design for a wide range of publications, including the Evening Standard, The Observer, the Sunday Times, The Independent, The Gentlewoman and Crafts magazine. She is the author of Happy to Be Happy: Making Slough Happy, the book that accompanied the BBC2 TV series. Liz's latest book, Dangerous Women: The Guide to Modern Life, is published by Orion and co-written with literary agent Clare Conville and poet Sarah-Jane Lovett.

Jana Kossaibati blogs at Hijab Style, the UK's first style guide for Muslim women (http://www.hijabstyle.co.uk). She is a medical student and has been running one of the UK's leading Muslim style blogs since 2007, aged

18. Jana has reported for *Vogue.com* and the *Guardian* and been featured on the BBC as well as on LBC radio.

Reina Lewis is Artscom Centenary Professor of Cultural Studies at the London College of Fashion, University of the Arts London. Her new book, *Re-Fashioning Orientalism: New Trends in Muslim Style*, will be published by Duke University Press in 2014. She is also author of *Rethinking Orientalism: Women, Travel and the Ottoman Harem* (2004) and *Gendering Orientalism: Race, Femininity and Representation* (1996). She is editor, with Nancy Micklewright, of *Gender, Modernity and Liberty: Middle Eastern and Western Women's Writings: A Critical Reader* (2006), with Sara Mills, of *Feminist Postcolonial Theory: A Reader* (2003), and, with Peter Horne, of *Outlooks: Lesbian and Gay Visual Cultures* (1996). Reina Lewis is also editor, with Elizabeth Wilson, of I.B.Tauris's *Dress Cultures* series, and, with Teresa Heffernan, of the book series *Cultures in Dialogue*. Reina was Principal Investigator on the project *Modest Dressing: Faith-based Fashion and Internet Retail* funded by the AHRC and ESRC as part of the Religion and Society Programme.

Daniel Miller is Professor of Material Culture at the Department of Anthropology, University College London. His books related to the study of clothing include *Blue Jeans* (2012) and *Global Denim* (2010), edited with Sophie Woodward, *Clothing as Material Culture* (2005), edited with Suzanne Küchler, and *The Sari* (2003), written with Mukulika Banerjee. More recent publications include *Consumption and its Consequences* (2012), *Migration and New Media* (2012), *Tales From Facebook* (2011), *Stuff* (2010) and the *Comfort of Things* (2008).

Annelies Moors is an anthropologist and professor of contemporary Muslim societies in the Department of Anthropology and Sociology, University of Amsterdam. She is primary investigator of a NORFACE research programme on 'The emergence of Islamic fashion in Europe' and of a NWO Cultural Dynamics programme on 'Islamic cultural practices and performances: New youth cultures in Europe'. She has published widely on Muslim family law, wearing gold, the visual media (postcards of Palestine), migrant domestic labour and Islamic fashion and is writing a book on face-veiling in the Netherlands. Her publications include *Women, Property and Islam. Palestinian Experiences 1920–1990* (1995), co-edited special issues of *Islamic Law and Society* (2003), *Fashion Theory* (2007), and *Social Anthropology* (2009), and five edited volumes.

Shellie Slade is founder of ModBod. Established in 2004, and based in Springville, Utah, ModBod's range of modest apparel and accessories sells online and through direct marketing and is also retailed in selected stores across America, including Costco, Nordstroms and Walmart.

Hana Tajima-Simpson launched Maysaa in 2010 (http://www.maysaa. com). Born to a Japanese father and English mother, Hana describes herself as a Muslim convert. Prior to setting up Maysaa, Hana blogged at *Style Covered* (from 2008), which she still maintains along with the Maysaa website.

Emma Tarlo is Professor of Anthropology at Goldsmiths, University of London. She has worked on the anthropology of dress, material culture and urban life, conducting fieldwork in India and Britain. Her publications about India include *Clothing Matters: Dress and Identity in India* (awarded the Coomaraswamy Prize in 1998) and *Unsettling Memories: Narratives of the Emergency in Delhi* (2003). More recently she has worked on contemporary Muslim dress practices, co-editing (with Annelies Moors) a special double issue of *Fashion Theory* (2007) on Muslim fashions around the world, preparing an edited volume on Islamic fashion in Europe (forthcoming) and publishing her own book on Muslim dress in Britain, entitled *Visibly Muslim: Fashion, Politics, Faith* (2010).

Elizabeth Wilson is Visiting Professor at the University of the Arts, London. She formerly taught at London Metropolitan University, Goldsmiths College and Stanford University California and has lectured at Stockholm University. Among her published works are *Adorned in Dreams: Fashion and Modernity* (1985, 2003), *The Sphinx in the City* (1993) and *Bohemians: The Glamorous Outcasts* (2000). She has also published three period crime novels, *The Twilight Hour* (2006), *War Damage* (2009) and *The Girl in Berlin* (2012).

Linda Woodhead is Professor of Sociology of Religion at Lancaster University (Department of Politics, Philosophy and Religion), and Director of the AHRC/ESRC Religion and Society Programme. She has written extensively on religion and change in contemporary Western societies.

FOREWORD

Linda Woodhead

It's a sign of how new and original the subject of this book is that it is likely to arouse perplexity as well as interest. Were it about 'veiling' or 'religious symbols' or even 'religious dress', there would be less confusion. There are sociologists, anthropologists, historians and specialists in the study of religion for whom the idea of studying material cultures and even dress cultures is not novel. There are also political scientists and legal specialists for whom the idea of studying controversies around the Muslim hijab or Sikh turban is familiar. What is discombobulating is the combination of religion and fashion. But it is this which constitutes the genius of the book, and the research on which it rests, and which allows it to make such an innovative and important contribution to a number of fields, including the study of religion.

To a much greater extent than studies which concentrate on established locations and more conventional manifestations of religion, this exploration of modest fashion enables us to see how religion has been changing – not declining or dying, but transforming. I have been arguing for decades that we have witnessed a tectonic shift in the religious landscape of the Western world since the 1980s – but we are only just beginning to take seriously this 'de-reformation' of religion. Old forms are shrinking; new forms have arisen to take their place. There are a plethora of new religious actors, drawing on new resources and technologies, joined in new forms of association, and busy modifying and reinterpreting traditional beliefs and practices from many parts of the world.

The fact that fashion is so marginal to historic, authorised and 'orthodox' forms of religion is precisely why it offers such a good sight-line into an area of new religious vitality. We as scholars may not have appreciated that fashion and religion can mix, but the research which this book presents leaves little doubt that fashion choices are central to the religious lives of many people. The findings also reveal a great deal about why this should be;

and the reasons are the same as those which make it hard for conventional approaches to religion to take these manifestations seriously.

A key point is that the fashion world is seen to be dominated by women – not just as producers, but as consumers. Yet 'real' religion is normally assumed to be dominated by men – who occupy the power positions of religion both 'really' and symbolically. One of the most striking features of the religious shifts of the last few decades is that women have been at the forefront. This is not unprecedented in the sense that women have long outnumbered men in the Christian churches in the West, but what is new is that many now operate outside such organised religion and have been busy creating – or reclaiming – their own forms of religion, both as producers and consumers. When I took part in a study of alternative, 'holistic', forms of spirituality in the town of Kendal in Cumbria at the turn of the twenty-first century, we found that 80 per cent of those offering and participating in mind, body and spirit activities were women (Heelas and Woodhead 2005, Sointu and Woodhead 2008). The visibility and significance of second- and third-generation Muslim women in Britain, and more widely in Europe, is also widely recognised. What is less often noticed is that many of the latter are actively engaged in interpreting and re-forming Islam in a way that marks a new departure in the history of Islam (Chapman, Naguib, Woodhead 2011; on women's new leadership in Islam outside the West, see Bano and Kalmbach 2012). In other words, the fact that women are independent, influential actors in fashion makes it an obvious rather than a surprising place to start looking for interesting religious activity, as this book confirms.

Of course, a major reason for women's high profile in both fashion and contemporary religion is that these are – or, in the case of religion in the West, have become – areas of low prestige. This is both cause and effect of the way in which these spheres are often trivialised or ignored. However, it also turns them into spheres where women can act autonomously and creatively, outside of male control and as leaders in their own right. By paying attention to the margins rather than the centre, research such as this turns power relations upside down and, by shifting the dominant gaze, allows us to see what otherwise falls below the scholarly horizon.

Another reason why fashion and religious reinvention work together is that they both have to do with 'everyday', material, quotidian, matters – and with the body. These are also coded as trivial in our societies, in contrast to 'real' religion which has to do with the extraordinary, sublime, transcendental and other-worldly – the high rather than the low, the spiritual rather than the bodily, the sacred rather the profane or mundane (Woodhead 2010). But the forms of religion which have been growing fastest since the 1970s are precisely those which have been most effective in offering routes to heal, empower and enchant everyday life and heal the body – Charismatic Christianity being the most notable example, but alternative forms of spirituality also illustrating the trend. Yet again, this book shifts our gaze, allowing us to see that things like dress, which are often viewed as most mundane, can equally be viewed as most vital, most basic to human life, relationship, identity and communication – with the sublime being the real luxury.

What this book's interest in fashion also gives access to is the growing importance for contemporary religion of consumer capitalism, the market and the internet. Again, because of a fixation with older forms of organised religion, whose primary relationship was with the state not the economy, scholarship has tended to view such domains as hostile to religion – the materialistic as opposed to the spiritual, the selfish as opposed to the selfless (e.g. Carrette and King 2004). The chapters which follow give the lie to this assumption. It is the market and the internet which have allowed modest fashion to break out of narrow religious community-based circles and go global, crossing the boundaries of a single religious community or tradition, and catering to all who have access to the universal cultures and currencies of shopping, money and internet access. The fact that blogs, websites and chat rooms cater for Muslims, orthodox Jews, varieties of Christians (including the Latter-day Saints), and non-religious women may surprise those schooled in the traditional idea that such groups are sealed off from one another by the walls of organised tradition, but is less surprising to those who realise that religion is now located not only in communities of face-to-face interaction and in centralised and hierarchical forms of religious organisation, but also in cyberspace, in virtual networks of elective connection and in occasional gatherings – ranging from Hajj to Glastonbury Festival to evangelical conventions. These are global not in the sense that they are standardised across time and space ('MacDonaldised'), but because different communities of taste, aspiration, value-commitment and so on can now link to one another across national and traditional religious and ethnic boundaries. It is not a matter of global homogenisation and 'broadcasting', but of new opportunities for de-differentiation and 'narrowcasting'. It is through micro-level convergences and conformities that a process of differentiated religious globalisation is effected. And how better to recognise those with whom we have something in common than by their dress and fashion sense?

There is little doubt then that this book upsets some orthodoxies. I have tried to explain why it upsets an old-fashioned, orthodox view of what religion is, who its main actors are and where it is located. But it also upsets a prevalent secular orthodoxy, widespread in Western societies, which holds that women who dress modestly for religious reasons are passive victims of patriarchal religious traditions and associated forms of male oppression – in contrast to secular modern women who are seen as liberated agents of their own self-determined pathways of fulfilment. As several authors argue, it is this 'othering' secular myth which makes the mainstream fashion industry – and the newspapers, magazines and other media which support it – reluctant to give any space to modest fashion. Far from being open, tolerant and liberated, their own prejudices and exclusions are revealed in the process. The chapters which follow remind us how constrained and uniform-like our secular fashion can be, and how narrow-minded our media. The entrepreneurs and consumers who are the subject of this book contend with all this, defying our stereotypes with their distinctive mix of free-spiritedness, piety, creativity and attachment to the ideal of modesty.

REFERENCES

Bano, Masooda and Kalmbach, Hilary (eds) (2012). *Women, Leadership, and Mosques: Changes in Contemporary Islamic Authority*. Leiden and Boston: Brill.

Carrette, Jeremy and King, Richard (2004). *Selling Spirituality: The Silent Takeover of Religion*. London: Routledge.

Chapman, Mark, Naguib, Shuruq and Woodhead, Linda (2012). 'God-Change', in L. Woodhead, L. and R. Catto (eds), *Religion and Change in Modern Britain*. London: Routledge, pp. 173–95.

Heelas, Paul and Woodhead, Linda (2005). *The Spiritual Revolution: Why Religion is Giving Way to Spirituality*. Oxford: Blackwell.

Sointu, Eva and Woodhead, Linda (2008). 'Holistic Spirituality, Gender, and Expressive Selfhood'. *Journal for the Scientific Study of Religion*, 47/2: 259–76.

Woodhead, Linda (2010). 'Real Religion, Fuzzy Spirituality', in Dick Houtman and Stef Aupers (eds), *Religions of Modernity: Relocating the Sacred to the Self and the Digital*. Leiden: Brill, pp. 30–48.

INTRODUCTION
Mediating Modesty

Reina Lewis

The title of this book, 'Modest Fashion', is received by many as a paradox rather than a description. Simply putting the terms 'modest' and 'fashion' together immediately invites questions, comments, criticism and, not infrequently, incredulity. This book contains much by way of comment, question and critique, but never incredulity since all of its contributors in their very different ways and from very different and sometimes opposing positions think that modest fashion is something that deserves to be taken very seriously indeed.

In the current terminology of the global fashion industry, however, the words 'modest' and 'fashion' are mostly regarded as antipathetic. When 'modesty' and 'fashion' are paired positively in the fashion press, such as the much-vaunted 'modest' wedding dress worn by Catherine Middleton in her wedding to the Duke of Cambridge in 2011 (designed by Sarah Burton at Alexander McQueen), these exceptions paradoxically reinforce the commonsense presumption of an apparent gulf between modesty and fashion. When, occasionally, seasonal fashion trends are lauded as modest the same exceptionalism applies: whilst it might periodically be chic to aspire to the more 'covered' 1950s and 1960s look popularised by the hit TV show *Mad Men*, or the retro 1970s hippy floral maxis of summer 2011, these occasional forays into covering are rendered cool precisely because they are distinguishable from the usual conventions of fashionable dress. That the actual garments spawned by these trends (whether tight fitting décolleté frocks, or floor-length skirts in loose see-through chiffon) are often not entirely conducive to modesty (however defined) is rarely acknowledged in the fashion media. Whilst it is true that most women most of the time dress in ways that are not especially revealing, prevailing fashion trends often produce garments and aesthetics with elements that do not suit consciously religious or modest attire. Indeed, in the West since the 1980s there has been a general drift away from baggy deconstruction towards more fitted 'body con' clothing aimed at an ever younger demographic with the result that many ('older', working) women can feel poorly served by the high street offering. In the now discernible modest fashion sector itself, designers and bloggers join individual dressers in lively discussions about how best to adapt high street clothes to seize the moment when mainstream styles become more modest-friendly.

The increasingly visible range of modest dressing being undertaken by women around the world today provides the stimulus for this book, exploring the development of modest dress and related commercial fashion circuits among Christian, Jewish and Muslim faith groups in the UK, EU and North America. Attending also to women not identified as religious, *Modest Fashion* brings together academics, journalists, designers, entrepreneurs and bloggers to consider modest dressing across all phases of the production– distribution–mediation–consumption cycle.

As with many trends the proliferation of fashionable modesty has been powered by the internet and related information communication technologies (ICTs). The reduced costs of e-commerce have facilitated the development of specialist brands manufacturing and selling modest fashion. At the same time, the early adoption of digital communications by, most notably young, women has provided a multitude of new platforms on which discussion and disputation about modest dress and behaviour can take place and be widely disseminated. There has been an exponential increase in commentary, ranging across 'independent' blogs, YouTube fashion tutorials and discussion fora as well as brand websites and corporate social media. The increase in forms of fashion mediation creates a parallel world of fashion activity for groups of dressers usually ignored by the fashion media and extends discourse about modesty into arenas beyond conventional religious organisations or authorities. Online commentary has also made more visible the participation in modest dressing of 'secular' women and of women who, whilst they might be 'of' faith, do not identify religion as their main motivation for how they dress. The emergence of modest fashion as a niche sector within the global fashion industry is not just about clothes: it simultaneously stimulates interest in and validates modesty as a sphere of personal and community activity.

One common denominator among different sets of modest dressers is age: modest fashion as it has developed in the last 30 years has been predominantly a youthful phenomenon, now in its second or even third generation. However, unlike other youth cultural forms, modest dressing is rarely regarded in the frame of youthful rebellion or experiment. Modest dressers tend to be regarded as representatives of essentialised, unchanging, collective religious identities rather than as individuated youthful style seekers. This is especially true for those whose appearance seems to mark them as of one particular faith, and most especially for young Muslims in the context of the securitising discourse prevalent after the 2001 events of 9/11. Yet, unlike many in their parents' generations who may have experienced consumer culture as oppositional to religious and ethnic cultures, the younger generation of modest dressers (including those now entering their later twenties or early thirties) have grown up with consumer culture and expect to be able to express their identity through what they buy and what they wear. These young women are able to style modish modesty by engaging with mainstream fashion rather than having to rely on 'ethnic' and 'traditional' clothing.

The ways in which modest self-presentation is achieved are myriad and so are the reasons that motivate it. For some women, modest dressing is clearly motivated by their understanding of their religion. For others, it provides a way to reinterpret community and ethnic norms in relation to contemporary life. For others, modest dressing is less about faith or spirituality than about pragmatic options for achieving social or geographical mobility, or for responding to changes in their lifecycle (such as having children, getting older, going to a new job). Modest dressing can mean different things to different women and can change meanings over the course of their lives.

This book therefore makes no attempt to demarcate what modesty is or which forms of dress or personal presentation most accurately embody it. It is the premise of this book that modesty is a mutable concept that changes over time and is diversely adopted, rejected, altered by or in some cases imposed on different groups of women (and, to a lesser extent, men) in different times and places. Each of the three faiths (and their different denominations and derivations) covered in this book has different regulations and customs about how to cover and comport the female body, often characterised by multiple interpretations and internal disputation. Just as there are no garments or ways of wearing them that are intrinsically modest or intrinsically the property of any particular faith or sect, neither are there any guarantees that particular forms of dressing will be universally recognised as modest by those that observe them. All clothing is inherently polysemic and open to interpretation by different wearers and observers. Garments may acquire meaning as modest or as a marker of a particular faith over time, but this is also subject to change and contestation. For example, in Western Europe and North America the increasing numbers of young women wearing the headscarf, or hijab, is often taken as the most visible sign of increasing religious identification among Muslims. But as Leila Ahmed (2011) and others have argued, the very identification of the hijab as Muslim can be seen as historically produced and politically intentioned, with Islamic revivalism effectively disavowing the headscarf's pre-Islamic origin and multi-faith regional usage in earlier periods to resignify hijab as both exclusively Islamic and as the key marker of female piety (see also Lewis 2004). The global discursive impact of this switch may effectively mark as non-devout those Muslim women who do not cover: regardless of their own sense of piety or religiosity, women can find themselves judged or anxious about being judged as less 'good' Muslims once the practice of head-covering (and in some circumstances covering the rest of the body and/ or face) reaches critical mass in their particular community or environment (see also Tarlo 2010).

The knock-on effects of this 'shift to the right' have been observed in other faiths too. The growing presence and influence of ultra-orthodox Jewish sects is often seen to have ramped up the levels of visible orthodoxy among other Jews, with many younger women in the modern orthodox Jewish tradition electing to cover their hair with wigs or scarves in ways unimaginable to their mothers, except perhaps for visits to the synagogue. That this may often be accompanied for many young feminist and progressive Jewish women by a level of soul-searching about participating more fully in potentially patriarchal religious conventions designed to control female sexuality goes largely undetected.

Often unwilling to 'wash their dirty laundry in public', religious groups, especially those in a minority situation, have often avoided making public their internal disputes. External observers lack the cultural competencies to distinguish one sort of modest dressing from another within a particular faith tradition and media representations often rely on stereotypical images to signal generic religious identities. It is only when disputes become so pronounced as to enter the wider political scene that differences within religious groups are more widely acknowledged. In 2012 as this book goes to press, for example, there has been substantial coverage (see Bronner and Kershner 2012) of divisions within the international Hasidic community in response to attempts by some far right Hasids in Israel to impose modesty regulations and gender segregation (notably on buses) on women outside of their immediate communities and vicinities (now also extending to

Brooklyn, New York, Duell 2012). Similarly, in the US, the 2011–12 campaign by Mormon Mitt Romney for the Republican presidential nomination put an unwelcome political spin on the resolutely apolitical agenda of the official multimedia PR campaign launched by the Church of Jesus Christ of Latter-day Saints (LDS) across the country in 2010 (Goodstein 2011). For a Church committed to proselytising, events that bring the LDS version of Christianity onto the world stage may not be unwelcome. But in the context of the long-standing hostility of other US Christians, and especially Protestant evangelicals, who regard Mormonism as heterodox (Cannell 2005), anxieties about how LDS is represented can be acute not just for centralised Church institutions but also for ordinary Mormons including those potentially visible as fashion entrepreneurs and bloggers. In Britain and the European Union new diversity legislation has brought to the fore challenges to secularity that arise more often from members of the majority Christian demographic than from the minority Muslim population, as might have been expected (see also Pew 2010). Presenting themselves as minoritised by a dominant secular society, Christian demands for protection of religious expression have often focused on dress (crucifixes worn with workplace uniform, refusing to wear trousers) and on the rights of Christians to avoid sanctioning homosexuality (as public officials, hoteliers, etc.). Often backed by evangelical campaigning organisations, taken cumulatively these cases produce a public discourse about Christianity that may in time prompt calls for 'moderate' Christians to disassociate themselves from 'extremists' similar to those faced by Muslims in 2001 after 9/11 and repeated after subsequent attacks, such as the 7/7 bombs in Britain in 2005.

The emergence of a niche market for modest fashion needs, therefore, to be situated in relation to the diverse ways in which religion has become more and differently visible in political and public life, a process that inevitably brings to the fore the multiplicity of competing religious practices and definitions. In this book alone, the reader will find an array of definitions of clothing, practices and beliefs chosen (and/or avoided) by the different individuals and groups represented here, with each chapter usually following the nuanced self-designations used by participants in online and offline interactions. The ambiguity that characterises the field extends beyond discussions of what constitutes modesty to include changing and conflicting definitions about the parameters of religions, the nature of the spiritual, and the boundaries between the religious and the secular. Given that, as Talal Asad describes (2003), secular modernities are marked by the foundational traits of the religious cultures from which they developed, it is not surprising that the recent advent of public religiosity into British cultural life is perceived as more of a departure than the ongoing presence of religiosity as the basis of social and political life in the United States. Similarly, the dramatic attempts to legislate Muslim women's dress in France, the Netherlands and Germany can be seen in relation to the specific place of religio-ethnic identity within their various nationalisms as courts try to arbitrate the legitimacy of different faith claims and their appropriateness for civic society.

The spread of ICTs and affordable broadband connectivity not only brings modest apparel styles and options into the orbit of more women, but also creates new publics able to traverse boundaries of faith, sect and nation with implications both welcome and unwelcome for the various participants in and observers of modest fashion. Illuminating contemporary dress debates with historicised analyses, contributors to *Modest Fashion* track emergent styles and taste communities and evaluate the role of innovative forms of fashion mediation and religious interpretation in three interrelated sections.

Part 1 focuses on overtly *Faith-based Fashion and the Commercially Fluid Boundaries of Confession*, outlining and evaluating online and offline manufacture and retail practices and related social media commentary and marketing. Annelies Moors focuses on the rapid development of Muslim fashion online from its origins in the 1990s to the wider Islamic consumer culture recognisable today. With developments in ICT popularising increased visual content, blogs and YouTube now top internet searches, augmenting material on webstores to produce a cross-referential online world of interactive Islamic fashion. Notably these new publics are more successful and get more hits when characterised by openness rather than prescription in how they promote behaviours of Islamic modesty. This, Moors notes, became especially the case after 9/11 when negative stereotypes of Muslim extremism prompted many to emphasise pluralism, peace and moderation as intrinsically Islamic values, a shift from previous tendencies to universalise modesty as a connection across faiths. In this light she notes that Muslim bloggers and brands emphatically avoid being perceived as making claims to Islamic authority, with many key bloggers (including two who feature in the industry panel discussion of chapter 9) issuing disclaimers about not wanting to arbitrate 'correct' forms of hijab, leaving decisions to individual wearers.

Widening the frame to include Jews and Christians, my chapter in contrast argues that taken cumulatively, online modesty discourse can indeed be regarded as a new form of religious discourse in which women are achieving recognition as religious interpreters and intermediaries. My account of how entrepreneurs from the three faiths have variously been able to create and supply a niche market situates the modest blogosphere in relation to the wider structures of fashion blogging and corporate digital communications to examine how bloggers and brands respond to challenges particular to their sector, such as avoiding alienating customers/ readers with different modesty interpretations, creating 'modest' visual representations of the female form. Whilst the ability of digital media to foster the creation of new modes for religious knowledge formation and transmission is often characterised as producing a domain of male activity, my chapter repositions women's often trivialised fashion knowledges to argue that the intrafaith, interfaith and faith/secular connectivities of digital modesty create new publics able to endow bloggers and designers with kudos as reputable arbitrators of style for the 'secular' world.

Also tracking cross-faith connections, Emma Tarlo focuses on how the internet has created new modes for the articulation of debates about modesty between ultra and orthodox Jewish and Muslim women, two groups whose conspicuous modest dressing is mostly seen to preserve community insularity. In contrast, she argues, internet discussion groups uniquely foster quite intimate communication between women of different faiths, often facing similar dilemmas about how to source clothing for fashionable modesty and how to arbitrate the boundaries of modesty within a prevalent etiquette of not overly judging others. Solidarity offered by cross-faith alliances of modest dressers may provide light relief for the frustrations of 'faux' modesty (the merely technical compliance with hijab or tzniuth by cartoon characters 'Hot Fatima' and 'Hot Chanie') and offer wardrobe solutions (hijab pins from a Muslim website recommended to Jewish wearers of hats). However, ideological tensions, especially about Middle Eastern politics, can also surface in cross-faith exchanges. So too can the movement of material goods through cross-faith consumption run up against the desire of many orthodox Jewish and Muslim women that their dress should preserve visible religious distinction.

The need among Hasidic Jewish women for dress to act as a marker of religious distinction is revealed by Barbara Goldman Carrel's study of ultra-orthodox fashion in Borough Park, Brooklyn, to be as much about demarcating internal social and spiritual status as about performing external religious difference vis-à-vis the majority 'secular' American population. Selectively appropriating mainstream fashion merchandise, Hasidic women have developed an 'old world' European 'royalised' aesthetic that emphasises quality and formal attire. Many repudiate the casual, 'sloppy' dressing of the American mainstream to promote a positive image of orthodox women as members of an elite religious lineage. Women's fashionable self-presentation may serve the community's need for positive external representation, a counterweight to the obvious non-contemporaneity of Hasidic men's dress, but too much interest in fashion also imperils women's commitment to their main role as the transmitters of Torah-observant values. Whilst cautionary tracts and tapes advise girls and women to avoid the 'evil inclination' of creeping fashion enthralment, many opt for a strategy of 'minimising harm' by providing tips on how to 'Hasidify' garments (via home sewing or local tailoring services) in order to render mainstream apparel suitable to be used as part of women's embodiment of Jewish religious elite distinction.

The distinctiveness and legibility of Hasidic consumption habits in relation to the wider frame of Jewish fashion also prompts Daniel Miller's exploration of the contested status of denim for religious and secular dressers as part of Part 2's discussion of *Modesty without Religion?*. Focusing on a textile rather than a garment, he notes how the periodic 'ban' on denim issued by ultra-orthodox Jewish rabbis in the US prompts horrified fascination in the mainstream British *Jewish Chronicle*. He argues that denim jeans have now reached such a level of global ubiquity that they are 'postsemiotic': jeans are now so common that they have lost their initially transgressive connotations and become effectively 'neutral', with denim operating in fashion terms as a non-colour that goes with anything. He speculates about why, despite its potential for modest humble self-effacement, denim poses a conundrum for some communities of modest dressers. Whilst migrants to London might value denim for its unmarked qualities, allowing them to fit in as 'ordinary' citizens, this is precisely why it is repudiated by many Hasids in New York for whom denim's unremarkableness runs into conflict with their desire for conspicuous dress as confirmation of their religious and moral distinction.

The ways in which modesty-related concerns online traverse and call into question the religious–secular divide are documented in Jane Cameron's online ethnography. She reveals that preoccupation with the problems of body image and self-presentation faced by women and girls in contemporary sexualised societies are core features of both religious (in this case Christian) modesty blogs and fora and of non-religiously-aligned parenting/mothering sites. This digital overlap prompts both potential alliances and disputes, with secular participants often frustrated by attempts by the religious Right to gain ownership of campaigns against the sexualisation of children, and religious participants made anxious by displays of intrafaith competitive piety. Navigating the internet's intrinsic connectivity requires particular care for participants who want to avoid being incorporated into ideological definitions of modesty to which they do not adhere, such as the non-religiously-affiliated blogger who turned down an ostensibly flattering request to have her picture included on a modest dress forum because of what she saw as its patriarchal attitude to women as the guardians of male sexual control.

The disputed and moralised binary between the religious and the secular and the difficulty of challenging religiously-held views from a non-religious perspective forms the basis of Elizabeth Wilson's polemic. Unlike the widespread tolerance of Hasidic men's conspicuously distinctive dress, Muslim dress (in which recent controversies about the niqab or burqa have melded into opinion about all forms of the 'veil') has become a flashpoint for a series of debates about gender, sexuality, patriarchy and immigration that often have little to do with religion but that tend to demonise Islam as uniquely attempting to regulate female sexuality. Challenging popular criticisms of Muslim dress that pose it as the opposite of fashion, understood as a rule-free zone of individuated expression, Wilson connects the history of European church and state sumptuary legislation to the prevalence of contemporary uniform codes that regulate bodily behaviour at work or at school. Following Ahmed (2011) on the Islamic rebranding of hijab as the idealised personal expression of faith, Wilson critiques the discourse of choice utilised by many hijabis by identifying 'choice' as one of the foundational myths of consumer culture that affects everyone regardless of their beliefs. Emphasising commonalities – the sexualisation of girls' clothing is welcomed neither by 'secular' feminists nor by religious adherents – over differences, she calls for a willingness to engage in discussion that is not hampered by the fear of 'offending' religious sensibilities. Critique should challenge puritanism and pornification at the same time, seeking alliances of the progressive across the so called religious–secular divide.

Part 3, on *Manufacturing and Mediating Modesty*, brings together reflection from entrepreneurs, designers, bloggers and journalists involved in the construction, transmission, practice and critique of modest fashion. Journalist Liz Hoggard provides an insider view of why it is so difficult to get modest fashion onto the style pages of daily newspapers, even though religious dress (notably the European burqa and niqab controversies) seems sometimes to monopolise the news pages. With editors reluctant to see everyday modest dress as a 'bone fide' fashion story, modesty may make it to the style pages when connected to celebrities, either dressing against type (voluptuous British chef Nigella Lawson in a burqini) or representing modern style fusion (Turkish First Lady Hayrünnisa Gül at Buckingham Palace in covered dress and killer heels). Hoggard identifies a widespread 'modesty double standard' in which some women are rewarded for dressing modestly (older women, First Ladies, teachers) whilst others are ridiculed for immodest behaviours (older women showing 'too much' flesh, 'vulgar' working-class women wearing tacky clothes at Royal Ascot). That the modesty double standard reinforces hierarchies of class and ethnicity as much as of gender was spectacularly called into question by the wearing of intentionally 'inappropriate' clothing on the feminist SlutWalks that spread around the world in 2011.

The challenges of making and marketing products for modesty form the basis of Chapter 9, the edited transcript of an industry panel held at the London College of Fashion in 2011. Liz Hoggard was joined by two leading Muslim style bloggers, sector initiator Jana Kossaibati of *Hijab Style* and Hana Tajima-Simpson whose popular *Style Covered* blog paved the way for her Maysaa clothing range. Coming from Utah, Shellie Slade discussed her company ModBod, in conjunction with academics Reina Lewis and Linda Woodhead. Motivated to mount a corrective to hijabis' over-representation in negative news stories, Kossaibati's blog had from the start a dual purpose: to provide a comprehensive hijabi fashion style guide and to create a safe space for hijabis to talk to each other. The international range of respondents to her English-language blog confirms that hijabi fashion moves beyond 'traditional' or regional dress and is increasingly served by new online brands. Driven by young entrepreneur-designers (many from the UK but also Malaysia, the Emirates and Turkey), Kossaibati predicts that the modest market will grow and expand into currently underserved sub-segments such as plus-size or maternity clothing. Despite the fact that nearly all of the specialist brands that pioneered the modest market originate from within a faith community, many are adjusting their products to meet the needs of different faith groups, as illustrated by LDS entrepreneur Shellie Slade whose products were initially designed to help pre-teen daughters achieve the then fashionable 'Britney Spears look' without revealing too much flesh. Intended for wear under/with other fashion items, the ModBod wardrobe solutions were soon demanded by mothers, and women from other faiths as well as women needing suitable body cover for work or sports. In the context of the inevitable challenges of fashion manufacture and retail, Slade's experiences elaborate the opportunities and pitfalls posed by religious community structures and cross-faith interactions. Approaching from a design-led perspective, Hana Tajima-Simpson recounted her business development in the language of a personal and creative journey. Building a successful blogger profile was a key precursor to the launch of Maysaa, a brand intended to reflect her convert's freedom to visualise hijabi fashion outside of inherited ethno-national conventions. The ways in which modesty is regulated outside the domain of religion was explored by journalist Liz Hoggard's press review of modesty related stories from that week's media. Given the popular presumption that modest, especially Muslim, dress is a sign of female subordination to male control, Hoggard demonstrated how the media itself scrutinises, regulates and judges 'secular' women on the basis of the 'respectability' of their self-presentation. The panel's discussion provides a unique glimpse into a market in the making, with regional distinctions emerging (not just for dress styles but for different types of digital connectivity) and stratification developing as established brands reposition their initially faith-branded products and younger designers (who reveal surprising solidarities between potential competitors) aim to take the fashion world head on.

CONCLUSION

The wide range of material covered in this book reveals a fast-changing cultural and commercial scene in which practices of modest dressing and associated behaviours are spreading, proliferating and diversifying, spawning new generations and subcultures as styles and practices diffuse between different religions and into the 'secular' mainstream. During the period of editing this book (2011–12), matters of modesty have several times featured positively across the spectrum of fashion industry activities: on the catwalk, American Muslim and Christian fashion models have self-identified as 'modest' without exiting the industry, some signing to a new modest modelling agency (Thompson 2012, Dumas 2012); in marketing, the value of the – Jewish, and to follow Muslim – modest market was recognised with its own category on the British online personal shopping guide SoSensational.co.uk; in the third sector, British Muslim designer Sarah Elenany was commissioned to translate her urban vision of stylish modesty into new uniform options for the Girl Scouts (Hough 2012). Developments such as these have the potential to normalise modesty, assisting modest-dressing women to be included seamlessly in the fabric of contemporary society.

For many participants, whether entrepreneurs, fashion mediators or consumers, the rising profile of modest fashion is a matter of celebration. Yet the very success of modest fashion as a new niche may threaten the religious distinctiveness on which for some it is premised. If the proliferation of modesty into the recognisable forms of female fashion participation (reading mags, blogs, browsing stores on and offline) can render as normal or unremarkable practices that previously signified self-conscious faithfulness, does this help to keep people in the faith? Especially young people, their parents hope. Or does it dangerously dilute religious identifications? The success of modest fashion raises ideological and spiritual issues for women who do not want to 'pass' or be appropriated into a secular fashionscape, just as secular modest dressers may resent being rebranded as religious.

Whilst it is commonplace to regard fashion as an inherently fickle enterprise premised on ever more rapid style cycles, religion is often regarded and sometimes represents itself as inherently stable, premised on immutable and ever applicable values. The development of modesty as a niche market and fashion discourse brings together these two temporalities revealing fashion to be a territory shared with faith and revealing modesty to be ambiguous and changeable. Within the always slippery frame of passing trends, a lack of distinction in the fashion market has immediate commercial implications: entrepreneurs risk losing their niche if the various needs of their modest consumers can be more than occasionally met by ordinary high street purchases. At the same time, the connectivities of modest fashion discourse move material goods and visual aesthetics from one faith sector to another, suggesting that attempts to secure particular dress styles as the property of a single faith are likely always to be undermined by the magpie nature of fashion. When ultra-orthodox Jews adopt *jilbabs* or Christian bloggers re-post Jewish guides on how to tie a *tichel* (headscarf) it is not that religious boundaries disappear but that they are reframed through their interaction with the temporality and mode of fashion. It may be that modesty is having a 'fashion moment' and will pass like other trends. But the significance of the accelerated, commercialised and cross-faith modest fashion activity witnessed in the early decades of the twenty-first century is likely to be more lasting than any wardrobe ensemble.

REFERENCES

Ahmed, Leila (2011). *A Quiet Revolution: The Veil's Resurgence from the Middle East to America*. New Haven, CT: Yale University Press.

Asad, Talal (2003). *Formations of the Secular*. Stanford, CA: Stanford University Press.

Bronner, Ethan and Kershner, Isabel (2012). 'Israelis Facing a Seismic Rift Over Role of Women'. *New York Times*, 15 January. http://www.nytimes.com/2012/01/15/world/middleeast/israel-faces-crisis-over-role-of-ultra-orthodox-in-society.html?pagewanted=all (accessed 30 April 2012).

Cannell, Fenella (2005). 'The Christianity of Anthropology'. Malinowski Memorial Lecture 2004, *Journal of the Royal Anthropological Institute*, 11: 353–56.

Duell, Mark (2012). 'Bloomberg Outraged at Ultra-Orthodox Jewish Bus where Women are Told to Sit at the Back'. *Daily Mail*, 30 April. http://www.dailymail.co.uk/news/article-2051399/Bloomberg-outraged-ultra-orthodox-Jewish-bus-women-told-sit-back.html (accessed 30 April 2012).

Dumas, Daisy (2012). 'High Fashion CAN be Modest, says Founder of a New Modelling Agency for Muslim Women'. *Daily Mail*, 9 February. http://www.dailymail.co.uk/femail/article-2097977/Underwraps-Muslim-model-agency-founder-Nailah-Lymus-says-high-fashion-CAN-modest.html (accessed 8 February 2012).

Goodstein, Laurie (2011). 'Mormons' Ad Campaign May Play Out on the '12 Campaign Trail'. *New York Times*, 17 November. http://www.nytimes.com/2011/11/18/us/mormon-ad-campaign-seeks-to-improve-perceptions.html (accessed 16 February 2012).

Hough, Andrew (2012). 'New Uniforms Help Muslim Girl Scouts to Be Better Prepared'. *The Telegraph*, 30 March. http://www.telegraph.co.uk/news/religion/9173946/New-uniforms-help-Muslim-girl-Scouts-to-be-better-prepared.html (accessed 30 March 2012).

Lewis, Reina (2004). *Rethinking Orientalism: Women, Travel and the Ottoman Harem*. London: I.B.Tauris.

Pew Forum on Religion and Public Life (2010). 'Muslim Networks and Movements in Western Europe'. September. www.pewforum.org.

Tarlo, Emma (2010). *Visibly Muslim: Fashion, Politics, Faith*. Oxford: Berg.

Thompson, Paul (2012). 'My Body is Only for my Husband: U.S. Christian Model Kylie Bisutti Quit Victoria's Secret because it Clashed with Her Faith'. *Daily Mail*, 8 February. http://www.dailymail.co.uk/femail/article-2097793/Kylie-Bisutti-quit-Victorias-Secret-clashed-Christian-faith.html (accessed 8 February 2012).

Part 1

Faith-based Fashion and the Commercially Fluid Boundaries of Confession

1

'DISCOVER THE BEAUTY OF MODESTY'
Islamic Fashion Online

Annelies Moors

The Modest Clothing Directory, started in 1998 by Dana Becker from Minnesota, USA, is a good starting point to discuss the online interface of modesty, Islam and fashion.[1] In an interview about her motives for starting this website, Becker explained how, after her conversion from Christianity to Islam, her search for appropriate styles of dress led her to the internet and she 'kind of became obsessed with looking for Muslim clothing companies online'.[2] Having located 40 of these webstores, her desire to share her knowledge with others pushed her to start the Modest Clothing Directory. This website did not limit itself to Islamic styles of modest dress, as from its beginning Becker had decided to also include links to other religions. In her words, 'Because I used to be a Christian, I just feel a kinship to Christian women who want to dress modestly.' She also expressed the hope that having such links side by side 'will give all religious women a sense that, despite discrepancies in theology and a lot of misunderstanding about each other, they are not that different' (Fellow 2005).

The Modest Clothing Directory does not only bring together a wide variety of forms of modest dress, but it simultaneously segments these into multiple categories. Working with a database that has entries such as location, religion and style, Becker divides the webstores into 'Western Style', 'Creed', 'Other Regional Styles' and 'Speciality Niches', each of which is then, in turn, subdivided. The Creed section, for instance, differentiates between Islamic, Jewish, Latter-day Saints, Plain Simple Christian, Catholic, Trendy Modest Christian and Messianic webstores. In the case of the Islamic ones, there is a further division into particular items of dress (abaya, *jilbab*, hijab, long skirts, long shirts), materials (denim), styles (trendy, career) and functions (Eid, swimwear and sportswear). Under the button 'reasoning behind site's organization' she explains why she includes the category of 'Creed'. First, as she points out, she does so because there are those who would like to 'patronize stores that run under the auspices of their own religions', and second, because it makes it easier for women to find the kind of clothing that fits the requirements of a particular faith. Presenting the example of the length of skirts for Muslim women, she points out that if they go to the Islamic section they stand a far better chance that these will be long enough.

Whereas Dana Becker includes a wide variety of modest clothing webstores in her online directory, in this contribution I focus more narrowly on Islamic styles of dress, yet include a wider variety of online formats, such as weblogs and YouTube videos. Starting in the late 1990s, Islam online has become an academic growth sector. In its early years, the emphasis was mostly on how such new media have played a significant role in the fragmentation of religious authority, with youth, women and minorities actively engaged in interpreting the foundational texts (Eickelman and Anderson 1999: 11ff.). In the aftermath of 9/11, in contrast, digital Islam increasingly has come to be seen as a field in which 'competing authorities attempt to out-do each other in terms of the strictness of their interpretation of legal norms' (Turner 2007: 32). Whereas temporality is important to understand these divergent observations, the specific dynamics of particular fields also need to be taken into account. The Islamic culture industry, that has more recently become the focus of research, has tended to go in yet another direction, producing 'a marketable image that is attractive and desirable' to a broad public (Gökarıksel and McLarney 2010: 6). This raises the question of how ethical considerations and aesthetical practices work to authorise particular forms of Islam online.

Focusing on fashionable styles of Islamic dress in cyberspace, I start with a brief overview of two conditions that have enabled the emergence of Islamic fashion online: that is the offline proliferation of fashionable styles of Islamic dress and the development of internet formats that present these online. I will limit myself to the most successful ones that draw the largest audiences in terms of views. In the next section, I investigate the work these various online formats do in producing particular publics. How do they mediate Islam and fashion, concepts that may intersect and overlap, but also stand in an ambiguous or even tense relation to each other? Whereas Dana Becker's Modest Clothing Directory brings together different faith communities as well as regional styles through the lens of modesty, I investigate whether and how modesty functions as a bridging concept in the field of Islamic fashion and end with a brief note on its intersections with regional styles.

THE EMERGENCE OF ISLAMIC FASHION: A GLOBAL PHENOMENON

Whereas in many Muslim majority countries European styles of dress had become increasingly widespread in the course of the twentieth century, especially amongst the middle and upper classes, the ascendance of the Islamic revivalist movement in the 1970s and 1980s encouraged a growing number of women to start to wear recognisably Islamic, covered styles of dress (Brenner 1996; El-Guindi 1999; Göle 1996; MacLeod 1992; Mahmood 2005). Initially, this meant a move towards a uniform and sober style, such as uniform full-length, wide coats in muted colours, that many hoped would do away with the sartorial distinctions between the wealthy and the poor (Navaro-Yashin 2002; Sandıkçı and Ger 2007). In the course of one to two decades, however, more fashionable styles started to replace these austere and purposely non-fashionable forms of Islamic attire. By the 1990s the Islamic revival movement had become more heterogeneous and had shifted from an anti-consumerist radical movement to a more individualised reformist trend with identities increasingly produced through consumption (Navaro-Yashin 2002). The emergence of an Islamic consumer culture engendered a greater heterogeneity of Islamic styles of dress and stimulated the fashion consciousness among younger, more affluent Muslim women (Kiliçbay and Binark 2002; Sandıkçı and Ger 2007; Abaza 2007). Aesthetic judgements, taste dispositions, cultural capital and financial means increasingly structured women's sartorial practices, and processes of aestheticisation and personalisation turned sober forms of Islamic dress into highly fashionable Islamic outfits (Sandıkçı and Ger 2005, 2010).

A move toward trendy, fashionable, yet recognisably Islamic dress was not only discernable in settings that had first seen a shift from Western fashions to austere styles of Islamic dress. Also in settings where covered outerwear had remained normative, the increased commodification of dress and the turn to consumer culture led to more rapid changes in styles. In the Gulf States, some started to transform the abaya from a non-distinct, shapeless, all-enveloping black gown into something more akin to a fashion item, with seasonally changing cuts and models, materials and decorations

(Al-Qasimi 2010; Lindholm 2010). Elsewhere, the abaya was introduced as a new fashionable item of dress, such as in Yemen where it replaced existing styles of all-covering dress (Moors 2007), amongst migrants in south India (Osella and Osella 2007) or in Indonesia (Amrullah 2008), where it was often introduced by returning migrants and students.

Europe and the Anglo-Saxon world, where Muslims are a minority, were relative latecomers to the field of Islamic fashion. There, Islamic fashion emerged inspired by the global Islamic revival, in conjunction with local histories of Muslim presence and in an environment that has come to be increasingly Islam unfriendly (Moors 2009, Tarlo 2010). Within this context, young women opt to combine a style of dress that is visibly Muslim and simultaneously contemporary or modern. Rather than buying their outfits from stores specifically targeting Muslims, many of them turn to the same chains their non-Muslim peers frequent, such as H&M, Zara, or Mango, where they combine items of dress in such a way as to produce covered yet fashionable outfits. These consumers can be considered as creative co-producers, who 'make do' with mainstream items and recombine them, engaging in forms of bricolage to put together an 'Islamic' wardrobe.[3]

ISLAMIC ATTIRE ONLINE: WEBSTORES, VIDEOS AND BLOGS

All kinds of Islamic attire, both the more and the less fashionable, are present in cyberspace. A quick Google search shows the enormous amount of information on Islamic attire available. The term hijab gives over 23 million hits, 'Islamic fashion' 624,000, and 'hijab fashion' 364,000. The exponential growth of the internet is intrinsically related to the development of new infrastructures. In particular, the new web browser technologies, such as the introduction of Web 2.0, have turned the web into a more participatory platform. Rather than only allowing for the static downloading of content information in browser windows, it enables uploading user-generated content (such as text, photos and videos) and hence is characterised by a far greater interactivity. This has enabled the development of social media and networking, sharing pictures and videos, podcasting, blogging and wikis.

Researching the internet is a challenge, as the availability of information online is always in flux and user-dependent. In order to provide some sense of how the online presence of Islamic attire has proliferated and diversified,

I start by describing two screengrabs of Google searches, one performed on 26 December 2006, the other almost five years later, on 26 October 2011. A comparison of the first ten hits points to interesting shifts in Islamic fashionscapes. The screengrab of 2011 presented two internet formats that the 2006 Google search did not show: Google pictures and YouTube videos, pointing to a stronger visual and multimedia presence. But Islamic attire online has also diversified in another sense. Whereas in 2006 all hits were webstores selling Islamic clothing, except for a web article about an Islamic fashion show, in 2011, in contrast, amongst the first ten hits were four webstores, three Islamic fashion blogs and a link to an Islamic fashion festival in Malaysia (in addition to Google pictures and YouTube videos). This indicates a decline in the relative popularity of webstores and a stronger online presence of visual material and YouTube videos.

WEBSTORES: GREATER INTERACTIVITY

As the above indicates, Islamic fashion webstores are the oldest popular online format, dating back to at least 1997.[4] On the one hand, they are a highly unstable presence. Dana Becker claims that on her portal, 233 Islamic clothing stores are currently open, adding, 'Did you know over 220 online Islamic clothing stores have opened and then closed since 1998? Only four of the original stores I put up are still running today!' Many of the webstores Akou (2007) mentioned are also no longer functioning. At the same time, there is, however, also a considerable number of webstores that have been online for over five years.[5] Amongst the most popular ones are Shukr (2002), Al-Hannah (2000), Islamic Design House (2006), Jelbab (2001), The Hijab Shop (2004), Artizara (2003) and Islamic Boutique (2002).[6]

Webstores vary greatly in their styles of presentation. They all provide contact information, but whereas some present a personalised narrative about their background and motivation (often pointing to conversion of the owner), others present themselves more anonymously as a company or a team. Many are located in the Anglo-Saxon world, but there is also a significant presence in the Middle East, and the Gulf countries as well as South-East Asia are a growth area. Sometimes their main function is to draw attention to well-established offline stores, while others have only an online presence. Many webstores sell mainstream styles of Islamic dress, but some are first and foremost a means for avant-garde designers to present their work to the world at large. Styles of presenting items of dress also vary considerably, especially in terms of depictions of the human body. Some have no problem with depicting attractively posing models, while others only depict part of the body, use drawings, or only show the merchandise (see also Akou 2007).

Whatever differences exist amongst webstores, one major trend is that they have moved from a simple presentation of items of dress, information about the owner, pages about payment and shipping, and perhaps a guestbook, to a far more sophisticated online presence. These webstores include moving imagery, such as embedded videos of fashion shows, sometimes with music, have their own blogs, and extensively link to social networking sites. Many have uploaded promotion videos on YouTube, have made a Facebook fan page and use a Twitter account. Islamic portals and fashionista blogs, in turn, provide numerous links to webstores, sometimes including a qualitative evaluation. In other words, webstores have become integrated in a dense web of connections that makes up the wider interactive world of Islamic fashion online. Two of the new formats have gained a particularly strong online presence: YouTube videos and blogs.

YOUTUBE VIDEOS: THE BEAUTY OF HIJAB

YouTube videos, as another online form of Islamic fashion, date back to at least 2007. The most popular YouTube video for 'hijab' is ♥*.~.*The Hijab*.~.*♥, with over 2 million views.[7] The video is presented as 'showing the beauty of the Hijab which refutes the common stereotype that all Muslim women are oppressed when in fact it is the very opposite'. On his YouTube channel profile, the producer presents himself anonymously as 'Muslim and proud' and highlights that,

> Our faith is all about peace and we are able to live side by side in peace as communities of the past have shown … Don't listen to the haters and their propaganda, they just want to spread hate and trouble. Muslims want peace not war and that's all that counts.[8]

The second video, with over 1.2 million views, is 'How to wear a Headscarf (Hijaab/Hijab Tutorial): Pink Waterfall', which the producer, Amena from Leicester, UK, presents as 'Hijaabs, hoojabs and accessories available from http://www.pearl-daisy.com'.[9] This YouTube video also functions to attract customers to her webstore; on her YouTube channel (*Amenakin*) she provides a wide variety of such video tutorials.[10] More generally, such tutorials that show different styles of fashioning headcoverings are a very popular genre of hijab videos. They can be considered as an upgraded version of the hijab tutorial pages with still photographs that some webstores still provide.

The third most popular hijab video is 'Beautiful Female Muslim Celebrities With Hijab', with over 900,000 views.[11] The producer states that the images are those of 'Female Muslim Celebrities from Indonesia and Iran'. He then explains the differences between Indonesia and Iran. Indonesia is a secular country, where the government does not impose wearing hijab but gives freedom to all Muslims to practise their faith as long as they do not do so in an extremist way. The pictures present some Indonesian Muslim celebrities who wear hijab in their everyday life. In Iran wearing hijab 'is a must'. There you cannot find Muslim women who do not wear hijab, and this includes 'female celebrities'. On his YouTube channel the producer strongly expresses his dedication to Indonesia: 'It's all about Indonesia. Enjoy!!! … Indonesian Youth Rise Up! … Together we stand up, move forward in self confidence towards prosperous Indonesia!'[12]

These three most viewed YouTube hijab videos very much set out to convey the message that wearing hijab is beautiful, using a discourse of aesthetics as a means to draw people to Islam (da'wa), while also highlighting that, in ethical terms, Islam is a religion of peace. Comments, however, vary greatly, and some can be very negative. Moreover, there are online videos that present a far more negative view about wearing hijab. When entering the search term 'hejab' (a common transcription from Farsi), the most viewed videos show how supporters of the Iranian regime violently attack women they deem insufficiently covered. That the field of YouTube videos is highly charged is also evident in the existence of a genre of hijab videos that aims at ridiculing women wearing hijab, such as those linking hijab with pornography.

BLOGS: STYLE AND ENTERTAINMENT

Another major feature of Islamic fashion online is blogging. Starting as publicly accessible personal journals, thriving on the sense of presence the blogger managed to create, this genre also rapidly diversified (see Chapter 2 in this volume). Some staunchly maintain an independent presence, while others have close ties to particular brands. In contrast to some webstore owners and many producers of YouTube videos, bloggers often provide detailed information about themselves. Brands often use such a personalised blog format also. Whereas in the field of webstores and YouTube video productions both men and women are active, blogging about Islamic fashion is an overwhelmingly female field.

The first blogs about fashionable styles of Islamic dress started in 2007; thereafter their number has rapidly increased. The three most visited and linked into blogs are *Style Covered*, *Hijab Trendz* and *Hijab Style*, while other popular blogs include *We Love Hijab* (formerly *Precious Modesty*), *Stylish Muslimah*, *The Hijab Blog* and *CaribMuslimah*, with *Fiminin* (based in Indonesia) as an upcoming blog.

Style Covered, with by far the largest number of sites linking in (876), and a huge number of Facebook page likes (66,603) as another indication of its popularity, is a prime example of a blog that very much centres on the personality of the blogger and at the same time also has a commercial function.[13] This blog was started in February 2009 by Hana Tajima-Simpson, a designer from a mixed Japanese-English background, who converted to Islam about six years ago. Looking for the right balance in clothing, she states that she never wanted

> ... to lose sight of my own personal style and self expression. The secret to it all is simple, if elusive ... feel comfortable. So this blog has become an outpouring of my inspirations, style, and general musings, it may be something, it may be nothing ... a little bit like fashion.

This blog has both a strong, at times unconventional, visual presence of Hana and a focus on the higher and more experimental end of fashion, with designers, such as Haider Ackerman and Alexander McQueen, present as a source of inspiration for those wearing covered styles of dress. She makes good use of the interactivity of the internet, inviting 'all you stylish sisters out there to send in your photos, tips, and general sources of inspiration'. Some of these are then published on the 'Send Tips and Pics' page. The blog has its own YouTube channel (*stylecoveredvideo*), with two of her 'how to wear' videos registering very large numbers of views.[14] Once her blog was established, she used it to start her own fashion line at maysaa.com, an online store that was opened in 2010. More than half of the visitors to her blog are from Malaysia and Indonesia (each in roughly similar numbers), and she herself has developed a strong link with Malaysia.

The two next most popular hijab blogs both were started earlier. Miriam Sobh began *Hijab Trendz*, which uses the catch phrase 'the original hijab fashion, beauty and entertainment blog for Muslim women', in April 2007 when she was on maternity leave.[15] She presents herself as a professional (an experienced broadcast journalist in Illinois and Chicago and the founder of the Association of Muslim Women Artists) and a long-time wearer of hijab. Whereas her blog provides ample information about herself, especially through the 'in the press' button, it is first and foremost a very extensive entertainment and lifestyle blog; content includes a 'hijabme' dressing game, 'how to wear' videos, a very long list of hijab-friendly shopping sites, podcasts and a forum. Her entries provide information about where to find good hijab-friendly attire in mainstream stores, how to recognise the webstores that have interesting offers, and engages with the question of how to put together a suitable outfit.

The *Hijab Style* blog presents itself as 'The UK's first style guide for Muslim women'.[16] This blog was started in 2007 by Jana Kossaibati, a student of Lebanese background, born and raised in the UK, who has been wearing hijab for many years. She describes her aims as follows:

> I created this blog with the intention of providing an indispensable resource for style-conscious Muslimahs in the UK. I will post links and pictures of modest clothes, where to buy them, and how to wear them. I also hope to explore the world of international hijab fashion, and showcase designers and trends.[17]

Her blog focuses less on her person than the two websites mentioned above; no picture is provided. Instead, she focuses on items of dress and styling, evaluating new brands and collections, and presenting ideas about how to mix and match. She also provides extensive information about new designers and stores, with a strong global take. She not only includes upcoming designers from South-East Asia and the Gulf, but also has, for instance, an entry on traditional Korean dress (*hanbok*) that 'lends itself well to modest dressing', with photos of a fashion show held in Seoul (see Figure 1).[18]

Islamic fashion blogs as a genre not only cover styles of dress that originate from the Muslim majority world, such as abayas, or that are similar to those styles, but also provide information about how to put together an outfit by combining items of dress not specifically marketed for Muslimahs. A good example of the latter is *Carib Muslimah*, a blog that makes use of Polyvore, a programme that allows the creation of different sets of virtual outfits (including scarves, shoes, bags and accessories) from different stores

1 *Hanbok*
featured on *Hijab*
Style blog, posted
3 November
2011, screenshot.
Accessed 19
November 2011.

to which a direct link is provided.[19] Such blogs resonate strongly with the
sartorial practices of young Muslim women who shop at chains such as
H&M, where they produce 'Islamic outfits' by combining mainstream items
to turn their outfit into a more covered style of dress.

As mentioned above, a comparison of the screengrabs in 2006 and
2011 indicated a partial shift from webstores to YouTube videos and blogs.
The shift towards more sophisticated and interactive online technologies
has engendered strong connectivities between webstores, videos, blogs,
Facebook pages and other forms of social networking. This has not only
brought about a tremendously increased density of the online presence of
Islamic fashion, but also a professionalisation and commercialisation of
formats that had often started as small individual endeavours. Moreover,
locational shifts have also become visible. Next to the Anglo-Saxon world
and the Middle East, the Gulf area and especially South-East Asia have also
gained a more prominent online presence.

PRODUCING A PUBLIC: MODESTY, FASHION AND ISLAM

What work do these various formats of online presence do? I do not consider the diverse ways in which Islamic dress and fashion are presented as merely expressing the convictions or tastes of the producers and the publics they address. Rather, I take these formats to be performative, engaged in the work of fashioning particular publics that are not discrete, bounded entities, but rather always emerging and in the making. Focusing on the blogs, videos and webstores that have attracted the largest publics, I investigate how these popular online formats engage with the Islam–fashion nexus and how they authorise their positions.

Dis/claiming authority: blogs and videos

As Jana Kossaibati, the *Hijab Style* blogger, reminds us, blogging about Islamic fashion is not quite the same as mainstream fashion blogging. It is never only about aesthetics and style. In her words:

> ... the types of fashion I explore focus on modesty and creative ways of achieving the coverage that is required for hijab, rather than from a purely aesthetic perspective. In relation to that, unlike regular fashion blogs, mine is not about the way I personally like to dress; it's not just about my style choices, but those that I share with the larger, worldwide community of Muslim women.[20]

Because of such a connection with the broader Muslim community, many bloggers feel the need to engage with and work through the relation between Islam and fashion. Whereas a wide variety of positions on this issue is present online, the more popular blogs tend to avoid taking a strongly normative stance on how to combine Islam and fashion. Rather than discussing whether and how 'Islamic fashion' is legitimate within an Islamic tradition, they present it as more or less self-evident and, by doing so, contribute to its normalisation.

Still, there are moments when a sense of unease emerges, such as when blogs and videos include 'disclaimers' (a term some producers themselves employ). *Hijab Trendz*, for instance, explicitly states in its disclaimer that 'Hijabtrendz is not a religious or political website, nor does it seek to promote any such causes. This site is merely for informational and entertainment purposes.'[21] It is, indeed, evident that many hijab fashion blogs are very much part of the world of Islamic entertainment, which also includes other

formats such as festivals, contests and concerts. The producers in this field
do not claim a position of authority in the field of Islam; rather, they do so as
professionals working in the world of entertainment and fashion. Yet, even
if bloggers themselves use such secular forms of authorisation, claiming
expertise in the field of fashion rather than in that of Islam, these forms of
entertainment are recognisably Islamic. As such, they may evoke responses
from those disagreeing with the aesthetic forms presented.

Other bloggers distance themselves more explicitly from claims to
Islamic knowledge and try to stay away from the often heated discussions
about the correct form of hijab that posts on these blogs engender. Take, for
instance, the Hijabi Style blog, where, under the heading 'Disclaimer: "Hijab
Fashion" Posts and Unkind Comments', this blogger writes:

> This site posts many fashion styles that are for Mahram/Ladies-only
> events. Please don't assume that everything posted meets the conditions
> for hijab, as some of it does not. We do our best to *asterisk* styles
> that do not pass the 'demure test' but it is your responsibility to ensure
> that what you wear meets the conditions for hijab in public. We are
> just posting ideas that we find beautiful or interesting. Allah(swt) knows
> best.[22]

Rather than taking up a position of religious authority, or at most pointing out
that the styles shown are not suitable for settings where men may be present
for whom women need to cover, this blogger places the responsibility for
choice of dress firmly on the shoulders of individual members of the public.
In this way, she attempts to pre-empt unkind comments on her posts and to
circumvent a debate on the nature and force of Islamic dressing rules.

Producers of YouTube videos, where comments can be extremely rude
and offensive, are also acutely aware of the controversies their videos may
cause. In the text accompanying the highly popular ♥*.~.*The Hijab*.~.*♥
video, the producer explains, in anticipation of hostile comments and in
order to legitimise the pictures in the videoclip, that this video has no
religious claims about true hijab: 'It is not a video that shows the true
essence of Hijab … It is not a religious video based on religious opinions
but a video made up of a compilation of different pictures of how some of
the Muslim women exist today.' After adding a note stating that 'NO hateful
comments will be allowed so don't bother posting them in the first place,'
he explains that most of the pictures used in the video are of models rather
than of Muslim women wearing hijab in order to show girls that they are

'just as beautiful' if they wear the headscarf, and ends with the argument that some styles may not be 'deemed as fulfilling the proper requirements of Hijab' but that they may be worn at all-female gatherings.[23]

Other blogs are less hesitant in actively engaging with the relation of dress and religion. This is, for instance, the case with *We Love Hijab* (previously *Precious Modesty*), also one of the more popular ones. Preferring to remain anonymous, this blogger started her first post with 'Asalamualaykum! Welcome to Precious Modesty!', and highlighted her Muslim identity when she introduced herself:

> I am a 24 year old Muslimah. I wear hijab and as you know, it can be hard to find modest clothes. Some shops offer 'modest clothing' online, but the clothes aren't modest enough for a Muslimah. What's so modest about something long and skin-tight?

This blogger at times engages in discussion about the normative evaluation of particular styles of dress. A post titled 'Hot topic: Camel hump hijab style?' starts with an embedded video of the renowned Dubai designer Rabia Z. showing how to tie a hijab very high in the back, with the blogger asking 'Is the hijab style in this video haram? What do you think?' Discussing the style, she then refers to a *hadith* that considers 'scantily dressed women, the hair on the top of their heads like a camel's hump' as cursed. Recognising that there may be different interpretations of this *hadith* she then states, 'Personally, I am a "to each her own" type of person. I feel that we should be judged by our intentions and since God is the only One who knows our intentions, He should be the only One who judges us.' In yet another turn, this is followed by an invitation to comment, which also brings in aesthetics: 'That being said: What are your thoughts on this hijab style and the trend of wearing things under your hijab to make it look really big? Do you even like the way this looks or do you think it looks strange?'[24]

If the most popular bloggers and video producers generally refrain from strongly normative statements, there are also those who follow a different approach and firmly distinguish between what is and what is not legitimate hijab. These videos are, however, far less popular and attract a much smaller number of viewers. One exception to this is the popular *This is not hijab* video, produced by and featuring Baba Ali (Ali Ardekani), an Iranian-American who grew up in a secular family but became a committed Muslim when he was 20 years old.[25] In this video he criticises various styles of covering – such as the short-sleeve hijab, the skin-tight hijab, or the transparent hijab – that 'are not hijab'. In an upbeat style reminiscent of that of Amr Khaled and Moez Masoud, and in sharp contrast to the serious ways in which traditional religious scholars present Islamic arguments (Moll 2010), he addresses the public in a highly informal way and uses humour as a means to persuade viewers of the requirements of true hijab. In other words, also in the field of strongly normative videos, those using an entertainment format are the more popular ones.

Foregrounding modesty

If some popular blogs and videos foreground entertainment and proclaim their expertise in the field of fashion and its aesthetics rather than in that of Islam, webstores regularly employ the term modesty rather than Islam in their catchphrases, which range from 'Modesty on the outside, beauty in the inside' (Lamis Online) to 'The art of modesty and style' (Rayannes Design – see Figure 2), and 'Modest clothing turning heads for the best of reasons' (Taqwa Iman on Facebook).[26] Usually, however, such stores would simultaneously underline their Islamic character by other textual and visual means, such as through the name they have chosen, the explanation they provide about themselves, references to the Islamic calendar, links to other Islamic products such as music and books, or the causes they support, like Islamic Relief. Visual imagery varies from the use of calligraphy and Arabic writing to the styles of presenting their produce (such as by avoiding the depiction of the full human body).

Primo Moda, based in the USA, is a good example of a webstore that is immediately recognisable as an Islamic fashion webstore through the styles of dress it presents, but does not use the term Islam to position itself. Instead, it defines its mission as 'to help trendy women of all ages dress modestly'. In the 'about' section, the owner employs catchphrases, such as 'Primo Moda, where fashions are hip, clothes come to life, colors are vibrant, and styles speak volumes' or 'Primo Moda, for today's woman, where modesty, style, beauty and individuality come together'.[27] Rather than Islam, fashion and modesty are the key terms. Moreover, some emerging webstores do not even use the term 'modesty'. Hana Tajima-Simpson, the designer for the Maysaa webstore, presents Maysaa as 'This groundbreaking online label brings you high fashion at high street prices,' and as pioneering 'not only in fashion but in social responsibility'; neither Islam nor modesty are mentioned, and whereas a prominent item sold is the snood (a tubular form of headcovering), other items are not presented in a way that evokes wearing hijab.[28]

2 Rayannes Design e-retail webpage, screenshot. Accessed 19 November 2011.

Other webstores employ the notion of modesty to extend their reach beyond the Muslim public.[29] From its inception in 2004, the owners of Artizara tried to use modesty as a concept to bridge religious differences. Under 'Our story' they present their motivation to found Artizara as 'to fulfill the Islamic clothing needs of socially conscious women who desire to dress stylishly yet modestly', and to bring 'to the mainstream marketplace Islamic women's clothing blending Islamic Art and World Style'. Underlining the fact that they targeted 'not only Muslims but women of all faiths, who have an interest in modest clothing or world style', they point out:

> Like our vision, our clientele encompasses people of all faiths and backgrounds. Artizara modest women's clothing is Christian clothing, LDS [Latter-day Saints] clothing, Jewish clothing, Islamic clothing and World Style Clothing. Just as modesty is a value that has no boundaries, the World Wide Web is a market that has no boundaries.

Not surprisingly, from early on Artizara linked in to the Modest Clothing Directory.

One of the most popular webstores, Shukr, uses a different approach and grounds its presence firmly in an Islamic tradition (see Figure 3). As the owner states, 'SHUKR was the first to introduce contemporary styled Islamic and modest clothing for a new generation. Our motto is: Put Faith in Fashion.™'[30] Explaining its vision, Islam is strongly foregrounded. This is evident when the choice of name is explained:

> SHUKR is an Arabic word found in the Qur'an which means gratitude or thanks. God mentions in the Qur'an: "If you give thanks (shukr), I shall certainly increase you" (Qur'an 14:7). The company SHUKR was named as a means of reminding ourselves and others of this important Qur'anic word and principle.[31]

Moreover, Shukr also states that it aspires to be 'a model Islamic business, by applying sacred Islamic values to a contemporary, multinational company', following 'fair trade and ethical labour practices' and by applying 'Islamic financial and investment principles, avoiding interest-based financing', while there is also an extensive explanation of the value of 'The Prophet Muhammad's Sandal'. Its commitment to Islam is further highlighted in how the relation between women's dress, modesty and Islam is discussed. To the question 'Some of your women's clothing is not modest enough. Why is that?' (with over 6,000 views), Shukr answers:

> We would like to let you know that SHUKR is attempting to provide modest, Shariah-conforming clothing appropriate for Muslims living in the West. This is a new enterprise and there are no universally accepted 'Islamic' or even sizing standards for such clothing. We are trying our best to work with Muslims living in the West, to find standards that are acceptable from a Shariah perspective whilst meeting the aesthetic needs of our customers. We have consulted a number of scholars and they have generally approved of the clothing. When they have had reservations about some of our items or photos, we have tried to rectify it.[32]

Webstores, then, employ the concept of modesty in different, sometimes ambiguous, ways. It may be used instead of references to Islam (Primo Moda) or as a means to connect between different religions (Artizara). Modesty may also be employed in relation to an explicitly Islamic framework (Shukr). Yet even if Shukr is one of the few popular webstores that explicitly refers to the sharia, it also brings aesthetics into the discussion.

3 Shukr e-retail webpages, composite screenshot. Accessed 19 November 2011.

Localising webstores

Webstores, blogs and other forms of online presence may be accessed worldwide, but the deterritorialisation of webstores should not be overstated. As international shipping fees often make up a substantial part of the costs of buying online, locality matters. Hence, an increasing number of webstores, such as Shukr or Islamic Design House, have different sites for different locations.

Locality also matters in how webstores engage with Islam, modesty and fashion. Many of them are based in the Anglo-Saxon world and partake in discussions about what kinds of Islamic outfits are suitable in such settings. One issue raised is the need to adapt to one's environment. Artizara, a webstore hosted in California, strongly supports this. Stating that 'There is no single form of clothing that can be referred to as Islamic clothing,' the owners allow for a wide variety of styles. Whereas under 'Islamic Clothing Guidelines' they refer to Qur'anic instructions, they also recognise that head coverings were not worn in all medieval Muslim societies. In short, they argue, 'We believe that with the unique way a Muslim woman dresses, she can assert her individuality while at the same time assimilating beautifully into whatever world culture or community she is a part of.'[33]

Shukr also provides extensive advice about Islamic styles of dress for Muslims living in the UK. After pointing out that Shukr has clothes for most occasions and preferences, it continues:

> However, as Muslims living in the West, much as we would like to express our Islamic identity, we have to take into account the way our dress will be interpreted and received by those around us – people at college, work, in the street, or even our families!
>
> … SHUKR's philosophy is one of being proud of our Muslim identity and being recognized as Muslims. This doesn't mean that we all have to get out our galabiyya's and jilbabs and refuse to wear anything else … Our ultimate aim is to create a line of clothing which is truly reflective of, and relevant to, the needs of Western Muslims. So our general advice is: be strong and proud that you are a Muslim, but have wisdom in what clothing you choose to wear out in public.[34]

Rather than only producing or importing Islamic garments that are copies of traditional styles of dress from Muslim majority countries, Shukr attempts to develop fashionable styles of Islamic dress that also match Western aesthetics, while simultaneously foregrounding its Islamic message.

This may be contrasted with a trend amongst emerging webstores in the Middle East and especially the Gulf area that sell fashionable abayas. As the abaya is considered a quintessentially Islamic garment, these webstores do not need to highlight the Islamic nature of this style of dress, as this is self-evident. Instead, they focus their efforts on how to turn the abaya into a highly fashionable garment. A host of designer websites and webstores have begun to promote such upscale abayas, which are also displayed offline at events such as the Islamic Fashion Festival or the Dubai Fashion Week. Some designers of 'fashion abayas' do not use terms such as modesty or Islam at all, while others include these in a narrative that is first and foremost about fashion. The website-cum-webstore started by Rabia Z., who studied fashion design in the USA

Welcome to Rabia Z.'s world of Fashion, where modesty is always in style...

4 Rabia Z. e-retail webpage, screenshot. Accessed 19 November 2011.

and lives in Dubai, is an interesting example of the latter. When one opens her homepage, the first words that meet the eye are 'Welcome to Rabia Z.'s world of Fashion, where modesty is always in style' (see Figure 4). Her long 'About' section also focuses extensively on her career as a fashion designer. Still, Islam is referred to when she describes how she started her career.

> Living in the USA during the tragic 9/11 events made Rabia realize the challenges faced by moderate Muslimas in their current global situation. Commencing her career in a moderate manner, Rabia Z. had a clear mandate – to design attire for women that were modest but modern – this was a service which she commenced through her online site in 2007.[35]

For fashion abaya designers in the Gulf area, Islam functions as the taken-for-granted context, just as the abaya is considered the Islamic style of dress

par excellence. Rabia Z.'s style of presentation affirms how particular aspects
are highlighted with respect to local contexts. Whereas her site generally
highlights fashion, in the context of references to the attacks of 9/11 Islam
comes in, attenuated by modifiers such as moderate and modern.

CONCLUSION

When Dana Becker started her Modest Clothing Directory in 1998, Islamic
fashion webstores were already prominently present as part of the broader
field of modest attire. In the 14 years since, both Islamic fashion offline
and internet technologies have seen major developments. Islamic fashion
has been a growth market, not only in the Middle East but also elsewhere
in the Muslim majority world, especially in South-East Asia, as well as in
Europe and other locations where Muslims are a minority. The growth of
internet connectivity has not only enhanced such a global presence, but
transformations in internet technologies, especially the development of Web
2.0, have engendered new interactive formats such as weblogs, YouTube
videos, Facebook and other forms of social media. The net effect of these
transformations has been that a densely intertwined and interactive web
of Islamic fashion online has emerged, which has become increasingly
commodified and professionalised.

   In the field of Islam online, some have argued that the internet has
enabled a fragmentation of religious authority, while others have pointed
out that especially the more militant or strictly-orthodox strands of Islam
are prominently present, with the Islamic culture industry, in contrast,
presenting 'the friendly face' of Islam online. Whereas there are websites
whose main didactical concern is how to distinguish between those styles
of dress that are Islamically permissible (halal) and prohibited (haram),
these do not draw the largest publics. Most Islamic fashion webstores – at
least those with a greater popularity – refrain from taking such a strong
stance, and this is the more so in the case of YouTube videos and blogs.
The webstores, already present before the turn of the millennium, tend
to foreground the term 'modesty' to present themselves to the public,
enabling the recognition of commonalities with other religions that value
modesty as a virtue, as well as with non-religious forms of modesty. In
other words, rather than considering modesty as a particularistic Islamic
value, they underline its universalism, in a way similar to Dana Becker's
Modest Clothing Directory.

The blogs and the videos, as newer online formats, also employ other techniques to bring together Islam and fashion. The most popular ones actively disclaim a position of Islamic authority, refrain from making statements about what is and what is not 'true hijab' and leave the responsibility for what to wear up to the individual viewer. Simultaneously, they highlight their expertise in the field of fashion and style, and use a language of pedagogy to educate their audiences about how to develop a harmonious and fashionable outfit. Such a focus on aesthetics – together with a presentation of Islam as a religion of peace and moderation – may be seen as a response to the framing of Islam as overtly strict, militant and oppressive to women. This does not, however, mean that these forms of Islamic fashion online cannot simultaneously be part of an ethical project. Employing a strongly aesthetic vocabulary, they actively participate in spreading the message of the beauty of hijab and hence of Islam. More generally, webstores, blogs and videos both present Islamic virtues, such as modesty, in a universalistic manner (and use them as a bridging concept), and authorise secular ethical projects such as fair trade as part of an Islamic tradition.

ACKNOWLEDGEMENTS

This work is part of the research programme Cultural Dynamics, which is financed by the Netherlands Organisation for Scientific Research (NWO).

NOTES

1   www.modestclothes.com. All websites referred to in this chapter were last accessed on 19 November 2011, unless mentioned otherwise.
2   www.heraldextra.com/lifestyles/modest-clothing-for-those-who-want-to-grin-but-not/article_a6f1c7c6-4238-5179-8846-8585bc3da096.html.
3   See de Certeau (1984: 29ff.) about 'making do' and bricolage, as referring to how people use cultural products for their own aims.
4   The oldest webstores I could find are Al-Hediya (Kuwait, 1997) and Al-Muhajabat (USA, 1997; in 2011 transformed into Hijab Jewels).
5   At least 27 of the webstores on the list presented in Akou (2007) still function, and Becker presents a long list of stores that are longer than five years online.
6   Using Alexa ratings (www.alexa.com), all of these are ranked under 1 million and have at least 100 sites linking in. They are presented here in order of popularity with Shukr as the most popular. All were started in the UK or the USA, except for Jelbab (Jordan) and Islamic Boutique (Egypt). Other webstores mentioned in this

article that also have an under 1 million rating but that have far fewer sites linking in are Pearl-Daisy and Rabia Z.

7 http://youtu.be/3xxAhtkcoEQ.
8 http://www.youtube.com/user/0arabxxrose0?feature=watch.
9 http://youtu.be/A8Eojhz1gdE. Pearl-daisy is also under the 1 million threshold (679,463), but has only 35 sites linking in, probably because this webstore was only started in 2010.
10 http://www.youtube.com/user/Amenakin/videos.
11 http://youtube/NpnPd1NA6D4.
12 http://www.youtube.com/user/lagodaxnian.
13 http://www.stylecovered.com/.
14 ALL IN LIGHT a tutorial registered 313,250 views, and How to wear a Headscarf-StyleCovered Hijab Tutorial: Pashmina Style 761,913 views. This places them amongst the highest ranking hijab videos.
15 http://www.hijabtrendz.com/. Hijab Trendz ranked 262,915, has 167 sites linking in, and 9,743 likes on Facebook.
16 http://www.hijabstyle.co.uk/. Hijab Style is ranked 409,836, has 199 sites linking in, and 72,321 likes on Facebook.
17 http://www.hijabstyle.co.uk/p/about.html.
18 http://www.hijabstyle.co.uk/2011/11/abaya-inspiration-hanbok.html.
19 http://caribmuslimah.wordpress.com/.
20 www.taqwaiman.com/Articles.asp?ID=146 (site offline at time of writing).
21 www.hijabtrendz.com/disclaimer/.
22 hijabistyle.blogspot.com/p/hijab-tutorials.html.
23 http://youtu.be/3xxAhtkcoEQ.
24 http://welovehijab.com/2011/02/18/camel-hump-hijab-style-video/.
25 www.youtube.com/watch?v=F4jQi0Gjy3M. This video has 650,568 views, which is still considerably less than the ♥*.~.*The Hijab*.~.*♥ video clip. Baba Ali is an IT professional and co-owner of UmmahFilms, which produces web series. This video is part of its 'The reminder' web series. See also Akou (2010).
26 www.lamisonline.com. Accessed 6 January 2007; http://rayannesdesign.com.au; http://en-gb.facebook.com/pages/TAQWA-IMAN-Inc/135478153672?sk=info&filter=12.
27 www.primomoda.com/clothing-store/pages.php?pageid=2. See also Tarlo (2010) for more on this webstore.
28 http://www.maysaa.com/about-maysaa.
29 For the quotations below, the Artizara website was accessed on 20 May 2007. The present-day site presents similar points of view, but does so less extensively.
30 www.shukronline.com/. This website also provides information about the background of its owner, Anas Silkwood. See Tarlo (2010).
31 www.shukronline.com/about.html. This is the USA version of the webstore. The UK version has a far more elaborate Islamic explanation of the name.
32 http://support.shukrattire.com/index.php?_m=knowledgebase&_a=viewarticle&kbarticleid=53.
33 See note 28.
34 www.shukr.co.uk/advice.aspx.
35 www.rabiaz.com/about.

REFERENCES

Abaza, Mona (2007). 'Shifting Landscapes of Fashion in Contemporary Egypt'. *Fashion Theory*, 11, 2/3: 281–99.

Akou, Heather (2007). 'Building a New "World Fashion": Islamic Dress in the Twenty-first Century'. *Fashion Theory*, 11, 4: 403–21.

—— (2010). 'Interpreting Islam Through the Internet: Making Sense of Hijab'. *Contemporary Islam*, 4:3: 331–46.

Amrullah, Eva (2008). 'Indonesian Muslim Fashion. Styles and Designs'. *ISIM Review*, 22: 22–23.

Brenner, Suzanne (1996). 'Reconstructing Self and Society: Javanese Muslim Women and "The Veil"'. *American Ethnologist*, 23:4: 673–97.

De Certeau, Michel (1984). *The Practice of Everyday Life*. Berkeley, CA: University of California Press.

Eickelman, Dale and Anderson, Jon (1999). *New Media in the Muslim World. The Emerging Public Sphere*. Bloomington, IN: Indiana University Press.

Fellow, Jill (2005). 'Modest clothing …: For Those Who Want To Grin, But Not Bare It'. *Daily Herald*, 10 July.

El-Guindi, Fadwa (1999). *Veil. Modesty, Privacy and Resistance*. London: Berg Publishers.

Gökarıksel, Banu and McLarney, Ellen (2010). 'Introduction: Muslim Women, Consumer Capitalism, and the Islamic Culture Industry'. *Journal of Middle East Women's Studies*, 6:3: 1–18.

Göle, Nilüfer (1996). *The Forbidden Modern: Civilization and Veiling*, Ann Arbor, MI: University of Michigan Press.

Kılıçbay, B. and Binark, M. (2002). 'Consumer Culture, Islam and the Politics of Lifestyle: Fashion for Veiling in Contemporary Turkey'. *European Journal of Communication*, 17:4: 495–511.

Kossaibati, Jana (2009) 'It's a Wrap'. *Guardian*, 30 March.

Lewis, Reina (2010). 'Marketing Muslim Lifestyle: A New Media Genre'. *Journal of Middle East Women's Studies*, 6:3: 58–90.

Lindholm, Christina (2010). 'Invisible No More: The Embellished Abaya in Qatar'. *Textile Society of America Symposium Proceedings*, p. 34. http://digitalcommons.unl.edu/cgi/viewcontent.cgi?article=1033&context=tsaconf.

MacLeod, Arlene (1992). 'Hegemonic Relations and Gender Resistence. The New Veiling as Accomodating Protest in Cairo'. *Signs*, 17:3: 533–57.

Mahmood, Saba (2005). *The Politics of Piety. The Islamic Revival and the Feminist Subject*. Princeton, NJ: Princeton University Press.

Moll, Yasmin (2010). 'Islamic Televangelism: Religion, Media and Visuality in Contemporary Egypt'. *Arab Media and Society*, 10. http://www.arabmediasociety.com/articles/downloads/20100407165913_Mollpdf.pdf.

Moors, Annelies (2007). 'Fashionable Muslims: Notions of Self, Religion and Society in San'a'. *Fashion Theory*, 11, 2/3: 319–47.

—— (2009). '"Islamic Fashion" in Europe: Religious Conviction, Aesthetic Style, and Creative Consumption'. *Encounters*, 1:1: 175–201.

Moors, Annelies and Tarlo, Emma (2007). 'Introduction'. *Fashion Theory*, 11, 2/3: 133–43.

Navaro-Yashin, Yael (2002). 'The Market for Identities: Secularism, Islamism, Commodities', in Deniz Kandiyoti and Ayse Saktanber (eds), *Fragments of Culture. The Everyday of Modern Turkey*. New Brunswick: Rutgers University Press, pp. 221–54.

Osella, Caroline and Osella, Filippe (2007). 'Muslim Style in South-India'. *Fashion Theory*, 11, 2/3: 233–52.

Al-Qasimi, Noor (2010). 'Immodest Modesty: Accommodating Dissent and the "Abaya-as-Fashion" in the Arab Gulf States'. *Journal of Middle East Women's Studies*, 6:1: 46–74.

Sandıkçı, Özlem and Ger, Güliz (2005). 'Aesthetics, Ethics and the Politics of the Turkish Headscarf', in Suzanne Kuechler and Daniel Miller (eds), *Clothing as Material Culture*. London: Berg.

———(2007). 'Constructing and Representing the Islamic Consumer in Turkey'. *Fashion Theory*, 11, 2/3: 189–211.

———(2010). 'Veiling in Style: How Does a Stigmatized Practice Become Fashionable'. *Journal of Consumer Research*, 37: 15–36.

Tarlo, Emma (2010). *Visibly Muslim*. London: Berg Publishers.

Turner, Bryan S. (2007). 'Religious Authority and the New Media'. *Theory, Culture and Society*, 24:2: 117–34.

2

FASHION FORWARD AND FAITH-TASTIC!
Online Modest Fashion and the Development of Women as Religious Interpreters and Intermediaries

Reina Lewis

The rise in religiosity among predominantly, but not only, young people around the world has been demonstrated spectacularly in the development of new styles of modest fashion as women in growing numbers use dress to express on a daily basis their religious identity or commitment. This has been especially prominent in (but not exclusive to) Judaism, Islam and Christianity, the three Abrahamic faiths with which this chapter is concerned. The internet has been indispensible to the advancement of both commerce and commentary concerned with modest fashion: women are now served by a growing e-retail sector selling clothing designed to aid modish modesty and advised by an ever-expanding range of modest style blogs. They can also take part in discussions on a variety of platforms, ranging from the fast-paced circulation of images and ideas on social media like Facebook and Twitter to the longer-running, in-depth, debates hosted on internet discussion fora (see Chapters 3 and 6). The deterritorialised nature of online sales and communication uniquely fosters the creation of new communities of modest dressers from different faith and secular backgrounds (including women from other and 'alternative' religions). There is also significant participation as consumers and discussants by women who are not engaged with faith, or who do not see it as the prime motivator for their modest self-presentation.

In this chapter I set out some of the key issues facing early initiators in the online modest sector in the 2000s and 2010s, looking at brands and blogs from each of the three faiths. To do this I am drawing on findings from the Modest Dressing project that studied English-language online activity from the UK, Canada and the United States.[1] Whilst it is the internet and related information communication technologies (ICT) that have made possible the emergence of modest fashion as niche commerce and commentary, the encounter with new ICTs has raised challenges as well as opportunities. This chapter addresses and brings together two elements of this complex relationship; one ostensibly connected to fashion, the other to faith. First, I explore the extent to which dilemmas raised by ICT for the modest sector are distinct from those generically experienced in the global fashion industry. Second, I use the largely women-led field of online modest fashion to insert a gender analysis into the often masculinist consideration of new forms of religious interpretation and authority enabled by online media. The blurring of the distinction between the independent and the commercial, now commonplace in mainstream fashion blogs, is shown to be especially significant, with modest fashion online rendering porous (and therefore requiring new ways to arbitrate) not only the divisions between the commercial and the non-commercial but also the boundaries between faiths and between faith and secularity.

THE INTERNET AND THE SPREAD
OF MODEST DESIGNS AND DEBATES

The internet is not neutral and is not used and experienced by everyone in the same way (and is unevenly available to the world population). Whilst the technologies of the internet may be new, like all media forms they do not arise without history: just as fashion blogs need to be seen in relation to their print antecedents in magazines and newspapers (Rocamora 2012), for faith-based user groups digital communication technologies need to be seen in relation to existing models for the development and transmission of religious knowledge. Early research into religion and the internet often focused on the distinction between *religion online* (understood usually to mean information about offline religion shared through online communication) and *online religion* (new religions developing and existing solely online, plus online-only material from offline religions; Karaflogka 2007, Brasher 2001). As time has gone on, it is possible to draw attention to the mutability of and overlap between religion online and online religion (Bunt 2009). Discourses about modest dress online and practices of modest dressing offline are similarly mutable. Arising primarily from existing offline religions, women's practices of and discussions about modesty are made possible, and sometimes called into being, by new modes of online merchandising and commentary.

Whilst offline shops, and to some extent home selling or mail order, had been meeting the needs of some consumers, this often depended on living in or near an area of religious or related ethnic demographic density. Though widely available, mainstream fashion retail appeared to have no interest in targeting modest dressers (unlike the now widespread provision of 'ethnic/religious' foods in supermarket chains). Into these gaps, rose the new online modest market and a new cohort of modest style mediators. Often themselves a member of (or parent to) this youthful modest style demographic, women dominate the field as designers, entrepreneurs and opinion-makers, more likely these days to perceive consumer culture as one of the means by which religious (and related ethnic; Comaroff and Comaroff 2009) identities can be achieved and expressed than to see consumption and religion as oppositional.

The development of e-commerce has been one of the essential conditions for the emergence of the rapidly expanding niche market recognisable today. As for any specialist market, e-retail allows companies to reach more consumers more cheaply, across more geographical territories. For the modest fashion sector, e-retail also has the potential to reach consumers outside the faith groups from which brands originate.

In the UK it has been Muslim brands that have led the way in the development of the niche market in modest clothing, online and offline. In the US and Canada, Jewish and Christian faith groups with dress requirements show similar developments in the commercial production and distribution of clothing. This is seen especially but not exclusively among ultra-orthodox and modern orthodox Jews, and some Christian groups like Mormons (the Church of Jesus Christ of Latter-day Saints, LDS). Whilst all three religions share a concern with which parts of the body should be revealed to which people and in which spaces, there is no consensus between faiths on modesty policy and there is considerable debate within each faith about if and how modesty should be expressed.

Saba Mahmood (2005), in her study of Islamic revivalist women in Cairo in the 1970s, describes how for many women the initial and repeated experience of dressing in hijab is fundamental to the construction of the pious self. It is not that the subject is faithful a priori to donning the clothing, which might then merely clad the physical self. Rather, it is through the act of wearing, being seen in and comporting appropriately the veiled body that the pious disposition is cultivated and exercised. As well as this particular cohort, women may dress modestly for all sorts of reasons (making a political statement, avoiding unwelcome male attention, accommodating community norms, gaining social mobility or status), but the types of clothes they use and how they are worn on the body is rarely insignificant. Neither are women's dress decisions arrived at in a vacuum: the historically specific ways in which women's forms of modest dress are enabled and constrained by social, cultural and economic contexts includes the range and availability of garments from which women can choose.

Whilst, for example, earlier generations of Islamist women in Egypt had to sew their own clothes because none were commercially available (El-Guindi 1999), contemporary modest dressers from Muslim and other faith groups are able to render the body modest through its appropriate comportment in apparel that derives from within the fashion system. Providing these items is the mission of many of the companies researched by the Modest Dressing project. Made possible by the advent of cheaper home internet connections and broadband, not only can women now find products designed with modesty in mind, but can also consult style guides and join in fashion discussions about how to style modesty just like their 'secular' counterparts. It is not, therefore, only the processes by which the modest appearance is achieved that can be in and of themselves spiritually, socially, politically and personally significant, but also the ways in which they are represented, disseminated and discussed. The medium of the internet has created opportunities for women not (or not directly) involved in commerce to publicise their ideas about modest dressing. The new modes of fashion mediation that result become a form of religious interpretation that fosters women's voices and perspectives.

The markets for modest clothing aimed at, and produced by, particular faith groups have expanded and segmented, facilitating access to modest fashion and stimulating interest in it. A new category of 'modest fashion' has emerged and become legitimised over the internet, operating through a mix of commerce and commentary that connects faith groups with each other and with the 'secular' world. It functions simultaneously as a taste making mechanism, an ideological category and a marketing device.

With nearly all the first generation of modest online retailers originating from a faith community, the desire to support modest dressing and

COTTON HIJABS
CHECKED
EMBROIDERED
EASY-WEAR HIJABS
NARROW BAND
PALESTINIAN SCARF
PARTY WEAR
REPEAT PATTERN
SPORTING RANGE
SQUARE HIJABS
SNEEL BORDER
SMART
SUMMER HIJABS
STRIPES
TASSEL FREE HIJABS
WILDLIFE
ACCESSORIES
LUXURY HIJAB PINS
BARGAIN HIJAB PINS
NEW HIJAB PINS
PINS
BROOCHES
NECLACES
BONNET CAPS
SPECIAL FEATURES
HOW TO WEAR
HINTS & TIPS
PIN DESIGNER
MIX & MATCH
PROHIJAB TV ADVERT
SEARCH BY COLOUR
BLACK/GREY
WHITE/SILVER
BLUE
RED
GREEN
YELLOW/ORANGE/GOLD
PURPLE
BROWN
PINK
INFORMATION
LOGIN
ABOUT US
HELP
FAQ

Making hijab part of Victoria Police uniform

Constable Maha Sukkar yesterday became the first Victoria Police officer to wear a traditional Muslim hijab as part of her uniform.

The 30-year-old former graphic designer was supported by her parents, who flew in from her native Beirut for her graduation ceremony, and friends from the Muslim community.

"At first we were worried by how people would respond but we really admired her courage and she has been an inspiration to us," said her best friend, Aiesha Hussain, at the ceremony.

The navy, lightweight hijab, specifically designed for Constable Sukkar, has Velcro to enable its release should she get caught in a physical scuffle...

www.TheHijabShop.com

http://www.theage.com.au/news/National/...

Jewish dad backs headscarf daughters

Laurent Levy is the father of two teenagers - Lila, 18, and Alma, 16 - who last week were barred from the Henri Wallon lycee in the northern Paris suburb of Aubervilliers.

He is a left-wing lawyer, highly articulate. And he is Jewish.

"Let us say I am Jewish by Vichy rules but not by the Talmud," he told me in a cafe in Montmartre where I met him with his daughters.

"Three of my grandparents were Jewish, but not the one that counts - my mother's mother."

"I have a historical identity as a Jew, but not a religious one. I am atheist."

Mr Levy has leapt with a passion to the defence of Lila and Alma - and of the right of all girls who wear the headscarf - to an education like everyone else....

http://newsvote.bbc.co.uk/1/hi/world/europe/3149588.stm

The headscarf reaches new heights

Wearing traditional Muslim clothes has not slowed an Indonesian woman's climb to the top of her sport. Matthew Moore reports from Jakarta.

When she chalks up to cheat gravity in

5 Hijab articles featured on The Hijab Shop e-retail website, screenshot. Accessed 20 April 2012.

related behaviours is broadly understood as part of a religious, social and community commitment. It is characteristic of the field that the distinction between the commercial and the confessional is flexible rather than fixed. Commercial websites include educational and inspirational material, glossaries of modest clothing and related practices, such as British online company hijabshop.com that hosts an extensive 'news' page using secular and Muslim providers to link to international hijab news and fashion stories (see Figure 5).[2] But entrepreneurs may have to be careful to avoid alienating potential consumers from outside (or from different elements within) their own community as online shopping brings them into contact with consumers using different modesty codes. Whilst all apparel companies need to distinguish their offering from that of their competitors, companies in the modest sector face a challenge of considerable delicacy in needing to advocate not only their style but also their version of modesty.

Some sites deliberately define modesty as multiple and fluid. Coming from the modern orthodox Jewish community, Gary Swickley at Kosher Casual (based in Israel, selling mainly in North America) is resolute in not trying to appease all sections of the wider Jewish community. He is keen to develop site infomatics and product ranges inclusive enough for potential consumers from all religious, spiritual and secular backgrounds: 'despite that our name is Kosher Casual, we really are trying to offer goods to pretty much everyone ... modesty has a lot of definitions and we applaud all of them ... and everyone draws the line where they want to draw the line and that's fine'.[3]

The relentless spread of social media and the blogosphere means that commercial websites are expanding their role in commentary as well as sales. Even in just over a decade it is possible to see two if not three generations of innovation, as what was once new becomes routinised: whilst posting educational information was fast established as a characteristic of the first generation of internet pioneers (Tarlo 2010), few hosted a blog. Now, even small modest fashion brands run a blog and use social media like Facebook (established 2004) and Twitter (2006) to drive traffic. More recent start-ups, like those discussed in my final section, are also likely to develop a blog prior to their launch, building brand awareness before products arrive. The small-scale modest fashion entrepreneur shares much with the marketing strategy of bigger companies. Whilst corporate bloggers remain just 1 per cent of the overall blogger population, the use of social media has become now so common in all (commercial and independent) blog sectors that 'the lines between blogs, micro-blogs, and social networks are disappearing' (Technorati 2010). As the need to maintain a presence on multiple digital platforms increases, more and more modest fashion companies are outsourcing elements of their digital communications to companies specialising in social media, sometimes from within the brand originator's faith community. Modest fashion brands replicate the marketing practices now common in the fashion and lifestyle sectors of trying to encourage consumers to identify with the brand not just the product. In this case, the identification fostered is both with the brand and with practices of modesty, rendering corporate online presence part of a new internet-based fashion discourse about modesty liable to transcend divisions of faith.

Online retailing provides companies with clues that customers are shopping across faith divides: 'I'm getting an order from Broken Arrow, Oklahoma, there's not too many Hasids living out there, so I can figure that' (Gary Swickley). With further demographic data garnered through offline marketing, many brands are willing to moderate their offering and communication strategies to accommodate diverse consumers. Based in the 'Mormon heartland' of Utah, ModBod was one of the early brands to manufacture T-shirts and 'shells' to be worn under clothing that would otherwise be too revealing to meet modesty standards and to cover the Temple garment worn by many LDS women. Aware similarly from online communiqués that she had Jewish customers, when offline expansion into branches of Costco revealed the size of the market, founder Shellie Slade began to produce high neck, long sleeve summer-weight Ts for regional Jewish customers.[4] Like most brands, ModBod welcomes cross-faith and secular consumers, but being identified by faith online can be uncomfortable, though not, as Slade explains below, for the reasons that an outsider might presume:

> I mean we're okay saying we're a Christian company, but maybe not just specifically a Latter-day Saint company, because of just like the Bible Belt and the, you know, the Protestants and the Catholics … A lot of times people in those religions will not view us as Christian … There were even points in time where we discussed having a PO box in Dallas or somewhere in Texas that was a little bit more central [to avoid the LDS association of a Utah postal address].

ModBod's decision to avoid announcing online their LDS affiliation reflects especially the hostility from US Protestant evangelicals that, whilst not always widely known elsewhere, received sustained attention in the international media when Mormon Mitt Romney was running for the Republican presidential nomination and then in the election itself in 2011–12.

THE INTERNET AS NEW MEDIUM FOR RELIGION

The significance of new media in developing and disseminating religious ideas is not new. Neither is it new that innovations in communication technologies (like the printing press and the development of the vernacular Bible) produce changes in the interpretations and practices of the creeds that they communicate. Religious institutions and – though not always in the same ways or to the same effect – their congregations have variously repudiated, harnessed, controlled and fought over new modes of communication and transmission. Preceding the relationship of religion to the internet was the early adoption by Protestant evangelical churches in the US of radio in the 1930s and television in the 1960s (Allner 1997, Brasher 2001), and the widespread use of audio cassettes in the *da'wa* movement in Egypt since the 1970s (Hirschkind 2006).

Women's online discourse about modesty contributes a distinctively gendered strand to the emergence online of new forms of religious discourse often regarded as a male sphere of activity – as is the case with men's well documented Islamic online presence. As Bunt (2009) and others have established, the internet has facilitated the development of new forms of religious interpretation outside of the hierarchies of conventional clerical religious authority. Characterised by flat, or lateral, modes of relationship typical of early internet pioneers, new interpretations circulate online and are implemented offline, validating new forms of religious authority. Muslims, and especially Islamists, have led the way among other faiths in seeing the potential of the internet for developing and spreading ideas. The first cohort of Muslims online was often drawn from the same cadres of Western educated engineers and techies that populated and established the protocols for the early years of the internet (Anderson 1999, Bunt 2009). Just as radio and television created televangelist stars and powerbrokers that now influence American government policy, the internet brings new groups and individuals to the fore.

New forms of religious authority online vary across the Abrahamic faiths depending on pre-existent religious structures of authority and forms of knowledge transmission and modes of ministry (Turner 2007, Campbell 2005). The centralised transmission of religious authority that characterises some Christian denominations contrasts with the decentralisation in Judaism and Islam where clerical authority is habitually achieved through disputation. For Islam in particular, Peter Mandeville suggests, the internet marks 'the intensification of a tendency toward decentralised authority that has always been present' (Mandeville 2007: 102).

Across the faiths, electronic and digital media have expanded and diversified existing religious publics, but there is, as Meyer and Moors warn, 'nothing inherently progressive about the new media' (Meyer and

Moors 2006: 5–10). New modes of communication can be harnessed as easily by majority as by minority religious cultures, to develop conservative or progressive communities. Facilities like fatwa-online or ask the rabbi can build reputations for self-appointed moral guides disproportionate to their level of religious knowledge (Biala 2009), just as they can advantage clerics of both elite and minority status (Bunt 2009). That digital platforms let more people express their opinion does not lead necessarily to a more tolerant public domain: for Kline, blogging has given 'new voice and new reach to the extremist strain in American society' (Kline and Burnstein 2005: 22). In the new intellectual elite of diasporic Islam, Turner suggests, the competition to gain followers in the context of the individualisation of religiosity typical of early internet generations often produces an 'inflationary expansion of claims to purity and strictness that has a compulsory upward trajectory' (Turner 2007: 132). The opportunity to construct an identity based on ever stricter religiosity can be appealing to second- and third-generation socially excluded Muslim migrants in Europe (Roy 2002), as can the opportunity to regulate the behaviour of others through corrective advice dispensed as part of the *da'wa* obligation of moral guidance.

My focus on modest clothing reveals that, as early adopters of virtual communication, women style mediators and entrepreneurs are themselves constructing innovative forms of religious discourse online, creating cross-faith interactions that span commerce and conversation. Women's products and ideas circulate in the blogosphere, discussion fora, on YouTube and social media, and through sales, developing networks with the potential to displace discourses about modesty into arenas beyond traditional religious authority structures. Whilst many participants are motivated to promote modesty, the field is not strongly characterised by the doctrinal judgementalism seen in other areas of religion online. Recognising diverse modesty codes and motivations, modern orthodox Jewish entrepreneur Naomi Gottlieb at Tabeez is not alone in arguing that, 'it's not really about religion. I mean there's a lot of people that are maybe atheists and they're being modest just because it's like a respect, like a dignity kind of thing.'[5] For her, as for others, the assertion of multiple modesties underwrites a challenge to community conventions as well as external perceptions:

> Modest doesn't have to be conservative. Modest doesn't have to be grey and black and old and stiff, that's really conservative … my clothing's anything but conservative. The brighter, the wackier, the more beads, the more colours the better, but it is modest.

NEW BLOGGERS:
STYLE MEDIATORS, SPIRITUAL ADVISORS

Women are using the internet to share ideas, rate styles, comment on mainstream provision and intervene in debates about modest behaviour, extending the opportunities offered offline by the establishment in print of faith-based style media in the first half of the 2000s. Where once education or careers in the creative industries were perceived as inappropriate for or inaccessible to religious – and immigrant – populations, the new lifestyle magazines provided initial professional opportunities for fashion mediators from within faith communities (Lewis 2010). The advent of blogging software in 1999 made the personal 'weblog', or blog, increasingly accessible with a concomitant expansion of the numbers and types of voices online (Kline and Burstein 2005). Dominated initially by political and technical content, fashion bloggers began topic-based blogs (from plus size beauty to vintage or ethical fashion) and took advantage of cheap digital camera technology to feature their own wardrobes in personal style blogs (Rocamora 2011). Religious fashionistas embraced the blog just as did their 'secular' counterparts, with the development of the modest blogosphere matching the chronology of the medium. One year after the first fashion blog in 2003, LDS modest blog front-runner Jennifer Loch came online with *JenMagazine.com* in 2004, the year that saw a huge increase of blog reading (up 58 per cent) and a 'greater-than-average growth' in blog reading by women and minorities (Pew 2005). Numbers increased steadily since then with Muslim trail-blazer Jana Kossaibati starting hijabstyle.co.uk in 2007. Critical mass appeared by 2009 with a second generation of modest bloggers like LDS Elaine Hearn's *Clothedmuch.com* and Muslim Hana Tajima-Simpson's *Stylecovered.com*. By 2010, Technorati's *State of the Blogosphere* was reporting that an 'important trend is the influence of the women and mom bloggers on the blogosphere, mainstream media, and brands ... [the] blogger segment most likely of all to blog about brands'.[6]

The presumption that bloggers are independent commentators is changing as the blogosphere segments and professionalises. As predicted (Kline and Burstein 2005), an A list of 'star' bloggers has emerged whose activities cross over to other media, whilst corporations have themselves sought to harness the potential of virtual commentary by developing blogs and social media as an integral part of company communications policy. Positioned initially as marginal or renegade voices, key bloggers have by now accrued cultural and political capital equivalent to their established print media counterparts: in politics think of the *Huffington Post*, in fashion of the *Sartorialist* and the many other bloggers now seated front row for the catwalk shows and featuring in the print and online editions of established fashion magazines. The careful manoeuvres required if bloggers are to retain integrity as independent commentators whilst taking up cross-over opportunities in fashion PR (Burney 2011) have particular nuance for the faith sector. Modest fashion bloggers enter a new media field characterised by an intense anxiety about visual representations of the female form and rarely able to draw on the genealogy of fashion imagery and comment that makes it so easy for the *Sartorialist's* output to cross over.

Maintaining a convincingly authentic – that is, uncompromised – blog voice is also critical to success for corporate blogs. Initially wary, many companies now accept blogging as a valuable mode of public relations, with blog writing emerging as a new area of media training for senior executives. In PR terms this means augmenting or replacing the one-way ('control and command') communiqué of the press release with a ('listen and participate') blog post (Scoble and Israel 2006). For those whose blogs represent the brand, keeping it real depends on developing a blog voice that is authentic, credible and participatory. The same rules apply to social media, now incorporated into modest commercial communications. 'I have my face on the Twitter because I read somewhere that always, even though you're a brand, it's good to have a person behind it,' says Sandy Dougall of Utah LDS brand Diviine Modestee, who has learned to include 'personal things that aren't too personal [to avoid company posts being perceived as] bordering on almost spam'.[7]

Writing on the development of online religious communities among different Christian denominations in 2005, Heidi Campbell could already confirm (as indicated in Pew 2001) that in contrast to initial anxieties that online connections would erode participation in offline churches, the two are most often complementary. With religious (mainly church) groups at 40 per cent constituting the most popular form of community or civic organisation in America, by 2011 the internet had become a routinised adjunct to religious community life, bringing online older and African-American women congregants, with social media remaining the domain of the 18–29-year-olds (Pew 2011). The challenges posed for organised religion by the affordances of digital connectivity are proving more likely to result in the 'transformation and reconfiguration of existing practices, beliefs, and infrastructures' than in their replacement (Cheong and Ess 2012: 2).

Whilst regulars in online discussion groups may seek a sense of community with 'brothers and sisters in Christ' that can extend their communion beyond brick and mortar churches, for many the needs of local churches to establish at the very least a basic online informational presence provided leadership roles for 'techies', with attendant opportunities to attain seniority and respect (Thumma 2000). With the information overload that is now an inevitable part of the internet experience, the role of the mediator and guide becomes especially important, suggesting to Bunt that 'a critical area in the future of CIEs [cyber Islamic environments] is not the provision of content but the provision of guidance and information management' (Bunt 2009: 288). The combination of technical savvy and editorial confidence this demands relates directly to developments in modest fashion discourse online.

Despite the religiosity of the population, the (American) mainstream media outside of religious syndicated radio and television provides little specialist coverage (Kline and Burstein 2005), giving an especial significance to blogs and social media. Because 'bloggers have impact in aggregate', the ability to publicise and promote a religious view, and to influence the mainstream media, can come not just from the pulling power of 'star' bloggers but from the quantity of small bloggers posting on the same topic (Kline and Burstein 2005: 22). The interactive nature of blogging means that participation by readers (or Twitter followers or Facebook friends) in discussion or simply recirculating the original post can create sufficient buzz to bring a topic to an audience beyond the initial digital readership.

The hypertextuality that characterises virtual communication means that it is rare for any website or blog to be experienced in isolation as readers click through from internet search engines or from links on other sites. But, as Anastasia Karaflogka (2007) discusses, for virtual communications in the religious sector the significance of this traffic can be especially telling. Official websites (and, latterly, social media) of religious institutions may permit users to link to them but try to maintain their authorised discourse by refusing reciprocal links out (on the Roman Catholic Church's removal of comment functions from its YouTube channel, see Campbell 2012). Other sites may actively seek mutual links, while others may mask institutional or political affiliations (Bunt 2009). In the corporate blogosphere, company blogs that do not permit links with other blogs may find that for readers who privilege connectivity as a sign of good faith, 'the lack of interactivity removes the authenticity from the conversation' (Scoble and Israel 2006: 51). Different gate-keeping practices – including member-only sites – are important indicators of attitude and presumed addressees when analysing online content.

The website of star LDS personal style blogger Elaine Hearn of Clothedmuch illustrates a mixed economy with links to official organs and the development of new forms of virtual classification (and internal regulation). Introducing herself with variations on the theme of, 'I'm Elaine and I'm a Mormon. I'm poor and I don't have a lot of clothes so this blog is here to help me be more creative with what I already have', the blog immediately offers to link the reader to Hearn's personal profile on the official LDS site through the highlighted word 'Mormon'.[8] On the LDS site, Hearn expands her blog strapline under the headers 'about me', 'why I am a Mormon' and 'How I live my faith'. These are categories provided by the LDS site and structure all the testimonies online. Like the rest of the LDS site profiles, Hearn's includes witness to the power of faith in her life and how it structures the shape of her day (Bible study every evening), but unlike them includes fashion as part of her mission: 'I was born in South Korea, not North, and immigrated [sic] to Philadelphia when I was a wee babe. I've since lived in Idaho and Utah. Now I am residing in Los Angeles with my husband making an imprint in the fashion world one modest outfit at a time.'

Hearn herself runs The Mormon Fashion Bloggers Directory on her website. Registration is free, open to all those that identify as Mormon and as fashion bloggers. By April 2012 the directory hosted 78 different blog links under the strapline 'We're Mormon and we like clothes'. Again the word Mormon links the reader directly to the homepage of http://mormon.org, directing traffic to the Church's official virtual communications hub in the same way that the button which each affiliated blog is required to display will direct their readers back to Hearn's site.

In contrast to the regulated discourse on the official LDS site, Jewish personal style blogger Nina at alltumbledown.blogspot.com provides information on her modern orthodox affiliation via the unregulated Wikipedia. Her internal page on modesty also offers a link to the Wikipedia entry on tzniuth (literally 'hidden') as well as to MyJewishLearning.com which describes itself as 'the leading transdenominational website of Jewish information and education'.[9] This range of information is entirely in keeping with the blog's ideological commitment to diversity of practice – 'there is no one way to keep kosher, just as there is no one way to be Jewish' – and to creativity when it comes to dress:

While my style isn't risqué, it isn't classically modest, either … You see, I'm on a mission: to make the restrictions the last thing people notice when I walk down the street. I'd much rather you see an inventive use of contrasting colors or textural elements than the fact that I'm the only one wearing long sleeves in August.[10]

Working within a framework of modest fashion, Jennifer Loch had known from the first that she would garner interest from different faiths when she started her online *JenMagazine* in 2004 and initially considered not making the site overtly LDS. In the end she decided

… okay, I want to do this for me and for the LDS community so I make it very clear that it's LDS based, but knowing that it's for anyone … as long as they know that what we're basing it on [are] the LDS modesty standards.[11]

A former model with fashion industry experience, Loch has self-trained in internet marketing and is careful about how to increase traffic to her site. Leading a growing trend in which popular and successful bloggers cross over into retail, *JenMagazine* has now spawned an online range, Jen Clothing.

The proliferation of blogs into commerce is matched by the dramatic increase in the rate and extent to which brands are reaching out to bloggers. Early topic-based bloggers in the sector like Jana Kossaibati of *Hijab Style* searched for modest brands and solicited promotional tie-ins. Now she is inundated with press releases and product offers. Blogger awareness that they can be exploited as free publicity by companies and that there can be pitfalls to handling freebies is growing, and providing guidance on how to negotiate this changing set of commercial relations further establishes the status of leading bloggers (Lewis forthcoming 2013).

As blogs become corporate and professionalised, there are particular challenges for the religious sector. Based in the Jewish ultra-orthodox enclave of Borough Park, Brooklyn, H2O Pink Label manufactures modest clothing retailed online and wholesaled offline. E-commerce is especially tricky for a brand originating in and aimed at sectors of the ultra-orthodox Jewish community characterised by highly regulated internet access and suspicion of the mainstream mass media (most ultra-orthodox schools stipulate on their entry requirements that households must not have televisions for example). Company directors Mindy Schlafrig and Miriam Rubin[12] explain that their rabbis have issued a generic dispensation for internet use when it is essential for business, but that leisure use of the internet is generally highly restricted (and/or often regulated via the growing numbers of internet software filters now available; Sanders 2010; in contrast, see also Zakar and Kaufman 1998, Stolow 2006). For H2O, participation in virtual media by their target consumers is sufficient for them to have hired an orthodox-run social media company, NowSourcing Inc., to establish a blog and a Facebook and Twitter account. With a website strapline of 'H2O Pink Label the cutting edge in modest fashion', the homepage testifies that, 'our goal has always been to provide women with modest clothing that is up-to-date without compromising tznius standards'.[13]

H2O's interpretation of modesty renders fashionability itself as problematic. The concept of tsniuth is not just about which bits of the body to cover – this is regarded as a non-negotiable minimum by adherents – but also demands modesty in body management that could render trendiness too attention-seeking. H2O keeps up with the global fashion industry, but cannot simply adopt every style that provides sufficient cover: it is just as bad to be conspicuously avant-garde as frumpily old-fashioned. Mindy Schlafrig says:

> We'll be starting a style sometimes two years after everybody ... we want to look nice and modern and not really old-fashioned ... We don't want to stick out either way. We like to look nice but we're not going to be the first.

The transmission and take-up of style becomes a factor in the staging of modesty in which demonstration of fashion savvy must be judiciously melded with deference to community norms (see also Chapter 4). The reach of 'mainstream' fashion discourse is such that even communities who might eschew the fashion media are aware of passing trends, but too enthusiastic an adoption of cutting-edge styles is likely to diminish spiritual capital.

THE ACCELERATED CYCLE OF MODEST FASHION: NEW GENERATION DESIGNERS AND MEDIATORS

The need to avoid offending the most conservative elements of a given community – even if they are not the company's target demographic –

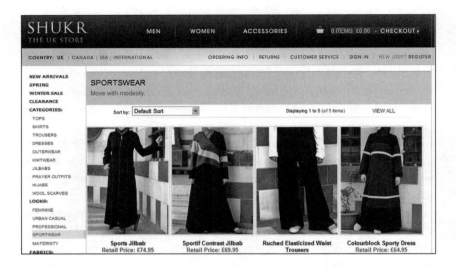

6 Sportswear, Shukr e-retail webpage, screenshot. Accessed 30 March 2012.

was a factor for many of the earlier generation of entrepreneurs. But as the modest market expands and segments, younger designers especially are increasingly able to create their own spot within the modest fashion niche.

Distinctive variations in communication strategies have already emerged, especially in relation to representations of the female body. New companies are launching modest brands with sophisticated online marketing techniques and high production values that are often far less tentative about selling modesty through the visual language of 'secular' fashion. New design-led companies are able to presume on a fashion-literate viewer who can read website visuals selectively rather than literally. New forms of religious and ethnic distinction are being created by younger generations who have the social and cultural capital to move between minority and mainstream fashion systems.

Most of the early modest company websites and blogs – regardless of originating faith – are notable for avoiding the sexualised imagery associated with the fashion industry. Religious delicacies about showing the human form are especially pronounced in relation to images of

7 Shells, H2O Pink Label
e-retail webpage, screenshot.
Accessed 30 March 2012.

women, and (sometimes to their own frustration, Tarlo 2010) bring companies, designers and communication teams up against competing regulations and practices within their own religious communities and those of others to whom they wish to sell. In particular some Muslim companies adhere to, or want to avoid offending those who do adhere to, interpretations of Islam that prohibit the representation of the human form. This has resulted in websites that crop the face and/or head from images (see Figure 6), or that avoid showing products on bodies at all, restricting visuals to product shots or to mannequins (see Figure 7). Of those companies that do feature their clothes on models, nearly all of all faiths avoid the sexualised poses that are fashion industry standard: 'models don't understand ... "So you don't want me to look sexy?"' (Naomi Gottlieb at Tabeez). These same challenges were faced by the new Muslim lifestyle print media in the early to mid-2000s and continue to prompt immediate and intense feedback from independent bloggers across the faiths. Commercial companies can be quickly criticised too for their representations of women and range of garments. Whilst bloggers might lose readers, commercial companies risk losing customers. More recent brands benefit from entering a developed and diversified field that makes possible a greater range of imagery. The garments may be similar in their potential for modest outfitting, but their presentation on the body is not necessarily bound by the lowest common denominator.

One such company, Maysaa, was launched in the UK in 2010 after a successful pre-launch web-based media campaign by designer and founder Hana Tajima-Simpson on her blog *Style Covered*. The start-up quickly began to punch above its weight with a well-designed website and a virtual magazine showcasing its still relatively few products in a high fashion mise-en-scène. In this, Maysaa moved distinctively away from the conservative visuals that previously characterised the sector. A jersey maxi skirt (Figure 8) is worn on the sales page with a sleeveless top, and displayed in her digital magazine on a model posed raunchily with décolleté:

> ... obviously we were aware that other people had a really strict policy on, can't show the head, can't show anything ... it's kind of ridiculous. [You] have to give the consumers some credit. Just because you show it a certain way doesn't mean that they're going to wear it that way. [T]hese clothes aren't just meant for Muslims, also they're not just meant for when you go out wearing hijab ...[14]

It would have been inconceivable even five years previous for a modest brand to risk this near-naked body – yet Maysaa is doing well with consumers who appreciate the value added of seeing modest clothing styled for fashion. American brand Eva Kurshid, launched a year earlier in 2009, is similarly committed to strong aesthetics, presuming a non-literal reading mode on the part of their fashion-forward consumers.

Friends since high school, Eva Khurshid founders Fatima Monkush and Nyla Hashmi are unusual for entrepreneurs in the modest fashion sector having both trained in fashion design. Able by 2009 to choose their niche within the modest sector, Eva Khurshid aims at professional women who favour on-trend glamour and workwear. The duo discovered in their first season that using the words Muslim or modest could hinder progress in their wholesale market, quickly realising '[that we]

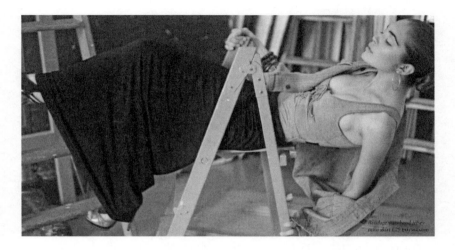

8 Maysaa digital magazine, September 2010, Issue 2, www.maysaa.com. Accessed 30 March 2012.

had to become very creative with how we describe the brand and how we define modesty'.[15] Now they rely on their 'tag line' of 'Sexy Rediscovered' to communicate their feminist ideal of 'empowering women and giving back control of what they define as sexy on their own terms'. Hashmi says that 'we want every woman to fall in love with our brand, whether they're Muslim, whether they're Jewish, Christian, whatever'. Reviewed favourably in Muslim magazines and blogs and in Christian modest magazine *Eliza*, nothing on their website indicates their modest or religious affiliation.

> NH: We're very proud of who we are and we [don't want to] pigeon-hole ourselves into just a niche market, we want to branch out and be sold in Bergdorfs, sold in Saks and Bloomingdale's … the visuals [help the company look like] it's very high fashion and [that's] what keeps us looking more in competition with the rest of the fashion world.

The field is opening up in terms both of product and address, with Eva Khurshid seeing their mission as both to promote fashionable modesty and 'to push the boundaries of what people wouldn't even expect to be "modest"'. Like Gottlieb, they want to challenge the presumption that only conservative women have the power to define modesty. Tellingly, both the design-educated Eva Khurshid team and daughter of artists Tajima-Simpson have highly developed visual literacy, regarding company visuals as essential to the communication of their spiritual as well as stylistic interpretations of modesty.

Website visuals are also key to Shabby Apple's appeal to the wider market (see Figure 9). Launching in 2007, Athelia Woolley and Emily McCormick avoided marketing the company as LDS 'because we felt like it would then turn away other potential customers'.[16] Like the other LDS brand ModBod, Shabby Apple could take this marketing decision secure in the knowledge that they could rely on word of mouth – 'LDS women talk about us to each other' – for consumers within their own community. This is not coincidental: LDS brands and bloggers benefit from the LDS ward structure of local (or life stage, young singles, students) congregational units. Many brands started with home selling and ward-based affiliate programmes and bloggers can form links online and offline through ward and peer group events, facilitating the reposting and retweeting so essential to reputation development.

Able to rely on word of mouth for LDS consumers, Woolley focused on a visually strong website with high-quality, well-styled photographs to appeal to the wider market. But briefing their favoured photographer,

> ... can be a problem because he's not LDS and he doesn't understand. So we've had to actually Photoshop some of the dresses [and] we send him emails like, your poses should be fun but not sweaty. It's just a delicate thing because we actually don't ever say that we're a modest company and [I'm] actually very personal about my LDS beliefs ... [I] don't really want to discuss that with him, I just want him to, like, know.

The use of what can seem to some as radically fashion-forward aesthetics is a significant intervention into the language in and through which female modesty can be defined, represented and disputed. Such developments mark a move away from the presumption of literalist modes of reading and etiquette that were previously standard practice for minority and ethnic and religious media, indicating a growing pluralisation of opinion and modes of expression.

9 Dresses, Shabby Apple
e-retail webpage, screenshot.
Accessed 30 March 2012.

CONCLUSION: NEW FORMS OF RELIGIOUS INTERPRETATION AND AUTHORITY

Religious discourse online is able to publicise forms of religious interpretation not usually given prominence, challenging existing hierarchies of religious knowledge with both new interpretations and new modes of transmission. The internet tends to fragment forms of religious authority, augmenting, sometimes replacing, hierarchical clerical communications (the one to the many) with self-selecting participatory networks (the many to the many) (Bunt 2009, Eickelman and Anderson 2003, Mandeville 2007). Writing on Islam, Bunt sees an inevitable standardisation of multiple rather than single interpretations, predicting that 'rather than a single ummah [global community of believers] idealised as a classical Islamic concept, in fact there are numerous parallel ummah frameworks operating in cyberspace, reflecting diverse notions of the concepts of community' (Bunt 2009: 31).

Muslim women's online-style mediation about modesty can be seen as part of one such parallel framework. Extrapolating from the Muslim context, I identify the development of modesty discourse across and between faiths and between religious and secular contributors as another set of communities or publics, in which, increasingly, multiple interpretations of modesty are coming to be the norm.

The activation of fashion as a mode for religious knowledge construction and transmission mirrors the widening of the 'religious' domain by the first generation of (male) Muslim online communicators, 'casting [religious] talk in idioms of speech and thought previously or otherwise allocated to separate speech communities' (Anderson 1999: 54–55). As diverse digital constituents come online, the range of discourses previously regarded as external but now included within religious content will increase. Framed through the logic of fashion – itself usually trivialised – women's online discourse about modesty can be seen as one such form of transmission, emerging as a predominant mode through which women are establishing themselves as religious interpreters and intermediaries. This is not to say that participants would themselves label their activities in this way (and many might think it presumptuous, grandiose or downright unfaithful). But taken in conglomerate, the impact of these new sets of discussions about modest fashion and behaviour and the increasingly diverse modes through which modest dressing is visually represented can be seen to create new discourses about how to experience and express religion in everyday life.

Whilst some forms of media may privilege the ideas and participation of particular social groups, 'messages also migrate from [one] medium to another' with new domains opening up in which to discuss religious ideas previously the preserve of elite clerical forms of transmission (Eikelman and Anderson 2003: 4). The fundamental reflexivity of digital cultures operates a 'logics that put [religious] authority in a different place than in the past' (Hoover 2012: xii). The rendering of the blog and of social media as platforms suitable for the development and transmission of religious discourse in the form of modest fashion facilities and guidance (commercial and non-monetised) constitutes new places and new publics for religiosity dominated by women. These new religious publics are appearing simultaneously among Jewish, Christian and Muslim women, and show increasing potential to migrate not just across media platforms, or between commerce and commentary, but also across boundaries of faith and secularity.

If indeed there are arising distinctive taste communities for modest fashion that transcend faith boundaries it is not surprising, in the context of e-commerce's capacity to reach diverse consumers, that many brands are now developing marketing strategies that are not only cross-faith but also faith-free. Though it may prove hard to maintain brand loyalty in face of consumer expectations that are both stylistic and moral, a neutral communication strategy could well become one of the characteristics of the sector as companies seek to establish their style vision as fashion worthy not just morally worthy: 'the word modest is not a good word for fashion. It's why as a consumer I never bought from a modest dress company' (Woolley at Shabby Apple).

Mainstream fashion bloggers were innovators of new genres of fashion commentary within a field already saturated by print media. That most mainstream fashion commentary ignored modesty as a fashion-related dress practice and that there was very little specialist print media provision meant that ICT was for modest fashion bloggers the means to invent not only new genres but also a new zone of fashion mediation (now itself becoming a news story for mainstream and fashion media).[17] In a sector where faith concerns bring bloggers and brands into close proximity and as multiple versions of modesty become the norm online there will be implications for the many manufacturers and bloggers and consumers who see their participation in modest fashion as spiritually and socially motivated and fulfilling. Itself an inherently ambiguous concept, once modest fashion is rendered viable as a fashion category it further becomes liable (like all fashion trends) to be endlessly modified, replaced, repositioned, recycled and appropriated. I predict a lively future for commercial and communal articulations of virtual virtue.

ACKNOWLEDGEMENTS

I am grateful to Agnès Rocamora and Emma Tarlo for their comments on earlier drafts of this chapter.

NOTES

1   This research was carried out as part of the project *Modest Dressing: Faith-based Fashion and Internet Retail*, funded by the AHRC/ESRC Religion and Society Programme, 2010–11, and further supported by the London College of Fashion, 2011–12. I am indebted

to the contributions and insights of my project colleagues Emma Tarlo and Jane Cameron. http://www.fashion.arts.ac.uk/research/projects-collaborations/modest-dressing/.

2 http://www.thehijabshop.com/information/article1.php. Accessed 18 March 2011.
3 This and all other quotations, Gary Swickley, personal telephone interview, 29 March 2011.
4 This and all quotations, Shellie Slade, personal interview, Pleasant Grove, Utah, 8 July 2010.
5 This and all other quotations, Naomi Gottlieb, interviewed by Jane Cameron, New Jersey, 16 July 2010.
6 John Sobel, 'State of the Blogosphere 2010 Introduction'. http://technorati.com/blogging/article/state-of-the-blogosphere-2010-introduction/. Accessed 7 July 2011.
7 This and all other quotations, Sandy Dougall, interviewed by Jane Cameron, Pleasant Grove, Utah, 8 July 2010.
8 http://mormon.org/me/1TRR-eng/Elaine. Accessed 15 April 2011.
9 http://www.myjewishlearning.com/aboutus/abindex.shtml. Accessed 28 September 2011.
10 http://alltumbledown.blogspot.com/. Accessed 4 August 2011.
11 This and all other quotations, Jennifer Loch, personal interview, Provo, Utah, 9 July 2010.
12 This and all other quotations, Mindy Schlafrig and Miriam Rubin, personal interview, New York, 13 July 2010.
13 All quotes from H2O website http://www.h2opinklabel.com/. Accessed 18 April 2011.
14 This and all other quotations, Hana Tajima-Simpson, personal interview, London, 3 November 2010.
15 This and all other quotations, Nyla Hashmi and Fatima Monkush, personal interview, New York, 12 July 2010.
16 This and all other quotations, Athelia Woolley, interviewed by Jane Cameron, New York, 13 July 2010.
17 See for example: http://www.dailymail.co.uk/femail/article-2049283/High-necklines-low-hemlines-The-rise-Mormon-modesty-blogs--fashion-bang-trend.html. Accessed 14 February 2012. http://www.styleite.com/media/mormon-modesty-fashion-blogging/. Accessed 14 February 2012.

REFERENCES

Allner, Michel (1997). 'Religion and Fashion: American Evangelists as Trendsetters and Fashion Innovators in Marketing and Communication'. *Modes and Modes*, 2:1: 145–55.
Anderson, Jon W. (1999). 'The Internet and Islam's New Interpreters', in D. Eickelman and J. W. Anderson (eds), *New Media in the Muslim World* (second edition, 2003). Bloomington, IN: Indiana University Press.
Biala, Tamar (2009). 'To Teach Tsniʻut with Tsniʻut: On Educating for Tsniʻut in National-Religious Schools'. *Meorot*, 7:2: 1–13.
Brasher, Brenda E. (2001). *Give Me that Online Religion*. San Francisco: Jossey Bass.

Bunt, Gary R. (2009). iMuslims: Rewiring the House Islam. London: Hurst.

Burney, Ellen (2011). 'Blog Party'. Sunday Times, 17 July: 16–17.

Campbell, Heidi (2005). Exploring Religious Community Online: We are One in the Network. New York: Peter Lang.

—— (2012). 'How Religious Communities Negotiate New Media Religiously', in Pauline Hope Cheong, Peter Fischer-Nielson, Stefan Gelfgren and Charles Ess (eds), Digital Religion, Social Media and Culture: Perspectives, Practices and Futures. New York: Peter Lang.

Cheong, Pauline Hope and Ess, Charles (2012). 'Introduction: Religion 2.0? Relational and Hybridizing Pathways to Religion, Social Media, and Culture', in Pauline Hope Cheong, Peter Fischer-Nielson, Stefan Gelfgren and Charles Ess (eds), Digital Religion, Social Media and Culture: Perspectives, Practices and Futures. New York: Peter Lang.

Comaroff, John L. and Comaroff, Jean (2009). Ethnicity, Inc. Chicago, IL: University of Chicago Press.

Eickelman, D. and Anderson, J. W. (eds) (2003). New Media in the Muslim World (second edition). Bloomington IN: Indiana University Press.

El-Guindi, Fadwa (1999). Veil: Modesty, Privacy and Resistance. Oxford: Berg.

Hirschkind, Charles (2006). 'Cassette Ethics: Public Piety and Popular Media in Egypt', in Birgit Meyer and Annelies Moors (eds), Religion, Media, and the Public Sphere. Bloomington, IN: Indiana University Press.

Hoover, Stewart M. (2012). 'Foreword', in Pauline Hope Cheong, Peter Fischer-Nielson, Stefan Gelfgren and Charles Ess (eds), Digital Religion, Social Media and Culture: Perspectives, Practices and Futures. New York: Peter Lang.

Karaflogka, Anastasia (2007). E-religion: A Critical Appraisal of Religious Discourse on the World Wide Web. London: Enquinox.

Kline, David and Burstein, Dan (eds) (2005). Blogs! How the Newest Media Revolution is Changing Politics, Business, and Culture. New York: CDS Books.

Lewis, Reina (2010). 'Marketing Muslim Lifestyle: A New Media Genre'. Journal of Middle East Women's Studies, 6:3: 58–90.

—— (forthcoming 2013). 'Establishing Reputation, Maintaining Independence: the Modest Fashion Blogosphere', in Bartlett, Cole and Rocamora (eds), Fashion Media. Oxford: Berg.

Mahmood, Saba (2005). Politics of Piety: The Islamic Revival and the Feminist Subject. Princeton, NJ: Princeton University Press.

Mandeville, Peter (2007). 'Globalization and the Politics of Religious Knowledge: Pluralizing Authority in the Muslim World'. Theory, Culture and Society, 24:2: 101–15.

Meyer, Birgit and Moors, Annelies (2006). 'Introduction', in Birgit Meyer and Annelies Moors (eds), Religion, Media, and the Public Sphere. Bloomington, IN: Indiana University Press.

Pew Internet and American Life Project (23 December 2001). CyberFaith: How Americans Pursue Religion Online. http://www.pewinternet.org/Reports/2001/CyberFaith-How-Americans-Pursue-Religion-Online.aspx (accessed 2 October 2011).

—— (2 January 2005). Data Memo: The State of Blogging. http://www.pewinternet.org/Reports/2005/The-State-of-Blogging/Data-Memo-Findings.aspx (accessed 2 October 2011).

—— (18 January 2011). The Social Side of the Internet. http://pewresearch.org/pubs/1861/impact-internet-social-media-facebook-twitter-group-activities-participation (accessed 2 October 2011).

Rocamora, Agnès (2011). 'Personal Fashion Blogs: Screens and Mirrors in Digital Self-portraits'. *Fashion Theory: The Journal of Dress, Body & Culture*, 15:4: 407–24.

—— (2012). 'Hypertextuality and Representation in the Fashion Media'. *Journalism Practice*, 6:1: 92–106.

Roy, Olivier (2002). *Globalised Islam: The Search for a New Ummah*. London: Hurst.

Sanders, Edmund (2010). 'Kosher Internet for the Pious'. *Los Angeles Times*, 20 November.

Scoble, Robert and Israel, Shel (2006). *Naked Conversations: How Blogs are Changing the Ways Businesses Talk with Customers*. Hoboken, NJ: John Wiley and Sons.

Stolow, Jeremy (2006). 'Communicating Authority, Consuming Tradition: Jewish Orthodox Outreach Literature and its Reading Public', in Birgit Meyer and Annelies Moors (eds), *Religion, Media, and the Public Sphere*. Bloomington, IN: Indiana University Press.

Tarlo, Emma (2010). *Visibly Muslim: Fashion, Politics, Faith*. Oxford: Berg.

Technorati (2010). *State of the Blogosphere*. John Sobel. http://technorati.com/blogging/article/state-of-the-blogosphere-2010-introduction/ (accessed 3 November 2011).

Thumma, Scott (2000). 'Report of Webmaster Survey'. Scott Thuma, Hartford Institute for Religion Research. http://hirr.hartsem.edu/bookshelf/thumma_article3.html (accessed 22 July 2011).

Turner, Bryan S. (2007). 'Religious Authority and the New Media'. *Theory, Culture and Society*, 24:2: 117–34.

Zakar, Susan M. and Kaufman, Dovid Y. B. (1998). *Judaism Online: Confronting Spirituality on the Internet*. Northvale, NJ: Jason Aronson Inc.

3

MEETING THROUGH MODESTY
Jewish–Muslim Encounters on the Internet

Emma Tarlo

In June 2010 an orthodox Jewish woman writing under the name 'Chassidmom' posted up a YouTube video she had found amusing and wished to share with other online members of *imamother.com*, a website based in North America targeted at married frum (religiously observant) women. Calling her posting, 'Miss Muslim Moral Beauty Context – HAHAHAHAHA!', 'Chassidmom' was clearly intending to provoke a good laugh amongst participants.[1] The video clip she wished to share was taken from a Saudi TV presentation of Saudi Arabia's first ever 'Moral Beauty Pageant', held in 2009, in which all the contestants wore long loose black abayas, gowns and face veils. The clip included an explanation of the idea behind the contest from the contest supervisor, an earnest bespectacled woman, also fully veiled:

> In our contacts with girls in general, we noticed that they follow false notions, due to the purposeless Western notions, conveyed by some TV channels. The girls are preoccupied with their external appearance only. This is how we came up with the idea of creating an alternative. So we thought of a contest for the title of moral beauty queen. The goal is, first and foremost, to spread virtue, even if through different means. In this contest, we focus on the theme of honoring one's parents. [Quoted from the English subtitles.]

Viewed from a distance not much was visible of the beauty contestants except their hands emerging from a sea of black cloth and it was no doubt this that amused 'Chassidmom' who wanted to share the image with fellow members of the online orthodox Jewish community. However her joke backfired, not because frum women objected to being exposed to the lives of veiled Muslim women in Saudi Arabia, but rather because they found themselves identifying with them.

'Maybe I'll be slapped for this,' writes one Platinum member on imamother.com, 'but why's this different than erm, choosing valedictorian in the frum schools, or the middos [good character] award or whatever?' 'Isn't this what we are concerned about for ourselves and our children?' asks another member. Seeing the turn of the tide, 'Chassidmom' offered an apologetic explanation: 'Ummm. Sorry. I didn't think of that. ☺ I just got a kick out of the "beauty" contest with a room full of burkas.' At this, she was reminded that this was a 'moral beauty' contest about 'inner beauty so to speak'. One woman commented: 'Listen, Religious people do their best, no matter what religion it is. We have to give credit where it is due, just as we expect it for ourselves.' Another commented that she felt such a contest 'wouldn't be bad in the frum world either'.

What is interesting in this debate is the ease with which strictly orthodox Jewish women in the United States could relate to the preoccupations expressed by Muslim women seeking to maintain strict and puritanical interpretations of Islamic dress codes and behaviour in Saudi Arabia. Their response contrasts strongly with the intolerant attitudes expressed about the same film clip in other online contexts such as Sundried Atheist Blogspot.[2] Here, perhaps predictably, far from provoking unanimous sentiments of identification, the film provoked mainly criticisms of Muslims, veiling practices and religion in general. Yet for the frum mothers participating in imamother.com, there was clearly a strong sense of recognition of the values and sentiments behind the 'Moral Beauty Pageant' which resonated with their own understandings of modesty, known in Hebrew as tzniuth. Recognising this shared preoccupation, Jewish women proved willing to look not just beyond the idea of external beauty as suggested by the contest but also beyond the physical presence of the veil.

This small ethnographic example of interfaith understanding and identification across religious and ethnic borders, which are often considered particularly sensitive or fraught, provides a useful starting point for considering the different ways in which articulations of modesty on the internet may be providing a new meeting point for Muslim and orthodox Jewish women whose levels of religious practice are often assumed to have segregating effects. A comparative study of how modesty is understood by religious women of both faith groups provides insights into the many points of convergence between Jewish and Muslim ideas of covering and body management. What is more significant, however, is the indication of recognition of these similarities by Jewish and Muslim women and the fragments of interaction that take place between them, for here we see religious communities which are often perceived to be insular evolving through processes of mutual recognition and interfaith engagement. Such interactions, however small, challenge many of the assumptions often made about both orthodox religious communities and religious dress practices as well as suggesting the benefits of developing new comparative frameworks of analysis.

That members of orthodox or revivalist religious communities should share features in common will hardly come as a surprise to anthropologists. The anthropology of religion has always had a comparative element and in recent years there have been various large scale attempts to compare the ideas and practices of 'non liberal' religious groups often bracketed together under the label 'fundamentalist' (Marty and Appleby 1994–2003). Yet what such studies fail to offer are insights into the extent to which members of such groups recognise these similarities and engage with them. The same is true for the anthropology of religious dress practices. Whilst anthropologists have recognised parallels in the functions and meanings of the dress codes of different religious groups, they have tended to study their actual dress practices in isolation. There have not to my knowledge been any previous studies which explore how religious dress practices and the ideas associated with them might in some cases offer possibilities of identification, communication and mutual understanding to members of different faith groups. Yet, as my introductory example seems to suggest, online discussions about *tzniuth* on orthodox Jewish websites and blogs may offer glimpses of more than a superficial level of interfaith recognition, sympathy and engagement.

DRESS, SEGREGATION AND RELIGIOUS DIFFERENCE

Hints of online interfaith engagement emerging in spontaneous and unexpected ways over the internet provide an interesting counterpoint to contemporary debates about conspicuous forms of religious dress in politics, the media and anthropology. Much contemporary public debate, policy making, legislation and scaremongering concerning religious dress practices hinges on the assumption that visible expressions of faith not only pose a threat to secular values but also endorse, and indeed encourage, social segregation. Here it is assumed that the dress of religious groups acts as a boundary-making device, preventing interaction with others and discouraging the development of shared values. It is precisely these criticisms that were levelled against Jewish migrants to Britain in the 1920s and 1930s. Their dress was taken as proof of their inability to assimilate and of their supposed inability to act as loyal British citizens. A similar accusation has been levelled against Muslims in recent years, culminating in the introduction of restrictions and prohibitions on the wearing of headscarves and face veils in a number of countries on the grounds that they prohibit the spread of secularism, suggest an unhealthy preoccupation with difference, encourage conservative values, are perceived as oppressive to women and pose a threat to multiculturalism or are, in part, responsible for its assumed failure (Bullock 2003, Scott 2007, Bowen 2008, Tarlo 2010). Here dress practices are thought to inscribe unhealthy levels of difference, encourage insularity and prohibit sociality beyond the assumed confines of one's own religious group.

Anthropological studies of what are considered orthodox or conservative religious dress practices are interestingly placed in relation to these discourses. Whilst anthropologists cannot, on the whole, be accused of showing intolerance to expressions of difference, they are often accused of the opposite tendency – of fetishising difference. Hence scholars writing about Muslim women have been accused of placing too much emphasis on 'the veil' as if it provides a privileged key to understanding all there is to know about Muslim women (Ahmed 1992, Bullock 2003). More generally, scholars studying dress practices of other conservative religious groups such as the Amish, Mormons, Mennonites, nuns and Hasidic Jews have tended to place much emphasis on how dress acts as a material and symbolic device for instilling group values, disciplining the body and mind, perpetuating tradition and reinforcing the distinctiveness and boundedness of what Oliver Valins (2003) calls 'stubborn identities'. These ideas are usefully codified by Linda Arthur in her introduction to the edited volume, *Religion, Dress and the Body* (1996). Drawing on the work of Bryan Turner, she summarises how dress serves to establish and maintain '(1) personal and social identities, (2) social hierarchies, (3) definitions of deviance, (4) systems of social control, and (5) patriarchal power in ethno-religious subcultures' (Arthur 1999). Whilst this provides a useful framework for understanding some of the social functions of dress in maintaining power relations within religious groups, it tends to uphold the idea that such

10 Headwear on sale in the Hat Salon in the Jewish neighbourhood of Williamsburg, New York. September 2010.

groups are characterised by their insularity and traditionalism. Dress is seen largely as a form of boundary maintenance, social control and repetitive reproduction. Yet, as recent studies of religious fashions suggest, apparently conservative or orthodox religious dress practices can be highly dynamic and innovative and often play off mainstream fashions. At one level this is evident from the extraordinary diversity of so-called 'Islamic fashions' developed by and for Muslims both in Muslim majority contexts (Sandıkçı and Ger 2007, Tarlo and Moors 2007) but also in Britain, Europe and America (Tarlo 2010, Lewis 2007, Tarlo and Moors 2013), or in the variety of stylish head coverings and glamorous wigs produced for the orthodox Jewish market, whether in Britain, the United States or Israel. At another level it is evident in the rise of fashion companies marketing 'modest fashions' to women of different backgrounds and faiths and in the shopping practices of modesty-conscious religious women, whether Hasidic Jews, covered Muslims or conservative Christians who buy many of their clothes in mainstream shops and department stores and adapt them to their own religious purposes (Fader 2009, Tarlo 2010). Clearly, religiously motivated dress and indeed the wearers of it are not always as insular, static and bounded as assumed.

But how significant is it that orthodox women of different faiths may shop in the same spaces and sometimes select the same garments? Brief encounters in the ladies' department of John Lewis in London or Macy's in New York can hardly be taken as proof of social or emotional empathy and interaction across religious boundaries. It could be argued that the anonymity of the department store obviates the need for social engagement beyond the simple act of purchasing a garment. Yet in the realm of internet commerce and discussion fora, anonymity functions somewhat differently. Here, paradoxically, physical distance offers the possibility of emotional intimacy. As many of the contributors to this volume show, many websites offer a combination of commerce, conversation and religious and moral education. In particular, online discussion fora on particular topics provide opportunities for high levels of engagement not only with friends but also strangers on themes of common interest or concern. And it is in this context that incidents of online interfaith interaction between orthodox religious women who belong to what are often considered some of the most insular segments of religious communities pose an interesting challenge to mainstream assumptions in politics, the media and anthropology. Here recognition of a shared preoccupation with modesty and with the challenges of finding visually appealing religiously appropriate forms of dress seems in some cases to unite rather than divide women, encouraging dialogue across faiths and stimulating mutual feelings of recognition and shared moral sentiment.

This chapter explores these possibilities through the study of debates about modesty taking place in Jewish websites which cater specifically to people who self-identify as Hasidic, orthodox or frum – categories which are by no means watertight, leading to a certain amount of terminological turmoil. Hasids ('pious ones') subscribe to strict forms of reformist orthodox Judaism popularised in eastern Europe in the eighteenth century and later transplanted to different contexts following the Holocaust. They are often referred to as 'ultra-orthodox' Jews but what is 'ultra-orthodox' to some is merely orthodox to others, reminding us that none of the popular terms – orthodox, ultra-orthodox, modern orthodox, traditional, traditionalist, revivalist, conformist, reformist and conservative – are clear cut. Furthermore the internet encourages further fluidity. In this chapter I have tried where possible to use the terms preferred by the people about whom I write whilst recognising that all strictly religious Jews try to observe the 613 mitzves (commandments) found in the Hebrew Bible. My contribution focuses in particular on conversations taking place with or concerning Muslims within the conservative end of the spectrum of the online orthodox Jewish milieu. It focuses principally, though not exclusively, on two websites: imamother.com, based in the USA and established by a Lubavitch woman with the stated aim of 'connecting frum women everywhere', and the American branch of chabad.org, the website of the Chabad-Lubavitch with a mission to 'unite and educate Jews worldwide'. It is no doubt significant that both websites are run by members of the Lubavitch which is considered the most outward oriented of the Hasidic sects owing to its emphasis on expansion through education and the recruitment of less observant Jews.

In keeping with the expansionist logic of the Chabad-Lubavitch, the websites chabad.org and jewishwoman.org (the women's section) are open to anyone who cares to browse them. The introductory pages are written in an energetic, enthusiastic and inspirational tone. The word Chabad is explained as 'a Hebrew acronym for the three intellectual faculties of chochmah – wisdom; binah – comprehension; and da'at – knowledge'. Chabad-Lubavitch is described more generally as being simultaneously 'a philosophy, a movement and an organisation' which aims to reach out to all Jews and sees itself as setting a good moral example for humanity at large.[3] The website offers a mixture of Scripture, advice, activism and information as well as spaces where people can ask questions and respond to articles on various topics. The women's section covers a range of issues on such themes as spirituality, health, childrearing, relationships and so forth, and contains a number of articles written by inspiring figures within the community.

Imamother.com offers a wider range of interactive possibilities but is less open to the general public, welcoming only 'married or divorced orthodox Jewish women'. To become a member, women have to fill out a form which, amongst other things, is designed to test their religious knowledge and credentials. If a prospective applicant identifies herself as a 'non orthodox Jewish woman', she is turned away with the message:

Imamother was created for orthodox religious women exclusively. If you are Conservative, Reform, Traditional, Reconstructionist, or simply not religious you are not eligible for entry. We define religious as keeping the following three mitzvos fully and completely. Taharas Hamishpacha – the laws of family purity and mikvah, Keeping Kosher, Keeping Shabbos. Thank you for visiting Imamother.[4]

Criteria of membership is then based on a set of orthodox practices though not restricted to particular sects. Members are requested to avoid highly controversial issues, insults, racism and the divulgence of unnecessary details of intimacy. The aim is to provide a place where frum women can 'relax, chat, debate, share tips and ask questions' in a 'private, authentic and modest' atmosphere. Not being an orthodox Jewish woman I did not attempt to become a member and restricted my research and analysis to areas of the website which are open to public access as opposed to chat rooms and user groups which are restricted to members only.

As with many of the Islamic websites I have written about elsewhere (Tarlo 2010), imamother.com provides a context where religious women can improve their religious knowledge and share their experiences of a whole variety of matters, including dress, child rearing, health, shopping, cooking and coping with work and family. Such spaces provide a supportive environment in which women share the trials and tribulations of daily life as well as asking advice of experts and of each other. In this sense they differ little from other online communities in which people are connected through a shared set of values and interests.

DEBATING MODESTY ON THE INTERNET

One topic that is much debated in the women's areas of orthodox Jewish websites and Islamic websites is the issue of modesty. In both cases understandings and definitions of modesty are varied, with multiple interpretations offered and discussed by religious women. Just as the Islamic notion of hijab refers to a whole set of ideas and practices regarding modesty, privacy and separation, so the Jewish notion of tzniuth covers a range of ideas concerning modesty, covering, dignity and privacy. Both religions offer scripturally ordained ideas on dress but interpretations of how these should be put into practice vary within and between faith groups.

Key areas of difference between orthodox Jewish and covered Muslim women's dress practices revolve around the questions of how, when and in what contexts parts of the body should be covered. Those orthodox Jewish women who perceive hair covering to be a *mitzvah* (commandment, obligation, blessing) cover their heads only once they are married, whilst those Muslims who perceive hair covering to be a religious duty or obligation advocate covering as soon as a girl reaches sexual maturity. Whilst orthodox Jewish women tend to choose from snoods, *tichels* (small headscarf), wigs and hats, with some Hasidic sects shaving their heads and wearing hats on top of wigs to signal their married status, most Muslims who cover favour headscarves. In addition, face veils are common in some countries like Saudi Arabia and Yemen and relatively uncommon in Muslim minority countries like Britain and the United States.

Both Jewish and Muslim women who maintain strict covering practices prefer to keep as much flesh as possible covered, with many Muslims exposing only the hands and face in public contexts where non-familial men are present, and strictly observant orthodox Jewish women taking care to cover the hair and wear clothes which cover the knees, elbows and collar bone. Whilst Muslim women in Britain, Europe and the United States often wear a blend of Western and Eastern styles and fabrics such as denim jeans, long skirts, trousers, tunics, robes and new styles of 'Islamic fashion' designed with Western Muslims in mind (Tarlo 2010), orthodox and Hasidic Jews on the whole follow relatively conservative styles of women's dress often considered 'European' such as tailored skirts and jackets with tights and simple elegant shoes. Strictly orthodox Jewish women also tend to avoid trousers as they are considered masculine attire and hence forbidden for women. The range of colours, styles and fabrics is therefore more restricted for strictly orthodox Jews than for many Muslims although a concern with fashion and elegance is nonetheless discernible (see also Chapter 4).

Reading through discussions of modesty on orthodox Jewish and Islamic websites, one is, however, far more struck by the many points of convergence than by the differences. Typically members of both communities place emphasis on modesty as a valuable female attribute to be cultivated and stress the importance of modest clothing as a means of upholding gender distinctiveness, maintaining boundaries between men and women, ensuring and guarding female privacy, containing sexuality to within marital relationships and reminding the wearer of her closeness to God and her membership of the religious community. The decision to cover one's hair is often represented as both a challenge and a blessing which brings spiritual rewards as well as marking levels of commitment. Women often describe head covering as one of the most difficult obligations to uphold, charting the difficulties they had when first deciding to cover in contrast to how they eventually grew into the practice. But many also stress that modesty is much more than just a matter of clothes: it is about an attitude, a way of life, an inner quality and mode of comportment.

'The laws of Tznius,' writes one woman in an online article entitled 'Taking it back', 'reflect the elevated way in which we perceive ourselves and at the same time, allow us to regain control of the way others perceive us.'[5] Her assertion resonates strongly with the way many Muslim women combine feminist and religious arguments in support of their dress (Tarlo 2010). Ideas of female empowerment are often used alongside the more traditionalist notion that women are 'precious pearls' which should be 'protected'. Wearing modest dress, many religious women argue, means that they will be judged not by their external appearance but for their internal worth. As Blima Moskoff puts it in her article 'Uncovering the mystery of Modesty', covering is not about 'hiding' but about 'exposing' her spirituality and 'inner self'.[6] This idea is further developed by those orthodox Jewish women who talk of nurturing and exposing the soul. For example, Robyn Cuspin argues: 'The laws of tzniut teach us that the body itself is clothing for the soul. By de-emphasizing the body we are declaring, *I am not a body. I am a soul wearing the body's clothes.*'[7] Whilst the stigma attached to visual distinctiveness sometimes features in both Jewish and Muslim accounts of enduring public insults, what features more strongly is the sense of pride in being recognised as a committed member of a religious community and in the continuity they feel with religious women of the past represented in sacred texts.

The complicated nature of the relationship between beauty and modesty is another common theme. Many religious women argue that modesty is about inner beauty. They nonetheless wish to find visually appealing ways of dressing modestly without wearing clothes which might be considered sexually provocative or revealing. As Esther Crisp, editor of thejewishwoman.org, put it, there is a fine line 'between being attractive and being attracting'.[8] Many women of both communities feel women are entitled to look attractive but should avoid looking alluring. In practice this generates a certain amount of anxiety and debate as women find themselves critical of the appearances of others but also critical of themselves for judging others by their appearances. Linked to this is an ambivalence towards mainstream fashions which are often portrayed as inappropriately sexual and revealing yet which may also act as a source of inspiration. Some are also critical of fashion companies and blogs which advertise 'Modest fashions' but offer clothes which do not fit their criteria of modesty. For example, when a Jewish frum blogger named Sharon invited readers of imamother.com to peruse her blog, www.Fashion-Isha, which she introduced as the 'coolest frum fashion life style blog', she found herself at the receiving end of a heated debate on tzniuth. Some praised the glamorous fashion and lifestyle spreads as inspiring; others were highly critical, feeling they represented a drop in standards. Taking a more analytical approach, one woman argued that 'Fashion is a tool for creative self-expression and as with any tool it can be used for good or evil. Each person and community has its own level of sensitivity.' After receiving nearly 200 comments, Sharon, the blogger, responded by thanking those who had 'defended' her. 'To the others,' she continued 'I am seriously listening and learning from your comments and I have even started questioning if I am justifying a lower level of tznius. So hopefully I will be able to make some small changes because there is no question that we are all here to grow and learn and improve ourselves.'[9] Sharon's concerns echo those expressed by some Muslim fashion designers and bloggers concerning the pull between a desire to experiment and the constraints represented by different interpretations and levels of modesty.

MODESTY – A MEETING POINT

How far are orthodox Jewish and Muslim women aware of their shared preoccupations and articulations of modesty? And to what extent do they express forms of interfaith recognition and engagement? One context where shared recognition clearly emerges is in Christian and Muslim responses to some of the articles on tzniuth (modesty) posted up on the chabad.org website. For example, Yael Weil's essay, 'Undercover: A Woman's Journey of Understanding Modesty', struck a chord with women of other faiths. In it the author recounts how and when she started wearing wigs and how covering the hair offered her a new self-image and sense of connection with the Divine. She discusses modesty in terms of inner motivations and speaks of the benefits of cultivating an attractive but non-provocative appearance. She also suggests that covering her hair infuses her with a 'continuous message of modesty', offering 'another step towards the ideal of a perfected personality'.[10]

Just as many Muslim women do not wear hijab, so many Jewish women are opposed to wigs but in this highly orthodox milieu responses to this article were mainly positive and included a response from a Muslim: ' Your article is so amazing. It's so true … I will most certainly take your words with me through life … May God fill all our lives with peace.' Another reader interjected,

> I am a Christian woman and have yet to hear the topic of modesty in a woman so well put as you have. Whether Jewish, Muslim or Christian, inner modesty is so important in keeping true to what is important before G-d … I celebrate this act and hope that this will be the way we should all be.

Similarly in the heated and contested debate following a short article on wigs entitled 'The Meaning of Hair Covering', written by Aran Moss, a rabbi based in Australia, we find interventions from a headscarf-wearing Christian woman who is 'thrilled to know that others are covered too', though sad to hear Jewish women squabbling about it, and an intervention from a Hindu in south India who is fascinated to learn of Jewish covering which she compares to Hindu practices.[11] Here there is also a more ambiguous discussion in which Muslim face-veiling practices are compared to Jewish ideas of covering.

Whilst many of the interventions discussed suggest recognition of common ideas behind covering practices and their perceived benefits, others express recognition of some of the tensions surrounding interpretations of modesty in practice. This was beautifully demonstrated through a cartoon posted up on imamother.com with the accompanying message, 'Apparently we're not alone in the "Hot Chanie" problem; there seems to be a "Hot Fatima" problem too!' (see Figure 11). The cartoon showed two hijab-wearing girls outside a mosque dressed in high heels, skin-tight clothes and lashings of make-up, criticising an inconspicuously dressed young woman who wears a simple loose skirt and plain long-sleeved top but does not cover her hair. 'How can she dress like that when her religion is Islam?' asks one of the lip-sticked hijabis![12]

Hot Chanie is the name given to what are perceived to be tartily dressed orthodox Jewish girls whose appearance obeys the technical requirements of tzniuth by covering the appropriate areas but is flashy and sexually provocative, contradicting the very meaning of tzniuth. Hot Chanie made her debut in the Jewish blogosphere in 2006 and has generated

11 Cartoon posted on the *imamother.com* forum, 31 January 2010. Accessed 10 November 2011.

pages of online chat, laughter, outrage, sightings and hilarity. The person credited with having invented her is Shifra, a popular Jewish blogger[13] who classifies herself reluctantly as 'modern orthodox'. When her blog reached 100,000 hits she attributed the success in part to *Hot Chanie*. Whilst *Hot Chanie* and her Muslim equivalent generate a certain amount of mockery, they also generate critical self-reflection amongst members of both faith groups concerning whether religious women have the right to pass judgement on each other when everyone struggles with issues of self-improvement.

In some cases, articles and blogs posted on the internet offer fragments of insight into encounters taking place in physical space. In a fascinating account entitled 'How did Daughter of the Enlightenment end up wearing a wig?', Jan Feldman, an associate professor of political science at Vermont, recalls how it was during her sabbatical year in Montreal that she first began to cover her head on a regular basis, aided in part by the fact that the city was 'full of women in hijabs and various head coverings' which made it easier for her to cover.[14] Here Muslim women's hijabs feature as reassuring, giving encouragement to a Jewish woman who wanted to cover but feared it would make her too conspicuous. But hijabs can also feature as disconcerting in some Jewish women's accounts. In a blog entry playfully entitled 'Tznius Showdown at SuperCuts', Shifra, of *Hot Chanie* fame, recalls her initial feelings of bewilderment at coming face to face with a hijabi hairdresser. My apologies to Shifra for not quoting her in full:

> Last week my daughter and I went to get haircuts at a local (but not too local) discount hair cuttery ... Now I know that many frum women would never get their hair cut in a public place ... [but] I go for the quick, cheap, anonymous back of the salon hair cut and I'm OK with that. This time, however, there was a bit of a twist. When it was my turn to have my hair cut my stylist turned out to be a sweet young Muslim woman in a **hijab**. For those of you from the midwest or living under a rock, a hijab is that head scarf that muslim women wear, covering their heads and necks. I, on the other hand, was wearing a **mitpachat** (hebrew for headscarf) or tichel (Yiddish for a headscarf) – also known as a *shmateh* (if you ask my mother) covering only my hair ... **It was a tznius showdown**!
>
> When I uncovered my hair I did feel more self-conscious about it than usual. Would this woman uncover her head for a haircut? I wondered. Would she consider ME immodest or worse a hypocrite? Did I care? If so why? ... When I did uncover my head the woman was surprised to find my hair was already fairly short. I told her I like to keep people guessing. She replied that friends were always surprised to find that she often changes her hairstyles and colors despite the fact that she keeps her hair covered up in public. As she washed and cut my hair we chatted about religion and head coverings (the when, where and how but most interestingly not the WHY) ... it was a very interesting conversation and a good haircut too![15]

There followed an amicable exchange of ideas, with the hairdresser demonstrating the benefits of a 'hijab pin' and Shifra demonstrating popular Israeli styles of tying scarves and concluding that the *tzniuth* showdown had been a draw! What is interesting about this posting is not only the obvious feelings of curiosity and empathy described by Shifra but also the many positive comments this encounter generated amongst her Jewish readers. 'Hairdressing meets interfaith dialogue. I love it,' writes 'Scraps'. 'Shame we can't all get along and appreciate differences and similarities,' writes 'Lakewood Venter'. 'It takes these types of conversations, I believe to help overcome prejudices, fears and misconceptions from all sides,' writes 'Sweettooth120'. Here real-life encounters in the physical world become expanded in the virtual world, enabling reflection on the proximity of Jewish and Muslim practices amongst a wider group of frum women as well as the sharing of practical and commercial tips. When one reader tried to drag the discussion into more complicated political terrain, commenting, 'if only we could get along so well in Gaza and the West bank!', Shifra was keen to clarify, 'Just for the record, this post was not meant to have any political overtones – it was more of a social/comparative religious type thing.'

From such fragments recounted online one also gets a sense of how material inventions and commercial ideas travel across and between faiths. This was Shifra's first encounter with the hijab pin and she joked about the possibility of marketing it to frum women under a different name. Soon one of her readers was talking about trying it out and suggesting that it should be called 'scarf pin' to make it sound more interfaith. A few pages later, a hijab-wearing Muslim woman posted up the link to a commercial hijab pin website.

In this case it was the novelty and practical potential of the hijab pin that had generated interfaith dialogue. In Linda Korn's article, 'Is that the J-Lo style: My Journey to Haircovering', it is trendy hats and scarves which, she claims, 'led to many great discussions with Jews and non-Jews alike', providing some sort of 'cross-cultural forum' at her workplace in Los Angeles.[16] If artefacts function as triggers for dialogue, then the websites marketing them also offer important conduits of knowledge about the dress practices of other faith groups as well as raising the possibilities of objects crossing religious boundaries. Whilst frum women would be unlikely to enter specialist shops selling Islamic or Christian goods in the physical world, they can enter the virtual world of religious commerce and chat with no more than the click of a button. So do orthodox Jewish women surf around on Islamic websites?

Whilst it is difficult to gauge the extent of interfaith purchases, there is certainly evidence that orthodox Jewish women are aware of Islamic fashion companies and Muslim blogs and are often keen to get ideas from them. One *imamother* member asks:

I know some say that fashion doesn't go along with tznius, but after seeing a Muslim blog on ideas about clothes/veils etc, I was wondering does something similar exist for tznius clothing. I am not talking about merchants' sites of tznius but a fashion tznius blog … does it exist?[17]

In this case she is recommended to take a look at *Frumfashionista* and *Modernly Modest* (both Jewish sites), but when a woman who describes herself as 'non-Jewish or non-practising' writes on the *Chabad.org* website asking for advice on where to buy modest clothes, given that the rabbinically approved *tznius.com* website offers little,[18] it is suggested she look at various websites, including Lilies of the Field, a Christian family business based in Kansas, and Shukr, an Islamic fashion company based in Damascus but catering to Muslims living in the West.

Similarly whilst some orthodox Jewish women are turning to Jewish companies such as Aqua Modesta, Sea Secret and HydroChic to find suitable forms of modest swimwear, others are turning to Islamic websites. Testimonials on the Ahiida website, which advertises 'burquinis', suggest that their products are purchased and appreciated by women from a range of backgrounds including Jewish and Christian women as well as people concerned with body shape or protection from skin cancer.[19]

In some cases we find orthodox Jewish women discussing clothes marketed on Muslim websites with considerable enthusiasm. For example, an *imamother* posting about the Egyptian headwear store, Wegdan.com (see Figure 12), generated a stream of appreciation from *frum* women, with several women picking out headwear styles they would like to wear. Here some anxiety was expressed as to whether it was acceptable for *frum* women to purchase garments from a Muslim site. At the same time there was much discussion of the compatibility of the designs with Jewish aesthetic sensibilities, with one woman commenting, 'Lots of [those scarves] can be worn "Jewishly".' There was much appreciation of the innovative and attractive ways the headwear was folded, plaited, layered, wound, stitched and tied on this website, making headcovering a glamorous and appealing option. 'I'm really blown away by the creativity and beauty of almost everything on the site,' writes 'Writermom'. 'Wow,' adds 'Fox':

> These are just what I've been trying to find for a long time! My old snoods look dated; I look goofy in turbans – even around the house; and I look even worse in pre-tied tichels. I need a kind of combination, which is what these seem to be. Has anyone ordered one yet?

'Pooh' speaks of waiting for her 'dh' [dear husband] to get home so that she can gauge his opinion 'aesthetically and halachically speaking' on whether she could purchase items from the site. 'I have gotten hijabs in the past to wear as tichels,' writes another contributor. 'I think those of us who wear

12 Headwear designed by
Wegdan Hamza, available
online through her website.

modest clothing should unite. I have a dream of opening a clothing store for
all women who dress modestly and calling it "Women of Valor".[20]

Seeing the appeal of her website to orthodox Jewish women, I emailed
Wegdan Hamza to find out more about her business. She told me that she
was born and raised in Egypt and that she had started designing headwear

in 1975 after she began wearing hijab. Her idea had been to make attractive designs that made it easier for women who wanted to cover their hair in the face of opposition from their families. She later spent six years in Canada where she expanded her headwear range to suit the Canadian market which consisted mainly of orthodox Jewish women and cancer patients. She was delighted that a researcher should take an interest in interfaith modesty since she sees headcovering as 'a link between all the Holy religions' which can help to 'reduce anger between mankind'. She was herself writing a book about headwear and its continuity in religions through the ages. It was interesting that although she does not make any verbal references to Jewish women on her website, readers of imamother had picked up on the Jewish-sensitive design and aesthetic. Here again one gets a strong sense of the interrelationship between interfaith engagements in the virtual and non-virtual world.

All of these examples, taken together, support the idea that the internet is offering unprecedented opportunities for even the most orthodox of religious women to engage with other faith groups and that ideas of modesty and modest fashion have become significant channels through which communication, ideas and actions flow. But it would of course be naïve to assume that such interactions are tension-free or that they signify the dissolving of apprehension between communities. What one senses is a combination of curiosity, appreciation and suspicion which lends a certain fragility to some of these encounters as seen from my final two examples.

The first concerns a discussion thread on imamother.com entitled 'Muslim blog featuring tzniuz!!'.[21] In it, a contributor called 'mama-star' writes, 'I googled "tichels" and look what I found!!' To her surprise the search engine took her to a Muslim blog entitled hijabchique where she came across a picture of a Jewish woman wearing a green tichel along with an article which explained about Jewish covering practices and ideas of tzniuth. The tichel was compared to hijab with suggestions of how Muslim women might adapt it.

The contributor 'mama-star' was enthusiastic about her discovery, pointing out how the Muslim blogger had talked about her 'orthodox Jewish sisters'. 'Bambamama' agreed: 'Yes, it is very nice that she refers to us as sisters ... would we reciprocate?' But after this the discussion deteriorated as Jewish women began to pick up on some of the comments posted by Muslims on the hijabchique blog. Whilst one woman writing anonymously had stressed that the two religions were very similar and asked why there was such a great divide between Jews and Muslims, another had interjected, 'Ummm – if you'd stop killing us, it might be a little step in the right direction.' Another commented that although she personally liked some of the items she had seen on Jewish modest clothing sites, she would probably never buy them out of fear that the money would go towards the Israeli oppression of Palestinians. A parallel reservation is expressed by a Jewish woman in relation to the otherwise desirable hijab under-caps available on the website, almuhajabat.com: 'I think I would have an issue with buying stuff made in Syria.'[22] Whilst some women of both communities were clearly keen to forge connections through shared recognition of the importance of modesty, others clearly wanted to keep divisions raw or avoid breaking down perceived barriers.

My final example concerns a discussion thread on the imamother website, entitled 'A Song on Tznius'. The posting read:

> This is really [a] beautiful song on Tznius …
> But …
> and it's a really big but …
> It's not from a Jewish source. It's from a Muslim source. But it's in English and beautiful and powerful and if one word – hijab – was changed to tznius, it would be the perfect tool to inspire about tznius …[23]

By clicking on a YouTube clip, it was possible to hear Ali Dawud Wharnsby (a Muslim convert of Scottish and Canadian descent) singing an inspirational lyrical song entitled 'Hijab'. It is a song in wide circulation in Muslim youth circles and is generally accompanied by a film showing images of women and girls in hijab in different countries and contexts. The lyrics recount the feelings of a Muslim girl who chooses to wear hijab in the face of criticism from those around her who tell her she is oppressed. The girl not only defends her choice of dress, declaring it to be an act of freedom and modesty, but also criticises the glitzy billboards and magazines advertising phoney fashions she considers demeaning to women. The song contains catchy phrases such as 'Faith is more essential than fashion, wouldn't you agree?', and describes the hijab as a 'mark of piety' for 'all the world to see'.

Responses from Jewish women on imamother were varied. 'They [the Muslims] are tsnius on the outside but what happens in the inside?' asked one suspicious observer. Her negative attitude was challenged by another:

If this teaches us anything, it's that some of them feel the same way that women here do … they dream of a life where somebody will understand their positive feelings about modesty and their desire to follow what they believe God expects of them. Why would you want to turn this into something negative? Finding something in common with other cultures, particularly this one, should be a good thing.

A third participant offered a more competitive model of piety: 'I will admit, I have heard Rabbonim say that there are two ways we should work on ourselves because the Muslims are 'one-upping' us: on tsnius and tfilah [prayer].' Whilst the previous participant persisted in arguing that 'finding common ground and values' could be 'enlightening, reassuring and encouraging', she was met with the bleak response: 'For what purpose? They want to kill us and we want to kill them!'

At this point the discussion thread was abruptly closed by a moderator and the following words inserted: 'Locked for review, should we be getting our chizuk and inspiration from unkosher sources?' That was in May 2008 and both the video clip and discussion thread have been locked ever since.

Whilst on the one hand, expressions of hostility, suspicion and difference can be attributed in part to international politics and events which push people into polarised positions, on the other hand the pressure to maintain differences is also boosted by the idea, valorised both by Jewish and Muslim women who cover, that as proud members of a religious group, they should remain visually distinctive and recognisable. This emphasis on being visibly Muslim or visibly Jewish serves to mitigate against the dissolving of boundaries between different forms of religious dress beyond a certain point. As we have seen, Jewish women look to how they can de-Islamisise goods sold by Muslims just as Muslim women look to how they can adapt Jewish styles to suit Islamic preferences.

CONCLUDING REFLECTIONS

A study of this kind which focuses almost exclusively on interfaith engagement over the internet inevitably has its limitations. Quite apart from the obvious, though sometimes exaggerated, fact that online identities can be fictional and that not everyone has access to the internet, there is also the fact that discussion fora are moderated spaces where debates are to some extent edited or, as the last example shows, may be censored or truncated.

As one participant in an online Islamic forum put it, the internet itself is 'a veil' which serves to conceal identities. Furthermore it is impossible to read from these encounters what or who has been excluded. We are restricted to analysing only those interactions that have left their traces in cyberspace.

It would be wrong, however, to consider that such debates and interactions are insignificant simply because they take place in cyberspace, for digital media have become an integral part of everyday life for many. Furthermore experiences which take place online may have transformative effects offline, just as interfaith engagement offline is recounted and reworked in cyberspace. The hijab pin example points to this two-way process. Demonstrated by a Muslim hairdresser to a Jewish client, it is later featured in the latter's blog where frum women experiencing various practical problems with keeping headscarves in place respond with interest, suggest giving the pin a more neutral name and incorporating it into their wardrobes. Here we see how a single unplanned encounter can, through its articulation on the internet, become magnified into something of greater significance with the potential to transform not only Jewish knowledge but also practices.

From an ethnographic point of view, online discussion fora and blogs are interesting for the intimate levels of debate they enable. In some ways, they represent an ethnographer's dream – access to the conversations and opinions of large numbers of people undisturbed by the disruptive presence of the researcher. This is not to say that the conversations that take place there represent some sort of unmediated, unselfconscious form of expression. It is clear, for example, that participants in imamother.com have a sense of belonging to a particular community which brings with it certain expectations of behaviour, etiquette and perspective, including constraints on what might be said and how. Yet it is precisely because this is a safe space for members of the community who by definition share much in common that members feel relatively free to express their opinions. Such fora offer access to the subjective perspectives of women it might otherwise be difficult to get to know.

What then should we make of the curious patchwork of fragments of interfaith engagement concerning issues of modesty and dress expressed within the specific domain of orthodox Jewish websites? Clearly it would be wrong to read too much into these encounters which are in some ways 'modest', and yet what they clearly show is an openness on the part of some orthodox Jewish and Muslim women to recognise and appreciate where their values, preoccupations and concerns converge and to learn from one another's struggles, practices and solutions. Modesty in this context offers a meeting point and this meeting is facilitated by the internet. When orthodox Jewish women in the United States discuss a moral beauty contest in Saudi Arabia in terms of its relevance to their own lives or when they listen to a song about hijab for the inspiration it might offer concerning *tzniuth*, or when a Muslim blogger advises Muslims on how to tie a *tichel*, we find small but compelling and emotive examples of connection between women who belong to religious communities which are often perceived as, and almost expected to be, oppositional.

Whether through recognising shared values and dilemmas, finding common solutions or surfing each others' websites and blogs in search of clothing, fashion tips and ideas, they enter each other's imaginative and material landscapes, however briefly, and, in many cases, challenge their own preconceived prejudices and ideas. Such encounters go against the grain of popular and academic representations of orthodox and conservative religious groups who are usually portrayed as insular, uncompromising, inflexible and secluded. They also go against politicised representations of religious clothing practices as intrinsically divisive. What we see here is a certain openness to others on the part of religious women which curiously is often lacking on the part of liberal thinkers in their portrayal of orthodox religious groups. Most importantly, we see the need for further studies which offer flexible methodologies and which do not just compare religious groups but also trace the relationships between them.

NOTES

1   http://www.imamother.com/forum/viewtopic.php?t=118337. Accessed 7 November 2011.
2   http://www.youtube.com/watch?v=Jl7bqYrICyA. Accessed 10 November 2011.
3   http://www.chabad.org/global/about/article_cdo/aid/36226/jewish/About-Chabad-Lubavitch.htm. Accessed 8 November 2011.
4   http://www.imamother.com/religious_staus.htm. Accessed 6 November 2011.
5   http:/www.being jewish.com/krese/tznius.html. Accessed 16 November 2010.
6   http://www.chabad.org/the JewishWoman/article-cdo/print/true/aid. Accessed 19 November 2010.
7   http://www.chabad.org/theJewishWoman/article-cdo/print/true/aid/527056. Accessed 19 November 2010.
8   http://www.chabad.org/the JewishWoman/article-cdo/print/true/aid. Accessed 19 November 2010.
9   http://www.imamother.com/forum/viewtopic.php?printertopic=1&t=152579&postdays=0&postorder=asc&start=0&finish_rel=-10000. Accessed 10 November 2011.

10 http://www.chabad.org/theJewishWoman/article-cdo/aid/397787. Accessed 22 October 2010.
11 http://www.chabad.org/theJewishWoman/article-cdo/aid/336035. Accessed 21 October 2010.
12 http://www.imamother.com/forum/viewtopic.php?printertopic=1&t=104185& star... Accessed 10 November 2011.
13 askshifra.blogspot.com. Accessed 11 November 2011.
14 http://www.chabad.org/theJewishWoman/article-cdo/aid/840073/je... Accessed 22November2010.
15 askshifra.blogspot.com/2006_06_01_archive.html. Accessed 11 November 2011.
16 http://www.chabad.org/theJewishWoman/article_cdo/aid/833177/jewish/Is-That-J-Lo-Style.htm. Accessed 21 November 2011.
17 http://www.imamother.com/forum/viewtopic.php?t=87758&highlight... Accessed 13 December 2010.
18 http://www.chabad.org/theJewishWoman/article-cdo/AID/958266. Accessed 19 November 2010.
19 See http://www.ahiida.com. Accessed 15 December 2010.
20 http://www.imamother.com/forum/viewtopic.php?printertopic=1&t=104185& star. Accessed 10 November 2011. See also http://wegdan.com.
21 http://www.imamother.com/forum/viewtopic.php?t=87742&highlight... Accessed 13 December 2010. See also http://hijabchique.blogspot.com/2008/11/tichels-introduction.html. Accessed 13 December 2010.
22 http://www.imamother.com/forum/viewtopic.php?t=60438. Accessed 7 November 2010.
23 http://www.imamother.com/forum/viewtopic.php?t=47962. Accessed 21 November 2011.

REFERENCES

Ahmed, Leila (1992). *Women and Gender in Islam: Historical Roots of a Modern Debate*. New Haven, CT, and London: Yale University Press.
Arthur, Linda (ed.) (1999). *Religion, Dress and the Body*. Oxford: Berg.
Bowen, John (2008). *Why the French Don't Like Headscarves*. Princeton, NJ: Princeton University Press.
Bullock, Katherine (2003). *Rethinking Muslim Women and the Veil*. Herndon: IIIT.
Fader, Ayala (2009). *Mitzvah Girls, Bringing up the Next Generation of Hasidic Jews in Brooklyn*. Princeton, NJ: Princeton University Press.
Jones, Carla (2007). 'Fashion and Faith in Urban Indonesia'. *Fashion Theory*, 11, 2/3: 211–32.
Lewis, Reina (2007). 'Veils and Sales: Muslims and the Spaces of Postcolonial Fashion Retail'. *Fashion Theory*, 11:4: 423–41.
Marty, Martin E. and Appleby, R. Scott (eds) (1994–2003). *The Fundamentalist Project*. Chicago, IL: University of Chicago Press.
Sandıkçı, Özlem and Ger, Güliz (2007). 'Constructing and Representing the Islamic Consumer in Turkey'. *Fashion Theory*, 11:2/3: 189–210.
Scott, Joan Wallach (2007). *The Politics of the Veil*. Princeton, NJ: Princeton University Press.

Tarlo, Emma (2010). *Visibly Muslim: Fashion, Politics, Faith*. Oxford: Berg.
Tarlo, Emma and Moors, Annelies (eds) (2007). 'Muslim Fashions'. *Fashion Theory*, 11:2/3.
———— (2013). *Islamic Fashion and Anti-Fashion: New Perspectives from Europe and America*. Oxford: Bloomsbury.
Valins, Oliver (2003). 'Stubborn Identities and the Construction of Socio-spatial Boundaries: Ultra Orthodox Jews Living in Contemporary Britain'. *Transactions of the Institute of British Geographers*, 28 (2): 158–75.
Warnsby, Dawud (2004). 'The Veil'. Enter into Peace. http://www.wharnsby.com/Lyrics/archives/000190.html.

WEBSITES

www.ahiida.com
www.chabad.org
www.hijabchique.blogspot.com
www.imamother.com
www.Islamonline
www.shiachat.com
www.shukronline.com

4

HASIDIC WOMEN'S FASHION AESTHETIC AND PRACTICE
The Long and Short of *Tzniuth*

Barbara Goldman Carrel

> When fibres, fabrics and ways of wearing are the medium for one's relationship to other people and the gods, we cannot have 'cloth' and 'religion' we can only have the materiality of cosmology. (Miller 2005: 7)

When I tell people that I'm interested in and write about Hasidic women's fashion, the response is most often something like, 'Oh, I didn't know there was such a thing!' or 'Well, I guess there's not that much to write about'. While it is true that Hasidic women are profoundly committed to modest dress and operate within strict religious, cultural and material guidelines, that by no means discounts their desire for fashion. Many Borough Park Hasidic women are indeed regular and savvy shoppers, rummaging the racks of their neighbourhood clothing stores in Borough Park, Brooklyn, and frequenting major department stores and discount fashion outlets all over Manhattan.

No, these women are not dressed in the latest revealing styles advertised by mainstream fashion media whether in print, on billboards or online. But they do pursue, purchase, parade in and promote mass-produced fashion from the American and European fashion systems. Most significantly, the female Hasidic shopper rarely selects the same ready-made garments or fashion elements that appeal to the New York City fashionista, nor will she consume the products she's purchased completely unadulterated. An investigation into Borough Park Hasidic women's selection (which clothing elements are preferred and why) and appropriation (both physical and ideological) of mass-produced fashion will reveal a culturally distinct clothing practice whereby these women construct (both physically and ideologically) their own unique female Hasidic fashion aesthetic in relation to mainstream American fashion.

FASHION

New York City's predominantly Hasidic Borough Park, Brooklyn, has become a global shopping mecca for many Torah-observant women due to the availability and variety of fashionable modest attire. Fashion abounds in Borough Park, both in the dress of the women walking down its main commercial thoroughfare of Thirteenth Avenue and through many of the women's clothing store awnings which line the street. Store names such as New Look Couture, Today's Fashion and The Chic Look are quite commonplace and unapologetically broadcast Hasidic women's appetite for fashion. Window displays, attempting to catch the eye of the ready-to-spend female shopper, blatantly and masterfully advertise their stores' merchandise through the construction and manipulation of fashion imagery. A women's novelty shop on Hasidic Thirteenth Avenue provocatively flaunts its merchandise by means of a fashion photograph of a bare shouldered woman seductively peering out from under her chic red-ribboned hat (see Figure 13). A peach-coloured scarf functioning as a 'dickey' (a fabric insert worn to fill in the neckline of another garment) is strategically placed over the photograph to partially cover the woman's chest, shoulders and collarbone so not to completely offend the religious community of orthodox and Hasidic men, women and children passing by.

The Bobover, one of Borough Park's largest Hasidic communities, originated in Poland and first settled in the United States on the West Side of Manhattan after the Second World War. Led by their third rebbe, Rav Shlomo Halberstam, the Bobover Hasidic community eventually made their way to their current home in Borough Park, Brooklyn, during the mid-1960s. A formal, conservative, 'Old World' aesthetic (see discussion below) radiates from the clothing of the women gathered in the Bobover *bes medresh*, or house of worship, located on the corner of 48th Street and Fifteenth Avenue in Borough Park. Many of the women are formally dressed in classically styled designer-like skirted suits made

13 Provocative fashion window display found on Thirteenth Avenue, a Borough Park commercial thoroughfare.

of dark fabrics and robust prints or in fitted blazers and skirts, or dresses, all with long sleeves and high necklines, fancifully embellished with gold embroidery, garnished yokes, gem detailing, or wide borders of contrasting patterns (see Figure 14). Stylish pillbox hats, stiff and precisely rounded, are familiar fashion fixtures. These head-coverings, although not necessarily 'in' by contemporary American standards, are often adorned with 'fashion' by means of a gold stick pin or shiny

14 Bobover
women dressed
for a wedding.

brooch. Even the most sacred symbol of the Hasidic woman's dress
code, her wig, can, at times, deliberately articulate fashion. Some wigs
are highly stylised with trendy, wispy bangs, ponytails enhanced with
coloured bows or crowned with dark headbands spattered with shiny
rhinestones, pearls or other fashionable hair accessories.

While fashion is unmistakably endorsed, and even celebrated, in both
everyday and ceremonial contexts, it is also reviled by many Hasidic
women in particular, and the Hasidic community in general. From the
perspective of dominant Hasidic religious and cultural ideology, the
American fashion system is a real and constant threat to the strength
and continuation of their community, seducing their women to pursue
materialistic, individual desires rather than the spiritual, communal goals
of the Torah and their people. Chaya, a Bobover Hasidic woman living in
Borough Park, equates women's craving for fashion to the deteriorating
downward spiral and disease of addiction: 'You're having a drug epidemic.
We're having a fashion epidemic.'[1]

During my early fieldwork, which largely took place in the early 1990s, many lectures (recorded and distributed on audio cassette tape) were marketed specifically to Hasidic women in an attempt to combat the influx of fashion. These lectures were often led by *rebbetzin*, or wives of rabbis, who play an important role in their communities, most particularly in relation to women's issues and observance. One lecture by London Rebbetzin Rubinitz confirms that the ultra-orthodox community of women were falling prey to the materialistic enticements of mainstream fashion. Employing the same metaphor of addiction as Chaya, she warns her audience of Torah-observant women that the entrapment of fashion can be a pretty slippery slope:

> One should look nice. One should look well turned out. And that's very different from the woman who has a brown dress on. And, on the brown dress, she has little gold, round buttons going all the way down. Because of that, her old brown pair of shoes in the closet were no good ... She had to go to the store to buy a brown pair of shoes which had a round, little gold buckle on it ... to match the little gold button [on her dress]. And then, on her pocketbook, there had to be a corresponding little gold buckle ... And then we have a little brown bow in the *sheytl* [wig] to make the thing complete.[2]

The enticement of fashion is often translated as the *yetzer hora*, or evil inclination, which lures young Hasidic girls and Hasidic women to purchase mass-produced clothing that not only materially accentuates the female body and feminine sexuality, but also symbolises the sin and indecency of American secular culture. Mrs Glazer, a sewing teacher at Bnos Zion, a Bobover school for girls, created a modesty handout for her students entitled *The Honor of a Jewish Girl is Inside*, to alert them to the evils of dominant American fashion and arm them with the ideological perseverance and technical weaponry to maintain their modest dress and Torah-observant way of life in the face of this powerful infiltrating 'outside influence'. Her handout personifies fashion as the villainous *yetzer hora* tempting young girls with the convenience of modern ready-to-wear clothing. She warns her students to be always vigilant:

> Many clothes and patterns today are made without zippers and buttons. 'It's so convenient, just slip it on!' That's the *yetzer hora* talking to us. These necklines will be cut low, and it is interesting to note that very

often the collar bone will be covered; it does indeed seem that all is well. However, if we focus our attention on the side of the neck, we find that it is exposed. (n.d.: 1–2)

Tzniuth dress, or modest dress, as the symbolic assertion of Hasidic identity, femininity and religiosity, is not only essential in the construction of Hasidic women's distinctive fashion aesthetic and practice, but is also the principal medium through which Hasidic women defend themselves against the 'subversive' power of dominant American fashion displays in particular, and the dangerous influences of American secular culture in general (Goldman Carrel 2008). Hasidic girls are taught at a very young age the importance of dressing in a manner which reflects their inner soul rather than emphasising any external manifestation of feminine physicality – sexual or otherwise – or drawing attention to themselves.

The religious requirements of modest dress to cover the *ervah*, or erotic, parts of the female body may be clearly understood and easily achieved. However, *tzniuth*, as a religious, cultural, aesthetic and even material ideal, is not only quite intangible and difficult to achieve but also open to divergent forms of collective and individual interpretation and expression. Hence, an acceptable mode of modest dress for observant Jewish women can vary considerably with regard to the acceptance of appropriate fabrics, the stylisation of stockings or socks and even the length of hems and/or sleeves between the Hasidic and orthodox communities, among different Hasidic communities and even within a particular Hasidic community or Hasidic family.

Tzniuth dress is further complicated in that many Hasidic women voice a very strong desire to present themselves as not only attractive in their modest dress but also fashionable (in a distinctively 'Hasidic way'). Ayala Fader, in her ethnography on the socialisation of young Bobover Hasidic girls into Bobover wives and mothers, entitled *Mitzvah Girls: Bringing Up the Next Generation of Hasidic Jews in Brooklyn* (2009), reports that, 'A goal for this generation of Hasidic girls and their mothers is to successfully participate in the embodied discipline of modesty which, girls are taught, need not preclude being with it ... [or] looking good' (Fader 2009: 147). She also relates that there is indeed a Yiddish word frequently used by Bobover girls to label those peers who fall short of presenting a fashionably modest look: the term *neb* is used to describe a girl who dresses unfashionably (Fader 2009: 132).

Mrs E, a 30-something-year-old orthodox Jewish woman I recently met in Borough Park, introduced herself to me as someone who was 'raised very Hasidic'.[3] She now lives in the predominantly orthodox Brooklyn neighbourhood of Flatbush with her husband and two young sons. Mrs E confided in me that in addition to wanting to appear attractive, fashion (along with cooking and food) is one of the few outlets an observant Jewish woman may employ to express individual creativity and/or mark economic, religious and/or social distinction within her community. Yet, the desire to be 'fashionable' extends beyond dressing creatively and appealingly for themselves, their husbands and the orthodox or ultra-orthodox communities. These women, living in such close proximity to the diverse and sophisticated fashion world of Manhattan, frequently acknowledge the importance of not being perceived as 'old-fashioned' or 'backwards' in the eyes the larger New York City population.

Hasidic women's everyday clothing practice, then, involves an extremely complex set of negotiations in an endless interpretive struggle between religion, custom and fashion. The goal for these women is to construct and achieve a mode of dress which is not only wholly (and 'holy') representative of Hasidism's 'hyperbolised' interpretation of a feminised Jewish modesty but one that is attractive, fashionable and truly reflective of their distinctive female Hasidic aesthetic, all constructed overwhelmingly from mass-produced garments engendered in the dominant fashion system. As Mrs E complained to me in one particular conversation, 'It's very difficult to dress fashionably and modest. There are not that many options.'

Özlem Sandıkçı and Güliz Ger identify a similar struggle in the 'beauty work' involved in Islamic women's headscarf practice in Turkey (2005). These authors demonstrate how these women experience comparable concerns in their desire to meet the material requirements of Islamic modesty and yet be seen as attractive and up-to-date: '[T]he headscarf and head covering practices embody the struggle between remaining faithful to the Koranic principles on religiously appropriate dressing and constructing a fashionable, beautiful and modern appearance' (Sandıkçı and Ger 2005: 61). Moreover, and much like the Hasidic women with whom I spoke, these authors found that many observant Muslim women living in Turkey today claim,

> ... that forming a wardrobe of matching clothes and scarves is more costly for covered than uncovered women who can 'go out in a pair of jeans and a T-shirt'. They argue that it takes a lot more time to search

for and is more difficult to find *tesettur* [religiously appropriate modest dressing] clothes that are beautiful and fashionable. (Sandıkçı and Ger 2005: 71)

HASIDIC WOMEN'S FASHION AESTHETIC DEFINED

Years ago when I was first introduced to Hasidic Borough Park, the manager of The Chic Look, a women's clothing store, spoke not only to Hasidic women's desire for fashion but also the existence of a unique Hasidic fashion aesthetic in relation to dominant American fashion trends when he said, 'These women want to be stylish. They really want to be "in fashion". But within their *own way.*'[4] At that same time, Suri, a newly married Hasidic girl in her twenties working in a neighbouring women's clothing store on Thirteenth Avenue, positioned her community's sense of decency in fashion above and in direct opposition to the lack of fashion in the provocative materialistic displays of New York City's mainstream female population. She asked rhetorically, 'These women in the streets … They're dressed to sell the body. Where's the fashion?'[5] Mrs E made a recent comment to me, similar to Suri's, which attributes a lack of discretion and fashion competence to most 'women in the street'. Mrs E is extremely forthcoming in divulging how utterly unimpressed Hasidic women are with the creativity and taste level of the average American fashion victim when she declares, 'These women who are supposed to be fashionable? I think they look lousy. They don't look nice. And those women who wear jeans everyday … That's boring. That's not original.'

Hasidic women's distinctive definition of fashion and their wardrobe choices were almost always presented to me in direct opposition to the dominant American fashion statements of the non-observant, non-Jewish secular world, as were most Hasidic lifestyle choices such as Jewish dietary laws. Ayala Fader offers an explanation for the Hasidic propensity to persistently position their customs in direct opposition to the ways of the non-Jewish, secular community: 'In some ways Gentiles and their immodest ways sustain and enable Hasidic women's claims to superiority and truth. Gentiles – their bodies, behavior and ways of speaking – are a continual warning of how not to be' (Fader 2009: 158). Departing words from Mrs Glazer's handout provide a scriptural reference point. She quotes the one Torah prescription on modesty most influential in shaping the female Hasidic fashion aesthetic in direct relation to the dominant American fashion aesthetic: 'Remember: "You shall not walk in their statuses". Not everything "in style" is our style!' (Glazer n.d.: 5).

So what is Hasidic fashion? And what are the meanings inherent in and promoted by the female Hasidic fashion aesthetic? First and foremost, as Mrs E reminds us, 'You cannot lump all Hasidic women into one fashion category.' Indeed, a multitude of material productions display the continuum of religious and cultural interpretations of *tzniuth* among and between distinct Hasidic sects, within individual Hasidic communities and even individual families (Goldman Carrel 1999 and 2008). It is important not to generalise one homogenous and static Hasidic women's aesthetic distinction to all Brooklyn Hasidic women. For example, the women of the Satmar Hasidic community living in Williamsburg, Brooklyn, may share the formal, conservative 'Old World' fashion aesthetic so characteristic of Bobover women, yet their dress is considered to be much more stringently modest. And the Lubavitch Hasidic women living in Crown Heights, Brooklyn, in general, are seen as promoting a more 'casual', 'American bohemian' fashion aesthetic.

Nonetheless, one defining characteristic of the dress worn by Borough Park's community of Hasidic women would be an unmistakable 'Old World' aesthetic. Fader concurs: 'These women have a clothing aesthetic that is most distinct from mainstream fashions. Other Hasidic women I met called this a "European look," again evoking an idealized pre-war European past' (Fader 2009: 151). Fader maintains that Bobover women and girls, through language and dress, aim to 'reproduce an idealized and imagined femininity of past generations' (Fader 2009: 121). This longing to replicate the life of their pre-war European ancestors perhaps stems from glorifying their ancestors' spiritual and religious commitment, as Chaya's comment so clearly demonstrates: 'In the old country, before the war, our people were on such a high level. The frum [Torah-observant] people were on such a high level of Judaism.'

Some adjectives commonly used by Hasidic and orthodox women to describe Borough Park Hasidic women's 'Old World' taste and culturally specific sense of style are 'tailored', 'formal', 'classic', 'neat', 'fine', 'elegant', 'refined'. Mrs E uses the terms 'conservative' and 'fancy' when characterising even the *everyday dress* of ultra-orthodox Torah-observant women:

In Borough Park, where there's mostly Hasidim, they're much more conservative [than the orthodox women living in Flatbush, Brooklyn].

Depends on which country they came from. The Satmar [women living in Williamsburg, Brooklyn] from Hungary are very fancy. But the Bobover women from Poland seem to have caught up with them.

Mrs E further distinguished the dress choices of Borough Park Hasidic women in opposition to non-Hasidic Torah-observant women and the dominant American taste for casual attire by instructing me that these women most certainly never wear 'trendy' or 'bohemian' clothing. Fader corroborates that Bobover women's construction of an appropriately Hasidic modest appearance in part involves an intentional aesthetic distancing from the typical informal clothing choices of the secular female consumer:

> casual clothing, like a hooded sweater, is considered less modest because of its associations with North American dress more generally, such as jeans, hooded sweatshirts and sneakers. Indeed, formal dress is one of the defining features of Hasidic femininity. (Fader 2009: 174)

During my original research, many women of the Bobover community stressed the word 'proper' in describing their dress. The desired representations of femininity for a Bas Yisrael (Daughter of Israel) might best be described as 'heymish' or homey (not homely, for heymish has positive connotations in the religious Jewish community), and 'balebatish' or respectable. These culturally-specific symbolic meanings in the female Hasidic aesthetic signify and further enhance the Hasidic woman's revered role of homemaker, where in Hasidic culture, the resident woman and her exemplary Jewish home are considered the cornerstones of and showpieces in the community. Bobover women stated that a requisite formal, proper and respectable aesthetic presentation guarantees respect and honour in the eyes of their extended families and the larger Hasidic and non-Hasidic Jewish communities, in addition to asserting this image to the New York City general public.

This 'Old World' formal aesthetic is partially generated through the selection of clean, straight silhouettes in dark solid colours, typically black or dark navy blue, and fashion accessories which all contribute to a 1940s-like style. Mrs T, a charming salesperson now working in the newly located The Chic Look, explains the reason for dark, solid, sombre colours when she says, 'Hasidic women do not wear colours that stand out. [For example,] no red.'[6] Apparel detailing and ornamentation are best described as elegant and regal. Gold, rhinestones, velvet, fur and ornate embroidery are some of the materials and design elements used to embellish the formal, classical silhouettes of Borough Park Hasidic women's everyday and ceremonial attire.

Choice of fabric is fundamental in demarcating Hasidic women's formal fashion distinction. Hasidic women pride themselves on purchasing clothing manufactured from quality fabrics. The former manager of The Chic Look once boasted to me that he never stocks his women's clothing store with polyester apparel because it simply 'will not move off the racks'.

Borough Park Hasidic women determinedly disapprove of one fabric in particular – the ubiquitous, all-American denim. Many non-Hasidic orthodox young girls and some non-Hasidic orthodox women do in fact wear denim. Moreover, not all Hasidic women renounce this fabric choice. Some Lubavitch women, for example, will wear denim skirts with appropriately modest hem lengths. An extreme condemnation of this material by one Hasidic community is illustrated by a series of 2007 incidents in Kiryas Joel, a Satmar Hasidic village in Monroe County, upstate New York. One family had their two vehicles vandalised and public notices were circulated urging them to leave this ultra-orthodox community simply because the wife habitually chose to wear blue-jean skirts and bright-coloured blouses.

This textile choice represents a most meaningful material distinction. Borough Park Hasidic women's condemnation of the American-made denim is almost always referenced in direct opposition to dominant American secular, meaning non-Jewish, tastes. Mrs T explains: 'Denim is more for [non-Jewish women's] everyday dress. That's not for the Jewish people. It's for Gentiles, farmers. It's not refined.' According to the Hasidic community, two significant distinctions are marked through this blue cloth. Denim is not only considered the fabric of the masses, but is also considered too informal and unsophisticated. Mrs E explains:

We don't wear jeans because ... And this is what I was told ... jeans originally came on the scene as a 'poor man's fabric'. We think of ourselves as princesses and that's why we don't wear a 'poor man's fabric'. (See below for further discussion on the Hasidic ideology of royalised femininity.)

HASIDIC WOMEN'S CLOTHING PRACTICE
AND THE FEMALE HASIDIC AESTHETIC

The female Hasidic shopper selectively consumes, physically appropriates and ideologically resignifies purchases she's made of mass-produced garments from both the American and European fashion systems. These practices constitute a culturally distinct form of subcultural clothing practice whereby Hasidic women construct their distinctive female aesthetic in direct relation to dominant American fashion in particular, and American secular culture in general. Their conspicuous mode of dress not only asserts their position within (both distancing from and competing with) the larger secular New York City population but also promotes culturally meaningful principles of Hasidic religiosity and womanhood (Goldman Carrel 1999 and 2008).

The dynamics and outcomes of Hasidic women's culturally distinct clothing practice are similar to the clothing practices discussed in Alexandra Palmer and Hazel Clark's *Old Clothes, New Looks: Second-Hand Fashion* (2004). These authors demonstrate how the recycling, reworking and reconfiguring of second-hand clothing interweaves both local and dominant modes of fashion to literally and figuratively reshape and ultimately *form new modes of fashion*:

> a transformation must take place in order for used clothes to become acceptable in another cultural context. The meanings of commodities are not fixed and new meanings are assigned relative to the consumer, not inherent in the process of production. (Palmer and Clark 2004: 100)

Just by walking into any of the women's clothing stores on the main thoroughfares of Thirteenth and Eighteenth Avenues in Borough Park, one immediately discovers the uniqueness of the Hasidic shopping experience. Strollers are often lined up with sleeping infants or toddlers just inside the entranceway of stores with little to no supervision while mothers comb through racks and racks of dark-coloured clothing. Toys are frequently strewn about on the floor in a corner to occupy children who are awake and out of their strollers.

The stylistic preference of these Borough Park women frequently involves the consumption of dominant American and European designer wear and fabrics as long as they can be modesty-appropriated. On my first trip to Hasidic Borough Park, The Chic Look's manager informed me that he principally stocked conservative apparel from mainstream fashion designers such as Calvin Klein, Ralph Lauren and Anne Klein. Ella, an orthodox Jewish woman living in Flatbush, Brooklyn, defends Hasidic women's passion for designer clothing by stating, as a matter of fact, that Jewish women have historically dressed in the 'best' clothing: 'Designers became a very big thing. [But] Jewish women were always dressed, in any country, in any place, unless they were being persecuted at the time, Jewish women were always dressed in the best clothes.'

Their consumer preference for designer fashion in part stems from the belief that Jewish women in general, and Hasidic women in particular, aspire to be dressed in the 'best' clothing made from 'quality' fabrics designed and manufactured by the fashion system's officially designated (conservative) elite. Because Hasidic men's dress patterns are so rigidly bound by custom and materialistically so dissimilar from contemporary menswear, Hasidic women's dress has become a symbolic vehicle for asserting social and economic position within the mainstream American society of which this community is an undeniable part. Chaya explains:

> It's all around. You work in Manhattan … If you're all day, nine to five, working with either Gentiles or irreligious people and you want to find favour in their eyes, and you don't want to look like some kind of unsophisticated person, so you try to [dress fashionably] …
>
> They're [Torah-observant Jews] also involved with other societies [non-Hasidic and non-Jewish] that they have to impress or that they have to deal with … In defence of these women [who are very fashion conscious], one reason is that when they go out to work, they're in the offices, they're in Manhattan. And the women have to compete with this. So this is sort of a legitimate reason that they have to look like this to compete.

When first visiting Hasidic women's apparel stores in Borough Park, I found fashionably-modest mass-produced clothing of dark solid colours which complied with prescribed hem and sleeve lengths, and neckline styles that covered the collarbone to meet *tzniuth* requirements without much ado. At that time, both store proprietors and Hasidic women complained of an overwhelming deficiency in the availability and selection of ready-made fashionably attractive *tzniuth* clothing. Indeed, most contemporary fashion wear neither satisfied the specific Torah prescriptions for physical coverage nor those governing appropriately modest fabrics, designs and/or colour choices. Interestingly, these stated shortcomings in mass-produced clothing and the transgressions of the American fashion system are what motivated (and continue to motivate) the distinctiveness of both Hasidic women's mode of dress in relation to the dominant stylistic displays of the larger New York City community of women and their consumption patterns in comparison to the mainstream American fashion shopper.

Hasidic women and girls employ a variety of physical techniques to nullify the profane material constructions inherent in ready-to-wear garments. The dickey historically has been perhaps the most uncomplicated practice whereby women and girls 'Hasidify' mass-produced clothing with plunging, V-neck, or other revealing necklines. The ever-present dickey can still be found today in some women's retail clothing and trimming stores, and tailor shops in Hasidic Borough Park. In lieu of purchasing a dickey, Mrs Glazer's handout on modesty offers her female high school students a multitude of sewing techniques to raise shoulder seams, reset sleeves and fashion homemade dickeys to compensate for low and squared necklines found in immodest off-the-rack clothing which, according to her, 'usually spell trouble' (Glazer n.d.: 3).

Many other home-based alterations which Hasidic women and/or girls may apply to physically appropriate immodest items of dress are outlined in Mrs Glazer's brochure. Her instructions are thoughtfully delivered with an irrefutable appreciation for her students' interest in fashion and concern for presenting a polished look. She provides instructions on how to 'Hasidify' skirts and sewing patterns for garments which are 'too tight', that is, in Hasidic terminology, 'too revealing', all the while preserving the original fashion essence of the garment. For example, she encourages young girls to convert mass-produced skirts with immodest slits into pleats, all the while ensuring that the stylish silhouette is retained (Glazer n.d.: 4). And, if it becomes absolutely necessary to eliminate a slit altogether, Mr Glazer sympathetically offers a fashion-saving, discrete way to accomplish that so 'your neighbor will never be able to tell' (ibid.). Most importantly, Mrs Glazer instils in her students and encourages a consciousness of their unique style. She writes, even though 'the skirt will look slightly different; it will now possess a chic [look,] uniquely ours' (Glazer n.d.: 5).

Garment altering techniques or what Mrs Glazer labels 'koshering' mass-produced clothing are served up with an enthusiastic 'team spirit' in the hopes of inspiring her students to maintain tzniuth and their female Hasidic aesthetic distinction:

... the hardships involved in finding clothing that we both want to wear and that we can wear according to *halakhoth* [laws of the Torah] are rampant everywhere! In an effort to help grapple with this problem, attached you will find ideas and suggestions that might come in handy. Altering a pattern, closing a slit, koshering a neckline – it's not difficult, and it can be done! Let's all do it together! (Glazer n.d.: 1)

Knowingly anticipating her students' reservations for grappling with mass-produced fashion evils, Mrs Glazer responds sternly with an indisputable command to safeguard their *tzniuth* wardrobe:

The typical argument will be: 'If the slit is eliminated, I can't walk in the skirt. It's too tight!!' You have answered your own question; a tight skirt that is uncomfortable without a slit has no place in your wardrobe. (Glazer n.d.: 4)

The shortcomings of immodest ready-made garments from dominant American clothing manufacturers have activated a range of unique commercial services in Brooklyn's Hasidic Borough Park which further contribute to and facilitate Hasidic women's distinctive clothing practice. When I first began my research years ago, many of the women's apparel stores I visited on Thirteenth Avenue either sold or donated supplementary pieces of fabric in order to 'tzniuthise' profane hem and/or sleeve lengths and revealing necklines. Garment pieces (mostly remnants of fabrics in assorted dark colours) were publically accessible, stored in bins or cubbyholes located in the back of many women's clothing stores. In addition to acquiring extra pieces of fabric, one of the buyers for a women's clothing store informed me that he intentionally sought out and stocked skirts and/or dresses with particularly generous hem and/or sleeve lengths to augment indecencies for that outfit in matching fabric, especially for summer wear when ready-made garments are so skimpy. Necessary alterations were then completed on site by store seamstresses, off site by neighbourhood tailors, or at home by skilful consumers.

More recently, and although not completely extinct, the all-purpose dickey has fallen out of fashion, most especially for the younger Hasidic female generation. On a recent visit to Hasidic Borough Park, I did come across a few women's clothing stores and a trimming/fabric store where one could purchase this bygone wardrobe necessity in one or more styles. However, as Mrs T from The Chic Look informed me, most women no longer utilise this dress accessory. Bins of supplementary fabric, at one time very common, also seem to be a thing of the past.

Augmenting physical deficiencies in mass-produced fashion wear, once accomplished almost exclusively by the dickey or fabric remnants, seems to have been replaced by a more convenient, stylish and 'modern' material alternative, 'layering'. Many women with whom I recently spoke, both Torah-observant female consumers and mangers of women's apparel stores along Borough Park's Thirteenth and Eighteenth Avenues, lauded the ease and range of aesthetic possibilities provided by a system of layering shells, tees, camisoles and long-sleeve or quarter-length-sleeve dresses under immodest off-the-rack clothing. As Mrs T puts it, plain and simple: 'Layering is a big thing now.' Reina Lewis observes that Borough Park women's embracing of layering reveals how 'Hasidic fashion both follows and adopts mainstream fashion trends and modes of production. Layering is a mainstream story adopted by diverse modest dressing communities … made possible by the advent of globalised fast fashion' (personal communication 2011).

On a recent visit to Borough Park, I witnessed rack upon rack in many women's clothing stores dedicated to layering pieces in a variety of fabrics, styles and colours – predominately black, varying shades of dark blue, whites and ivories. Today, there are retail stores in many Torah-observant communities both in Brooklyn and worldwide as well as online entirely devoted to, or specialising in, selling layering components for the religious Jewish community of women. The Shell Station is one such vendor with retail establishments catering to Hasidic and orthodox women in Flatbush, Borough Park and Williamsburg, Brooklyn, in Lakewood and Monsey, New York, and in Israel, with 'an exclusive collection of shells' for 'Ladies, Women, Maternity and Kids' (see Figure 15).

Interestingly, although Mrs E at first universally proclaimed, that 'Everyone layers now,' she tempered her comment by saying, 'Not everyone does it. Some Hasidic women don't think it's dressy enough.' She provided the example of a specific context in which some Hasidic women she knows would not layer under an immodest garment with a recent purchase for her sister-in-law's upcoming wedding. She explained that she decided on a dress designed with an immodest open V-back. In order to 'tzniuthise' this dress, she procured the services of a woman who acquired some 'very expensive fabric', dyed it to match

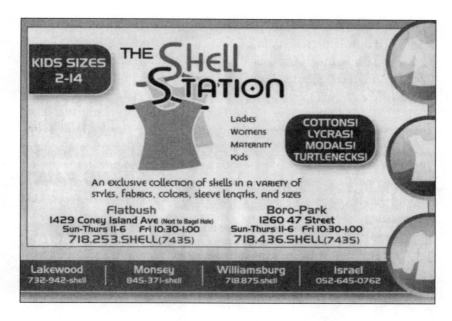

15 The Shell Station advertises the
abundance and variety of layering
garments, *Esra Magazine*, November 2011.

her dress and then fashioned a shell for her to wear underneath. Mrs
E clarified to me that some of her Hasidic relatives would not wear
layered attire to a wedding simply because they deem it too casual
and not formal enough.

One commercial service operation that has managed to survive
the commercial invasion of layering and continues to flourish is the
dressmaker and/or tailor dedicated to serving both the Hasidic and
non-Hasidic Torah-observant communities of women in Borough Park
and beyond. They are particularly skilful in constructing appropriately
stylish 'tzniuthised' custom-made versions of mainstream American fashion,
particularly for *simchas*, or ceremonial occasions. Many religious women
of economic means pay for custom-made Hasidic versions of high fashion
black tie apparel, especially for children's or grandchildren's weddings,
due to the undeniable lack of evening wear with adequate coverage sold
in mainstream department stores or average American women's better
dress shops.

When I first entered Toby's Dressmaking years ago, I was surrounded by high couture representations of fashion torn from the latest issues of dominant fashion magazines such as *Vogue*, *Harper's Bazaar* and *Modern Bride*. Toby, the resident 'expert dressmaker', proudly pulled out a photo album with pages and pages displaying her extraordinary skills at fabricating 'Hasidic Haute Couture' or 'Hasidified' versions of dominant haute couture (see Figure 16). On a recent visit back to Toby's (now Toby's Fashions), she informed me that she no longer displays her album of tailor-made modest fashions nor posts fashion magazine tear-outs on the wall. When I asked her how she stays up-to-date with current fashion trends, she responded, 'I just know. I watch television. I look at magazines.'[7]

16 Toby the Dressmaker's Hasidified version of a mainstream bridal gown.

IDEOLOGICAL APPROPRIATION AND
THE FEMALE HASIDIC AESTHETIC DISTINCTION

In addition to *tzniuth* and the physical appropriation of apparel born of the American and European fashion systems, religious notions of Hasidic women's spiritual and feminine distinction are mapped onto Hasidic women's clothing by means of a 'discourse of royalty' which serves to mediate the profane materialistic significations associated with dominant secular fashion. This ideological resignification, both by Hasidic women and the subcultural Hasidic fashion system, validates and publicises Hasidic women's spiritual distinction in relation to their male counterparts in particular, and the Hasidic community's spiritual superiority, and hence social distinction, in relation to dominant American secular (non-Jewish) culture in general.

In his ethnography of *Growing Up Hasidic* in the Bobover community, Robert Mark Kamen asserts that 'the Bobover Hasidim see themselves as part of an elite continuum; they are direct descendants of the men and women who received the law on Mount Sinai' (Kamen 1985: 7). Kamen maintains that this religious or spiritual ideology of elite distinction derives from the orthodox Jewish belief that 'at Sinai, God gave the Jews Torah, or divine purpose. The Jews were chosen, it is believed, to uphold Torah because *they alone among nations possessed souls capable of this awesome burden*' (Kamen 1985: 4; emphasis mine).

This Hasidic ideology of spiritual superiority, and hence social distinction, is substantiated in the following portion of Rebbetzin Rubinitz's audio taped lecture:

> The Torah says ... you're a special treasured nation ... *Kahal Yisreal* [the People of Israel] are supposed to be the *Kohanim* [high Jewish priests] of the world ... We are different from the *Goyim* [non-Jews]. We have different standards. We have different ideals in life ... We have a higher goal, a higher purpose ... [God] chose us because he saw within us, the potential to ... be something higher than the rest of the human race.[8]

Not only does Hasidic religious ideology bestow an elite spiritual distinction to the Hasidic people in general, but Hasidic women, in particular, also hold an esteemed spiritual position within the confines of their seemingly patriarchal Hasidic world. In her ethnographic comparison between newly orthodox Hasidic and non-Hasidic women (*ba'alot teshuvahs* or those 'returning' to Judaism) throughout the United States, Debra Kaufman (1991) writes that despite some commonality in their traditional interpretations of Jewish womanhood,

> Hasidic women were more likely than non-Hasidic women not only to affirm their honoured place in the theology, but to assert that their sensibilities might even be *superior* to those of men. Indeed, some *invert the gender hierarchy* by claiming that the highest levels of spirituality are reached through female life-cycle experiences. (Kaufman 1991: 54; emphasis mine)

Hasidic women assert that one of their unique and honoured contributions to the world is their innate spirituality which, in general, is considered to be more reflective of God and 'godliness' than men's spirituality due to women's biological capabilities. A Lubavitch Hasidic women's publication, *The Modern Jewish Woman: A Unique Perspective*, elucidates further:

> Woman's body ... reflects in a sense more of the aspect of G-d's essence than does man's, as Chassidus [teachings of Hasidic *rebbes*] explains. For woman has the ability to create within herself a new life, a new creature, a 'something from nothing,' and this parallels and derives from the power of the essence of G-d to create *ex nihilo*, to create from utter nothing. This is one of the ways in which woman is in a more sensitive spiritual position than man. (1981: 25)

Femaleness as a reflection of godliness is also unmistakable in the theosophic doctrine of Hasidism. Moreover, this feminine imagery of godliness is often articulated through a 'discourse of royalty'. For example, the *Shekhinah*, or the Presence of God on Earth, is considered to be the female manifestation of God which, according to Gershom Scholem, in his classic *Major Trends in Jewish Mysticism*, 'is not only *Queen, daughter*, and *bride* of God, but also the *mother* of every individual in Israel' (Scholem 1995: 230; emphasis mine). Israel and *Shabbos* (Sabbath), two of Judaism's most important symbols, are also 'feminised' and often referred to in 'regal' terms throughout Hasidism's mystically oriented doctrine. Elliot Wolfson, a scholar of kabbalistic texts and traditions, asserts that Israel, the feminised symbol for the entire Jewish nation, is cherished as 'the royal crown of God, the King'.[9] And *Shabbos*, articulated and religiously observed as 'a taste of the World to Come' is signified and celebrated as the *Shabbos Queen*. Fader provides yet another example. During her fieldwork, she attended a lecture for brides where the speaker proclaimed, 'Like a Torah, a Jewish girl ... should be adorned in a way that befits her holy, royal Jewish nature' (Fader 2009: 164).

Fader highlights Hasidic women and girls' use of the term *aydlkayt*, or 'refinement', as a royalised aesthetic goal which not only affirms but also justifies their materialistic inclination for the 'the finer things in life': 'The refinement (*aydlkayt*) attributed to Jewish women ... compares Jewish women to royalty. Some Hasidic women suggested to me that Jewish women's "royal souls" require or seek out expensive finery' (Fader 2009: 164). With specific reference to mode of dress and adornment, Fader maintains that Hasidic women and girls 'even claim that it is part of their royal, Jewish nature to seek out the highest-quality clothing or jewelry, legitimizing their taste for expensive goods' (Fader 2009: 178). Mrs E's previous comment on her community's condemnation of denim further substantiates, unequivocally, the existence of a royal ideology which in part fuels the construction and display of Hasidic women's distinctive fashion aesthetic: 'We think of ourselves as princesses. And that's why we don't wear a poor man's fabric.'

This 'discourse of royalty', or the symbolic expression of Hasidic women's regal feminine spirituality and their community's superior religious position, is employed by the orthodox and ultra-orthodox Jewish fashion system to resignify dominant American and European mass-produced fashion. The royalisation of Hasidic women's fashion is both produced by and communicated through the names and advertisements of women's clothing stores, both on the streets of Borough Park and online by webstores specialising in Jewish women's modest attire. This subcultural practice not only nullifies the profane material essence of mainstream (secular) fashion, but also simultaneously constructs, validates and further promotes Hasidic women's distinct regal aesthetic.

Royal Lingerie, a women's lingerie store on Thirteenth Avenue in the heart of Hasidic Borough Park, unquestionably utilises a 'discourse of royalty' to sell a sense of nobility through their bras, panties, camisoles and loungewear to majestically adorn the modest Jewish queen rather than merely cover her. A Borough Park bridal shop markets itself as Royal Bride (see Figure 17) as assurance that their soon-to-be-married female patrons will be 'crowned with royalty' when purchasing from their 'unique and unparalleled collection of imported and domestic bridal gowns'. The Tznius Princess (see Figure 18), another bridal shop in Brooklyn catering to the religious community of Torah-observant women, pictures a modestly

17 The Royal Bride advertises royal distinction, *Esra Magazine*, c. 1990–93.

dressed princess bride-to-be in an overflowing 'Haute Couture' gown cascading down an elegant stairway she's ascending towards aristocracy, class and fashion.

The royalisation of fashion and products of adornment can also be found online, with webstores that specialise in selling modest apparel for the devout Jewish woman. It is important to note here that these websites are most probably owned by members of the orthodox Jewish community rather than the Hasidic community. Yet, this religious ideology of spiritual distinction for the Jewish woman in particular, and the Jewish People in general, is not unique to the Hasidic community.

18 The Tznius Princess promotes modest haute couture, *Esra Magazine*, November 2011.

As stated above, it is clearly evident in orthodox Jewish ideology as well. Moreover, although Hasidic women do not regularly shop online (most ultra-orthodox homes in Borough Park do not have full or unrestricted internet access), Mrs E did inform me that some Hasidic women do, on occasion, use their husbands' office computers to 'cybershop'.

Fortune Wigs (www.fortunewigs.com), selling the most conspicuous item of the religious Jewish woman's wardrobe, resignifies this otherwise outdated fashion item to articulate affluence, luxury and wealth for those who choose to purchase and parade in one of their many fashionable headcoverings. Raza Designs online (www.razadesigns.com), who boast a transnational, religiously inclusive consumer base, provides a collection of 'elegant and casual loungewear, hostess gowns, robes, vintage gowns, caftans, evening gowns, wrap robes, modest clothing, modest shabbos clothing, muslim garb, shabbos robes, frum clothing, jalabeas and peignoir sets'. Raza employs a marked 'discourse of royalty' in branding and describing many of her majestically inspired *Shabbos* robes. For example, the 'Queen of Diamonds' (see Figure 19) is richly fabricated in black velvet and gold diamonded tapestry, then adorned with a regal gold sash centred down the garment. The royal narrative reads, 'Exquisite! You're a Queen. Treat yourself royally.' Other modest *Shabbos* garments in Raza's inventory labelled with noble distinction are the 'Queen of London' and 'Royalty in Purple'.

In addition to the presence of a blatant regal vocabulary employing words such as 'royal', 'queen' and 'princess', written declarations of taste distinction – 'excellence', 'class', 'elegance' and 'exclusivity' – are broadcasted through women's clothing store awnings and retail advertisements towards the construction and promotion of a privileged and refined mode of Hasidic fashion. These written markers of exclusivity and elite taste distinction provide insight into what is considered fashionable and therefore valued by this community of religious women in particular, and their community as a whole.

The Top Shop, a self-proclaimed leading vendor of 'Exclusive Ladies Fashions' in Borough Park, shamelessly offers their Hasidic female clientele the highest quality, select merchandise. Another women's clothing store on Thirteenth Avenue adopts a minimalist awning employing three discriminating words, Unique Distinctive Classic, to draw those customers who desire a selective, timeless wardrobe. Coat Plaza announces itself as 'The Elegant Discounter', attempting to appeal to the shrewd sophisticated woman interested in refined, chic outerwear at a reasonable price. An apparel heaven with racks of modest ready-made garments produced by the top players in the fashion field awaits the Hasidic woman who enters through the gates of Designers Paradise.

Many online wig retailers describe their *tzniuth* competence, design skills and selection of head coverings in superlative terms to portray an expert image to solicit the patronage of discerning religious female customers wishing to adorn themselves in distinction. Yaffa Wigs (www.yaffawigs. com) promotes *'excellence'* through her *'exquisite'* wigs made from *'only the finest virgin European hair available'*. She promises that her incomparable wigs are 'certain to *exceed every expectation*'. Miri (www.miriwigs.com), another wig

Queen of Diamonds. - 1056-V2T72

$150.00 - Regular Sizes
$160.00 - Plus Sizes

Exquisite! You're a Queen. Treat yourself royally
You deserve it. This piece is such an elegant
silhoutte. The faux coat meets at
the waist and the sash ties it all together. The sash can be worn tied in front or back to accentuate a fitted contour.
Black Stretch Velvet & Gold Diamond Tapestry
90% Polyester 10% Spandex
24" Zipper This garment can be rented for theater groups or costume parties. Please make a note in the comment
area that you are interested in a costume rental and we will contact you.

Specify size: [Size ▼]

Size Chart How to measure

Select Option: [Option   ▼]

Specify length of the dress or sleeves (in inches) and we can
hem your dress at extra $15.00 and sleeves for extra $8.00.
(Hemmed items not returnable.):

Hem: [   ] " Sleeves: [   ] "

About Hemming
(*Absolutely no Returns after alterations.)

Quantity: [1   ]

[ADD TO CART]

19 Royal distinction offered by the luxurious Queen
of Diamonds *Shabbos* robe, Raza Designs e-retail
webpage, screenshot. Accessed 22 November 2011.

designer dedicated to the cyber community of Torah-observant women, boasts of their unique expertise, exceptional hair creations and select clientele in equally superlative terms:

> Miri began as an elite establishment. Utilizing unique knowledge of wig design, Miri wove the finest of hair … Soon it became known that Miri was synonymous with perfection … And so we began providing discerning customers with exquisite hair pieces and custom designs. For over a decade, Miri has been available to a select few but now Miri has fashioned an exclusive line for a new, important, highly-exclusive client – You![10]

CONCLUSION

It is my hope that this ethnographic example of Hasidic women's clothing practice and distinctive fashion aesthetic will extend existing definitions and understandings of the relationship between fashion and local and/ or subcultural practices, forms and meanings. Hasidic women's mode of dress is assembled largely from mass-produced, ready-to-wear mainstream merchandise. It is not presented as a conspicuous 'uniform'. Nor is it 'exotic' or 'iconic' in form or substance. Yet, a closer look at Hasidic women's clothing practice does in fact reveal a distinctive mode of consumption and appropriation which ultimately produces a distinct alternative (local or subcultural) mode of fashion and aesthetic.

Hasidic women are selective in their consumption of dominant fashion apparel. They often physically alter and/or manipulate their mass-produced dress purchases to meet the hyperbolised definition of Hasidic feminine modesty. Dominant fashion is not only physically transformed; Hasidic women and the orthodox Jewish fashion system resignify dominant fashion with culturally specific meanings of Hasidic womanhood, royalty and social distinction. Their distinctive mode of clothing practice ultimately produces a unique Hasidic female fashion aesthetic created through an active (and reactive) dialogue with dominant American (non-Jewish, secular) fashion and American (non-Jewish, secular) consumer culture.

NOTES

1 Interview with Chaya Klein in her house in Borough Park in the autumn of 1992.
2 Tape recorded lecture by Rebbetzin Rubinitz from the early 1990s.
3 Conversation with Mrs E in Borough Park tailor shop, October 2011.
4 Conversation with the manager of The Chic Look, women's clothing store in Borough Park, early 1990s.
5 Conversation with Suri, a woman working in a women's clothing store in Borough Park, early 1990s.
6 Conversation with Mrs T, working at The Chic Look in Borough Park, November 2011.
7 Conversation with Toby at her dress shop, October 2011.
8 Tape recorded lecture by Rebbetzin Rubinitz from the early 1990s.
9 Elliot Wolfson, 'Jewish Mysticism and Hasidism'. Lecture, Department of Hebrew and Judaic Studies, New York University, autumn 1991.
10 Miri Wigs, http://www.miriwigs.com/about-us/. Accessed 9 January 2012.

REFERENCES

Fader, Ayala (2009). *Mitzvah Girls: Bringing Up the Next Generation of Hasidic Jews in Brooklyn.* Princeton, NJ: Princeton University Press.
Glazer, Rifka (n.d.). *The Honor of a Jewish Daughter is Inside.*

Goldman Carrel, Barbara (1999). 'Hasidic Women's Head-Coverings: A Feminized System of Hasidic Distinction', in Linda .B. Arthur (ed.), Religion, Dress, and the Body. Oxford: Berg.

——— (2008). 'Shattered Vessels That Contain Sparks of the Divine: Unveiling Hasidic Women's Dress Code', in J. Heath (ed.), The Veil: Women Writers on Its History, Lore, and Politics. Berkeley, CA: University of California Press.

Kamen, Robert Mark (1985). Growing Up Hasidic: Education and Socialization in the Bobover Hasidic Community. New York: AMS Press.

Kaufman, Debra R. (1991). Rachel's Daughters: Newly Orthodox Jewish Women. New Brunswick, NJ: Rutgers University Press.

Lubavitch Educational Foundation for Jewish Marriage Enrichment (1981). The Modern Jewish Woman: A Unique Perspective. Brooklyn, NY: Lubavitch Women's Organization.

Miller, Daniel (2005). 'Introduction', in Suzanne Kuechler and Daniel Miller (eds), Clothing As Material Culture. London: Berg, pp. 1–19.

Palmer, Alexandra and Clark, Hazel (eds) (2004). Old Clothes, New Looks: Second-Hand Fashion. Oxford: Berg.

Sandıkçı, Özlem and Ger, Güliz (2005). 'Aesthetics, Ethics and Politics of the Turkish Headscarf', in Suzanne Kuechler and Daniel Miller (eds), Clothing As Material Culture. London: Berg, pp. 61–82.

Scholem, Gershom G. (1995). Major Trends in Jewish Mysticism. New York: Schocken Books.

WEBSITES

Fortune Wigs, www.fortunewigs.com. Accessed 5 May 2011.

Miri Wigs, www.miriwigs.com. Accessed 9 January 2012.

Raza Designs online, www.razadesigns.com. Accessed 22 February 2011.

Yaffa Wigs, www.yaffawigs.com. Accessed 29 September 2011.

Part 2

Modesty without Religion? Secularity, Shopping and Social Status through Appearance

5

DENIM
The Modesty of Clothing and the Immodesty of Religion

Daniel Miller

WHEN RELIGIONS STRIVE TO BE IMMODEST

For as long as I can recall, amongst both my family and many other families we know well, there has been an assumption that to be a member of the UK Jewish community it is practically compulsory to read a weekly newspaper called the *Jewish Chronicle*. The *Jewish Chronicle*, or JC as it is colloquially known, was founded in 1841 and reading it has become something akin to those many more formally sanctioned rituals and duties that come with religious identification. When meeting with other Jewish families the conversations often centre on things we have read in this paper. Being Jewish, this translates as bonding around the very different ways we all vehemently disagree with and are outraged by much of what we have read in this week's JC.

I have no systematic evidence, but from my own personal recollection I would note that there is a particular storyline that reoccurs every few years. This will concern some ultra-orthodox Jewish group in New York or Israel and their decision to ban adherents of the group from wearing denim. The implication refers to the women of this group, since there is no chance that men in ultra-orthodox Judaism would in any case have been wearing denim. I have always been curious, not just about the fact that any group might choose to do this but also why this newspaper should intermittently choose to report that they have done this. The readership of the newspaper is largely mainstream readers such as myself, including members of liberal, reform and orthodox synagogues and those unaffiliated to a formal congregation, with varying degrees of religious observance. The stories about denim reflect a sort of fascination that the mainstream has with what is seen as the rather extreme or outlandish behaviour of the ultra-orthodox. A fascination which has grown as we have come to realise that this branch of Judaism, so far from fading away as we once assumed was inevitable under conditions of modernity, seems to be growing in numbers and influence. But this still begs the question of why focus upon denim, a question this chapter seeks to answer.

DEFINING MODESTY: SELF-EFFACEMENT OR CONSPICUOUS DISPLAY?

From the perspective of the issues being discussed in this volume, the act of banning denim by highly religious groups raises a whole series of interesting questions about the very word 'modest' and what we mean by it and what is at stake. I think it shows that there are actually many different meanings to the word modest, some of which are in direct contradiction to others. I want first to consider the semantics of the term itself, and then turn to the recent history of denim to suggest that quite apart from concerns emanating from religion, there can be relationships between forms of clothing and modesty that have extraordinarily profound consequences for both the understanding of society and even for philosophy.

If we imagine telling a member of the general public that we are engaged in a study of modest clothing, I assume that the meaning of the term modest within that phrase would have seemed straightforward enough. It pertains to concerns shared by most of the major world religions – Christianity, Islam and Judaism, Hinduism and others – about how much and what parts of a woman's body should be covered. This had become an ongoing tussle between secular emancipation, which encouraged the rendering explicit of female sexuality, and the response within each religion as to what if any of this was acceptable within their canons of religiosity. So for clothing to be modest would be almost entirely related to the degree to which it countered that increasing exposure and provided means by which women's bodies would first of all be covered, and furthermore covered in a manner that the underlying contours of the body were also obscured. As such, religion would share this concern for modesty with other cultural parameters, such as the protection of elite women in some societies from the public gaze. One of the aims of the chapters in this volume is, however, to show that things may not be quite as clear cut as this.

The problem with the newspaper articles about banning denim amongst ultra-orthodox Jews is that this simply cannot be the meaning of modest in such instances. In fact denim skirts are really quite common amongst orthodox but less extreme groups, because a full denim skirt does this job of covering up the body quite effectively. Denim is generally quite a thick textile which has less tendency to cling to the body at least in terms of its inherent qualities as textile. It is a dark colour favoured by orthodox groups and for all these reasons there have been times when seeing a young woman wearing a long full denim skirt in the area of north London where I live has been precisely a sign that she was indeed an orthodox Jewess dressed modestly and appropriately.

There are certain rules within Judaism with regard to cloth and clothing which again are the subject of other chapters here, including the rules of *shatnez* which forbids the mixing of linen and wool, possibly as of plant and animal derivation. There is also the more general issue of *tzniuth* which is central to the debates around modest fashion because it refers to the meaning of modesty as discussed above. But neither of these apply to denim. In fact it is quite hard to find any direct reference to what is the issue here. But in trawling through the internet I discovered a site called *www.backoftheshul.com* which has several discussions around these topics. In one case an individual had posted the following remark: 'I agree that skirts with other fabrics can also be not tznius but since denim is more the look of the *goyim* [Yiddish for Gentiles] that is what may bother the rabbis.'[1] I would say that this is also my assumption with regard to why denim is sometimes subject to a ban. It detracts from the desire to look different from non-Jewish or less religiously orthodox Jewish groups.

The ethnographic setting for such behaviour and concerns has been excellently drawn by Ayala Fader (2009) in her book *Mitzvah Girls: Bringing Up the Next Generation of Hasidic Jews in Brooklyn*. This book provides a richly textured analysis of the socialisation of young women into ultra-orthodox Judaism with considerable attention to the nuances of language, clothing and the everyday. Within the text there is a telling passage that bears on our problem:

> Chani, a teacher in the Bobover boys' nursery school, for example, told me that her twelve-year-old daughter once modelled a denim skirt for her father, asking if he would allow her to wear it outside. He looked her over and said, 'a nice dark skirt, long enough, sure, no problem.' He was unaware, the teacher told me, laughing, that denim is considered

modern because it is the material of the jeans Gentiles wear. When the young girl displayed her skirt for her mother, Chani told her emphatically that she was not allowed to wear the denim skirt. Her daughter said, defensively, 'But Totty, Daddy said it was all right,' at which Chani explained to her husband that denim was too modern for their family. Once he understood he agreed with Chani, and their daughter did not wear the skirt. (Fader 2009: 152)

If this is the case then curiously it pitches one meaning of the word modest against another. The phrase 'to be modest' is actually equally used with the implication of humble self-effacement, the desire not to draw attention to oneself and to remain inconspicuous. The problem is that many of the examples of modest clothing studied by the modest clothing project are actually remarkably immodest if we turn to this equally prominent meaning of the word modest. Islamic women in hijab or orthodox Jewish women wearing black ankle-length skirts in the middle of summer could hardly look more conspicuous on the streets of London. It is almost impossible not to stare at them, which one might think is the exact opposite of the ideal of being modest. If the aim of these ultra-orthodox Jews is to look different from everyone else, then it follows that they are going to end up looking conspicuous. In walking around areas such as Hendon in north London there is no difficulty at all in identifying the women from these communities. They do indeed stand out.

So we can see there is a potential conflict here between the two main uses of the word modest: to be covered up and to be inconspicuous. And we would expect and find that this tension is something that will sometimes be evident to those involved in the practice of modest clothing. But this still leaves two quite different explanations for what is happening in such cases. It is entirely possible that being conspicuous and stared at is simply an inadvertent side effect of being covered up. A woman wearing a hijab in Iran or Iraq would not thereby invite stares. It is merely the context of London, where most women dress in ways that these religions consider immodest, that results in this unfortunate contradiction and those involved simply have to accept that this is an unavoidable consequence. In many cases this is undoubtedly true and the women concerned reflect on the problem.

But the quote from *backoftheshul.com* and the example of Chani exposes another possibility here. The implication of this evidence is that the religious authorities are actually seeking for conspicuousness rather than trying to avoid it. In other words, at least with respect to the dominant meaning of the word modest, it seems that some ultra-orthodox groups are actually striving to be immodest rather than modest, to ensure that their adherents stand out in the crowd as different from others. There are some reasons for thinking this is not uncommon. Many strongly religious groups seem to embrace anachronistic clothing, but this conservatism seems also a way of ensuring that they stand out as marked members of that particular group as opposed to others, for example the Amish, but also the use of anachronistic Eastern European garments by Jewish men in London. Similarly the degree of covering associated with nuns in Catholicism is a means by which they become recognised rather than invisible. So there are grounds for suggesting that under the general rubric of studying how groups express modesty there is also a need to acknowledge that in some respect this is equally framed as a study of how those same groups strive to be immodest. They wish to assert a superior moral sensibility and to some degree flaunt this to the general public as a conspicuous assertion that could properly be described as immodest. There are of course differences of degree here. Of the various ultra-orthodox groups, the most extreme in this regard would be the Chabad (Lubavitch), whose particular history of visual culture (Katz 2010) has led them to see conspicuousness as an integral part of the objectification of faith.

But that still leaves open another question raised by the initial example of ultra-orthodox Jews banning denim; which is, why denim? Why out of all the fabrics and clothing types that could be banned in order to assert maintained difference have they chosen denim? What does this suggest about our relationship to denim? Following the logic of my argument so far, if denim is refused by religious groups who are striving to be immodest in the sense of conspicuous then the problem with denim may be that they perceive this textile to be particularly modest, a modesty that they wish to differentiate themselves from.

WHEN CLOTHING STRIVES TO BE MODEST

This is the point of articulation between the research project called modest fashion and a research project that I have carried out over several years along with Sophie Woodward on the meaning of denim. Sophie and I started what we called the Global Denim Project in 2007 (Miller and Woodward 2007) by proclaiming denim to be an example of what we called the 'blindingly obvious'. Which implies that we simply don't seem to be able to focus on this thing in front of us. There is a vast academic literature on haute couture and journals with titles such as *Fashion Theory*, but it seems that the less likely we are to actually wear something the more attention it gets in journalism and academic writing. By contrast, there is not a single paper in *Fashion Theory* about denim blue jeans which is the single most common garment we actually wear. Standing on street corners when travelling the world and counting people as they walked past suggested to us that in most countries today about half the people on any given day are wearing denim blue jeans. We wanted to know why.

There is a well-known history to blue jeans, from workers' wear to youth rebellion. Sullivan (2006) provides the conventional history, and Comstock (2010) a reinterpretation of some of the evidence. But it was clear in our studies that a middle-aged man in London does not wear such jeans as symbolic of youth rebellion or to look American. History did not explain the present spread of jeans. There is a glib tendency to assume commercial presence must indicate something called 'capitalism' as the cause. But this is nonsense. Certainly pretty much all our blue jeans are supplied through mechanisms that exist within capitalism: production, distribution and retail. But this is the 'how' not the 'why' of blue jeans distribution. For capitalism to be the cause requires an argument that jeans are more profitable than the alternative. The opposite is clearly the case. Most other garments are quickly out of fashion and thrown away when wear and tear is evident. The dominant form of blue jeans have remained largely impervious to fashion, are worn more often and for longer. Furthermore, the increasing sales of jeans at least in the UK are mainly associated with the cheapest supermarket varieties. So commerce does not explain their prevalence.

There are now several publications which have arisen from the Global Denim Project which look both to general explanations for why denim is worn today and local explanations relating to specific regions and populations (Miller and Woodward 2010, Woodward and Miller 2011). Interested readers are referred to these other publications and the arguments will not be rehearsed here. But in addition to these global studies, Sophie and I made the commitment to also study jeans through a more concentrated ethnographic-like project within London. It is aspects of this research that seem most relevant to the issue of modesty and it is those therefore that I will briefly summarise here. For this purpose we used the same technique I had devised originally for the shopping research of taking randomly selected streets and working with whoever happened to be living there.

Within this ethnography the relationship between being religious and wearing or avoiding blue jeans arose on many occasions. Although we picked the area pretty much at random based more on our respective convenience of transport and a general sense that we were looking for a place that had nothing special about it, actually there was quite a high proportion of migrants in the area. Taken as a whole, migrants, or their children, represented two-thirds of the participating population, making migrants typical rather than atypical of our participants. This is important since they tended to be more clearly devoted to their religions. The dominant group in this respect would be migrants from South Asia, though these included people from pretty much every part of South Asia and religions including Hinduism, Islam and Sikhism. The other group were migrants from Africa and the Caribbean who were Christian but often more specifically variants of Christianity associated with these regions such as evangelical Pentecostalism or Jehovah's Witnesses.

Looking closely at these discussions we can see both versions of modesty as having a bearing on jeans wearing. On the one hand, young Asian girls were certainly interested in various forms of figure-hugging and skinny jeans. Indeed they often described themselves in terms of their legs being thinner than most other English girls and this is something that they may or may not want to accentuate. Wearing figure-hugging jeans could then cause conflicts and there were cases of girls who told us that their brothers or parents had forbidden them from going out in such jeans. This also becomes important in wearing clothes for either a mosque or a temple. One of the most common garment forms for those of South Asian origin is the salwar kameez which amongst young people has been spreading recently at the expense of the sari (Banerjee and Milller 2003). The kameez is often a much longer blouse-like garment than the typical English shirt and is always worn outside. As such it covers the wearer often almost to the knees. What several young women reported was that they felt they could wear what otherwise would be regarded as unseemly or inappropriately tight jeans to places of worship since mostly these were covered by such as a kameez, so there was no issue of their bodies being exposed. At the same time by wearing tight jeans they felt that underneath they had retained their commitment to personal autonomy and expressive sexuality. I would see such examples as entirely concurring with the main conclusions of the *Modest Dressing* project.

However, when we turn to the other case, in particular an individual who belongs to the Jehovah's Witnesses, we see a rather different issue arising. This was with respect to a woman who was not so young and where there seemed no reason for thinking she had the slightest interest in blue jeans that were particularly exposing or immodest from the point of view of overt sexuality. Nevertheless attendance at her church was almost the only occasion on which it was seen as unsuitable for her to wear denim blue jeans. It was in fact a common question within our research to ascertain whether there were any occasions when jeans were not suitable. Putting together this case of the church along with the single most common answer which was weddings and to a lesser extent funerals, plus the prohibition in some workplaces but only when people were directly serving the public, it was clear that there was a common theme to these cases. The problem with jeans had nothing to do with modesty in the sexual sense; it was that they were too modest or 'humble' a garment, showing thereby a lack of respect for occasions or circumstances where an explicit mark of respect was called for. In other words, these were occasions when people were expected to make some effort and wear clothes that signified such respect, and jeans therefore seemed inappropriate. So in this case we are dealing with the other meaning of modest as inconspicuous and unmarked. Our evidence was that different Christian denominations would have had a range of attitudes to these issues, from favouring jeans in order to aspire to a more modern inclusive look, to banning them as disrespectful or too informal.

So once again we need to look at what it is about jeans that leads them to be what one might call conspicuously inconspicuous, possessing a modesty of such extent that it can lead them to become inappropriate at these marked occasions such as a wedding. What transpired in our research was that jeans seemed to have become an embodiment of a state we could call being ordinary, and indeed the title of our subsequent book is *Blue Jeans; The Art of the Ordinary* (Miller and Woodward 2012).

If jeans are half of what people wear on a day-to-day basis, generalisation is obviously going to be a problem. In fact most people possessed jeans that were branded or expensive or specially fitted which were often worn for special occasions. These might be particular styles such as skinny jeans, or smart Armani jeans. But while we could find these inside people's wardrobes, most day-to-day wearing is dominated by the most mundane and also often the cheapest of everyday jeans and it is these that start to give us a picture of what it means to look ordinary. The word ordinary means nondescript, nothing special, that jeans don't signify this or that. This is curious since the anthropology of clothing really developed out of semiotics – that is, the study of how differences in clothing are used to mark social or cultural differences such as male against female, rich against poor, formal against informal and so forth.

Once upon a time, jeans were thoroughly semiotic. We collected some wonderful stories from some of our older informants. One thinks he was among the first men in the area to obtain a pair of blue jeans, from a US soldier during the Second World War. Another told us how his aunt was beaten up by other women around 1958–59 because she had the effrontery, as a woman, to wear a pair of jeans. At first then in Europe jeans meant America, but this is now historical. There was once a relationship to transgressive or rebellious youth. But a policeman in the street told us how no one would see jeans as significant today; they prefer to look for 'hoodies' in order to predict trouble. Given the continued importance of class in Britain, it is extraordinary how jeans have lost any correspondence to income or status. Indeed, today the maid is just as likely as the mistress to wear an expensive Victoria Beckham brand of jeans.

Once, jeans were seen as appropriate to particular age groups, but not any more. We found cases of toddlers being dressed in jeans while still wearing nappies. Even more impressive was the extent to which older informants who had actually never worn jeans when young now saw them as entirely acceptable garments in their retirement. So there was no age left that signified when jeans were either more appropriate or less appropriate than any other age. Similarly, with regard to any other parameter of distinction and identity. There was some distaste for very large people wearing jeans, though this is evidently no longer true in the US, but it seems that once that prejudice fades there will be nothing left in terms of social distinction that can be signified by wearing jeans.

If we put all this evidence together there seems a pretty good case for viewing jeans as the first ever post-semiotic garment; the clothing that signifies nothing at all about the person who is wearing them. One of the ways we established this was through a couple of key questions. Apart from saying that jeans were comfortable, the other main reason people kept giving us for why they wear blue jeans is that they 'go' with everything. There is pretty much no garment, shoe or accessory that you can't wear alongside jeans today, which makes it a lot easier to get dressed in the morning. So the first question we would ask was, 'If you had some other trousers that were exactly the same colour as blue jeans but just not made from denim, could these trousers also go with anything at all?' People would think about this for a while and then come to the conclusion that they couldn't. So then we would ask, 'If you had another pair of trousers made from denim but not blue, say green denim or pink denim, could those go with absolutely any other clothes?' Again people would think about this for a while and conclude they could not. What this demonstrates is that there is absolutely nothing about blue or about denim that makes us think that all other clothes can go with denim blue jeans. This is a purely cultural construction and derives entirely from the fact that denim blue jeans are now post-semiotic and thereby effectively neutral. They are deprived of the ability to clash with anything they are matched with. Denim blue jeans today are more black than black. This post-semiotic condition is clearly specific to the London ethnography. When New York Jews ban denim, this demonstrates that, for them, jeans remain palpably semiotic.

It is this post-semiotic status of jeans that explains the problematic relationship between jeans and attendance at a Jehovah's Witness religious service. This is an occasion when men would be expected to wear suits. But Jehovah's Witness, rather like other highly prescriptive religions, may even expect men to wear suits more generally. They thereby conform to that pattern of using anachronism to make themselves conspicuous in relation to the general population around them. Just like forbidding jeans for church-wear, jeans for day-wear are also too 'modestly' inconspicuous to meet the community's desire to stand out in public. This is a religion that wants to remain 'immodestly' conspicuous in order to proclaim its identity and moral superiority. This is not a group that hides itself from the rest of us; it is intensely proselytising.

So at this point we seem to have a simple distinction between the potential post-semiotic neutrality of denim jeans and the needs of some religions to announce or proclaim themselves and their associated moralities and ideologies, in which context, jeans are rendered unsuitable. But at this stage I want to move the analysis still further and suggest that the problem of jeans may not just be their lack of signification but the way in which they thereby as a form of material culture become themselves a practice with moral and ideological consequences. In which case the threat to these religions becomes still more complex. To understand this we need to ask why this neutrality of jeans might matter, and why it might matter in particular to such immigrant populations in London.

In our ethnography of jeans we did not focus on religion per se, but rather on the issues of identity and migration about which there is a huge literature (e.g., Basu and Coleman 2008, Benmayor 1994, Guibernau and Rex 2010), and that, in a sense, is our problem. Identity implies identification, which situates migrants in arenas of choice: either to conform to and blend into the culture represented by the host society, or to retain the cultural values of their place of origin. Alternatively, they can take their stance from the radical politics of Ken Livingstone, formerly leader of the Greater London Council, with its avowal of a positively ascribed multiculturalism and anti-racism, including an appreciation of various forms of syncretism and fusion. For many years, London was regarded as a centre for progressive politics regarding migration, identified specifically with the left-wing aspirations of Livingstone. Within discussions of multiculturalism there has been some shifting in recent years from a focus upon ethnicity to that of religion, especially in respect to Islam (Baumann 1999, Madood, Triandafyllidou and Zapata-Barrero 2006).

Having now carried out five ethnographies in London, I have become increasingly aware that, for many migrants, the presumption by others of this valorisation of identity can be experienced as a burden and an imposition. Migrants are supposed to retain roots or to represent an identity. But many of them say that one of the major advantages of living in London, with its unusual degree of ethnic dispersal, is that it offers a superior opportunity for escaping from identity. For example, when I recognised that a participant in an earlier project (Miller 2008) was from Brazil, I became interested in knowing about the aspects of his life that pertain to that Brazilian identity. I tried to start conversations about when and whether he ate Brazilian food or if he had Brazilian friends, to which he responded by stating, 'If I wanted to be fucking Brazilian I would have stayed in fucking Brazil.' The great advantage of London, with its combination of diversity and dispersal, is that when migrants decide to loosen an affinity with a place of origin, they do so not because they feel under pressure to identify with London itself or with being British, which they might feel if living in another part of the United Kingdom. After all, in these streets to come from London is a minority, not a majority, position. To the chagrin of many more conservative or right-wing politicians, there is in the United Kingdom relatively little explicit celebration of a specific British or English identity, compared, at least, to identification with a local football team. By the same token, migrants may not feel anything but a remnant or token association with the place where they spent their childhood or where their parents were born. Many do, indeed, have an intensely strong relationship with a place of origin, one that may grow even if they were born in the United Kingdom. But the growing tendency for many people is simply not to identify with identity.

Once jeans achieve this post-semiotic status they become an ideal resource for immigrants who wish to transcend identity. The way such individuals achieve this is very rarely through any political, activist, or, indeed, even conscious trajectory. In a few cases migrants recall wearing jeans because they felt pressure to fit in with the host community, but mostly this was during the initial phase of migration. The broader ethnographic evidence suggests that few people feel pressure to lose identity in order to conform. If anything, the contrary is the case, as there has been a clear change toward a cultural valorisation of difference as something to cherish and celebrate on marked occasions but not necessarily to allow to intrude on everyday life and the sense of self. This is evident in the remarkable changes in the representation of difference in popular media such as television and in schools, which have led to the position, exemplified by the Brazilian migrant noted above, that identity, rather than being an embarrassment, has become something of an expectation if not a burden. This is a state for which London may well represent the vanguard, as a place that is a kind of particular nowhere, that is, a place in which one does not have to identify with London in order to get away from other forms of identity. So most migrants today do not wear jeans either to fit in or as a mark of authentic difference. They see wearing jeans as outside such issues of identity. For them, in their ordinariness, jeans have lost their connotations of assimilation or of distinction. The term that is overwhelmingly dominant in explaining jeans-wearing is comfortable.

In fact migrants now use jeans to become ordinary in much the same way that non-migrants use them to become ordinary. To avoid status competition at school in the absence of a uniform, parents encourage their children to wear jeans. In college, when students wish to become part of a community without being marked, they wear jeans. When coming home from work to relax, our participants wear jeans. Jeans can be dressed up without being too dressy but also dressed down. They resolve contradictions and deflect offence or argument. They allow people to relax into a comfortable state of ordinariness, which is not to be denigrated as a failure to become special but as an achievement in itself. The woman who could not wear jeans to her Jehovah's Witness church comes across as a rather typical informant with respect to the discussion of jeans as comfortable. The jeans she has a real attachment for, and identifies with, are the jeans that she has worn for ten years, and that have subsequently become soft and intimate and personal. It's not just that they signify a state of relaxation – they genuinely contribute to her ability to feel relaxed. One also senses that they are part of the way she feels comfortable in that wider social sense as just another person living in this area.

Migrants may compare this comfort with its lack in their place of origin, seeing it as something made viable by the heterogeneity of London. As a migrant from a Gulf state noted, 'You know, here you can go out wearing ASDA (Walmart) jeans and Tesco jeans and you wouldn't worry. Nobody would ever say anything to you. But over there it's a big thing what you wear.' Many may be aware from television that jeans are ubiquitous at a global level, but they do not assume they have the same (in)significance outside of the United Kingdom, or even outside London.

Let me be clear: I am not saying that all jeans-wearing in London signifies the ordinary. If that were the hypothesis, it would be a thousand times wrong. Vast numbers of jeans quite obviously are worn because they are particularly stylish, have expensive labels, or effectively represent some aspects of identity and status. There are designer jeans, extraordinarily skinny jeans and highly decorated jeans; jeans so tight that women break their nails trying to button them up. The point is that such jeans are a minority of all jeans worn. The same people who routinely wear jeans that are here categorised as ordinary often possess and on appropriate occasions wear designer jeans or jeans that achieve a particular effect. But none of this should detract from the significance being claimed for the majority of blue jeans, which are now worn in a manner that clearly strives to objectify a state of ordinariness. I presume that, as long as blue jeans are worn by the majority in the majority of countries they will always retain that flexibility, such that some will be used to express the marked, the special and, indeed, the extraordinary. For a natural science, that use would represent a contradiction. An ethnography, by contrast, can and should assert the importance of an ordinariness that can constantly be disproved but that remains the dominant usage by the population being studied.

MODEST CLOTHING AND IMMODEST RELIGION

In this conclusion I want to take this to one final still higher level (see Miller 2010, Miller and Woodward 2012), reflecting other publications where I argue that denim blue jeans represent a challenge, not just to theory in anthropology, but to the main trajectory of Western philosophy. Because from Kant through to Hegel and onwards, philosophers have hoped that the enlightenment would lead us to gain a consciousness of morality that would help us achieve moral lives through that consciousness as the embodiment of ethics and reason. Kant and Hegel both follow from the Protestant theological debates they were brought up in. But the shift from religion to philosophy was based on making explicit the grounds for morality. After all, both Kant and Hegel emerge from an essentially theological set of debates steeped in centuries of Christian discussion about the nature of morality itself. Two traits may be particularly significant. The first is that they stand for the role of consciousness itself. To be moral is closely linked to human intentionality, where we choose to be good having explicitly considered the options of being otherwise and make that personal commitment in a state of as full a knowledge of what we do as possible. Not all theology was as concerned with intention and consciousness, but Kant and Hegel certainly were. The movement to philosophy meant a disavowal of mere ritual and mere custom. Also these religions share with many other religions a general antipathy to materiality, something that had been reaffirmed in the Protestant repudiation of Catholicism, championing the belief in the inherent superiority of the transcendent and of the mind as opposed to being reduced to the materiality of the everyday world.

By contrast, blue jeans represent morality as located within material culture studies. This emerges from theories of practice as in Bourdieu (1977), not from theories of consciousness; from collective action, not from individual intentionality. It is clear from the analysis of jeans, migration and identity, that in some ways denim has a moral or even ideological impact, certainly in the furtherance of equality. But this is not an act of consciousness. There are no activists telling us we should be wearing blue jeans. No one says to their children, 'When you grow up I want you to be ordinary.' What our work on jeans suggests is that to the degree that they represent a particular moral position, this is largely unintentional and unconscious. So morality as effected through material culture would be anathema to this tradition of theology and philosophy represented by Hegel and Kant.

Could this in any way be related to the banning of jeans by ultra-orthodox Jews? I would suggest that at the very least there is an analogy here, but perhaps there is rather more. I am not suggesting that rabbis who try to ban denim know what they are doing. I don't think they would ever regard jeans as representing an alternative route to morality. At the level of consciousness, I agree with *backoftheshul.com* that they simply see a threat from the ubiquity of denim to their desire to assert the specificity of their religious adherence. But it is possible that at an unconscious level the fact that denim may in fact represent such a radically different form of morality, and indeed modesty, may be part of what has made them uncomfortable with denim. It is possible that the very term 'modern', used by Chani to describe that which it is important to avoid, carries something of this connotation.

Judaism is very different from that trajectory of Protestantism that is reflected in the philosophy of Kant and Hegel. While Christianity is very clear about the relationship to consciousness and intention, Judaism is much more 'conflicted'. Alongside Islam, this is much more a religion of practice, so that this implicit working of material culture is actually much closer to the way these religions operate. I think there is a constant tension within Judaism over explicit and implicit adherence to morality which may explain in part why the attitude to denim itself is clearly contradictory. In Judaism some orthodox groups see denim skirts as ideal, while others try to ban it. My point is merely that there may be something much deeper at stake than we appreciate. This may help answer my initial question, which was not why do some orthodox groups ban denim, but why does this intermittently seem to be so newsworthy that my community newspaper, the *Jewish Chronicle*, chooses to cover this as a story? Is there a sense that this is more important than might at first appear?

All this is mere speculation on my part. But none of it is necessary with regard to the larger position of this chapter. I do not wish to make any strong claims here. It remains the case that when people use the term 'modest' in relation to modest clothing, mostly they are concerned with finding clothing that is modest in respect to the prevention of immodest exposure of the body. The aim of this chapter is merely to reflect on the implications of that other meaning of the same word, regarding the desire to be humble and inconspicuous. With respect to this equally common usage of the word modest, it is possible to reverse the trajectory of our explanation. At least in the case of denim blues jeans, it seems that it is the orthodox religions that are trying to cultivate what we could term immodest claims to being conspicuous and morally superior and who therefore repudiate a form of clothing precisely because it has been more effective than any historical precedent in becoming the material culture of modesty and self-effacement.

NOTE

1   'Closetpartyanimal' posting on 26 February 2007. http://www.backoftheshul.com/
    viewtopic.php?f=3&t=1633&start=20. Accessed 9 December 2011.

REFERENCES

Banerjee, Mukilika and Miller, Daniel (2003). *The Sari.* Oxford: Berg.

Basu, Paul and Coleman, Simon (eds) (2008). 'Migrant Worlds, Material Cultures'.
    Mobilities, 3 (3) (special issue).

Baumann, Gerd (1999). *The Multicultural Riddle: Rethinking National, Ethnic, and Religious Identities.*
    London: Routledge.

Benmayor, Rina (1994). *Migration and Identity.* Oxford: Oxford University Press.

Bourdieu, Pierre (1977). *Outline of a Theory of Practice.* Trans. Richard Nice. Cambridge:
    Cambridge University Press.

Comstock, Sandra Curtis (2010). 'The Making of an American Icon: The Transformation
    of Blue Jeans during the Great Depression', in Daniel Miller and Sophie Woodward
    (eds), *Global Denim.* Oxford: Berg, pp. 23–50.

Fader, Ayala (2009). *Mitzvah Girls: Bringing Up the Next Generation of Hasidic Jews in Brooklyn.*
    Princeton, NJ: Princeton University Press.

Guibernau, Montserrat and Rex, John (2010). *The Ethnicity Reader: Nationalism, Multiculturalism
    and Migration.* Cambridge: Polity Press.

Katz, Maya Balakirsky (2010). *The Visual Culture of Chabad.* Cambridge: Cambridge University
    Press.

Madood, Tariq, Triandafyllidou, Anna and Zapata-Barrero, Ricard (2006). *Multiculturalism,
    Muslims and Citizenship: A European Approach.* London: Routledge.

Miller, Daniel (2008). *The Comfort of Things.* Cambridge: Polity Press.

— (2010). 'Anthropology in Blue Jeans'. *American Ethnologist*, 37:3: 415–28.

— and Woodward, Sophie (2007). 'A Manifesto for the Study of Denim'. *Social Anthropology*,
    15 (3): 335–51.

— (eds) (2010). *Global Denim.* Oxford: Berg.

— (2012). *Blue Jeans: The Art of the Ordinary.* Berkeley, CA: University of California Press.

Sullivan, James (2006). *Jeans: A Cultural History of an American Icon.* New York: Gotham
    Press.

Woodward, Sophie and Miller, Daniel (eds) (2011). 'Unravelling Denim'. *Textile: the Journal
    of Cloth and Culture*, March, 9.1 (special edition).

WEBSITE

www.backoftheshul.com/viewtopic.php?f=3&t=1633&start=20

6

MODEST MOTIVATIONS
Religious and Secular Contestation in the Fashion Field

Jane Cameron

This chapter looks at those issues other than the specifically or overtly religious that motivate women to dress modestly. The internet has been providing a medium through which women with the desire to dress fashionably yet compatibly with their religious beliefs can discuss and debate their motivations for dressing modestly. Individual blogs and brands exist which make explicit links between modest dressing and religion. With the proliferation of Christian modest fashion blogs and the plethora of debates on modesty and dress to be found on various Christian fora, it becomes apparent that modest dress is a topic of interest for people from a variety of Christian denominations. While there are many women on Christian fora that profess to dressing modestly, some contest that for them this is not necessarily a Christian or religious matter. There are also a number of women taking part in forum debates who are not religious but who do self-identify as modest dressers.

In addition to religious conviction, other key issues that emerged from the *Modest Dressing* research project[1] as motivating factors for dressing modestly included practicality, body image and life changes, including ageing. Concern with the increased sexualisation of children's clothing was also a prominent topic of discussion in relation to finding fashionable yet appropriate attire for young girls. These issues have all been raised and discussed within religious fora on modest dress. They also appear regularly in the mainstream news and fashion media and have been debated on non-religious fora and blogs, as well as being explored from a distinctly secular perspective in scholarly research into women's clothing choices. While various factors influencing the decision to dress modestly remain the same across the board, with women donning the same modest attire and sharing the same 'secular' body and dress dilemmas, disparities are detectable within the discourses on modesty. Modesty is a highly contested concept and evidence in fora debates and blog discussions suggests that it is the ideology behind the concept 'modest' that not only creates a divide between the religious and non-religious but discordance within different Christian communities. It is beyond the commercial domain of the web, within the perceived neutral territory of discussion fora and personal blogs, that these diverging perspectives are articulated.

WALKING THROUGH THE WEB

Conducting a study online presents challenges for the ethnographic researcher more accustomed to offline fieldwork, and influences how exactly one gathers research data. Traditional or offline ethnography tends to involve living with those being researched, integrating oneself into the community and undertaking both participant and non-participant observation. However, undertaking what I am calling here 'online non-participant observation' enabled me to circumnavigate a problem that many researchers working in the field encounter, which is the very presence of the researcher. The presence of a researcher along with the types of questions that are asked, which are always influenced by the researcher's own frame of reference, knowledge and assumptions, naturally has an impact on what information is revealed. Online the researcher and her questions are removed, leaving the material that is there unmitigated by an 'outsider's' line of questioning. The fora that I accessed were open to public viewing and only required a registration if I wanted to contribute to the conversation. Because my aim was to observe the conversations taking place, I did not undertake any registration.

This type of online non-participant observation is more commonly known as 'lurking' (Hine 2000) which, while arguably having unethical undertones, was employed to access whatever was already public and not alter material or enter into the debates in any way. 'Lurking' has invited much debate from those researchers entering into the relatively new territory of online ethnography. It is variably used by scholars in order not to disturb the naturally occurring discussions taking place or only at the beginning of studies in order to gather information that guides their research questions before they enter into the virtual field to engage with research subjects (Garcia et al. 2009). There are also those who assert that ethnography, either online or offline, implicitly involves participation (Miller and Slater 2001). For Miller and Slater, having an offline component was integral in contextualising the material gathered online as part of their ethnographic study. To this end the research that I carried out on the *Modest Dressing* project was not strictly 'ethnographic' as I felt that my presence and questions would not only disturb the 'field' but were also not necessarily required. What was of interest to me was that a dialogue on modest fashion often centring on the very questions that we wanted to ask was naturally occurring in the fora. A disadvantage to this particular approach was that because I was not entering into the debate I could not seek clarification on any posts that were unclear. Postings could only be read and interpreted as they appeared. The dialogic nature of the discussion fora often solved this problem for me: if a response to a post was considered to be a misinterpretation of the original comment the original poster would often return with a response to clarify what they meant. Several of the questions and queries that I had as a researcher were therefore actually being asked by many of the fora participants.

Another limit to this approach is that data such as age and gender are not always immediately apparent or verifiable. Post content would often give indications about gender, marital status and so on, but other information such as precise geographical location or specific denomination (if they affiliated with one) was not always stated. This can be an advantage for those taking part in discussions online where the level of detail provided that would identify someone is determined by the individual. The anonymity that the internet affords someone may grant them the security to discuss issues and topics that might not be so easily raised offline. Conversely, for the researcher it means that details that would normally contribute to the analysis of material are limited. There is no real way of determining who it is that is actually posting a comment, something that our online research strategies have to take into account.

Locating the various modest fashion brands and blogs discussed in this chapter was undertaken using simple Google searches with terms such as 'modest dress' and 'modest fashion'. Using tools such as Technorati (a blog search engine), boardreader (a forum search engine), and those provided by Google that are freely available online, it was easy to identify key brands and bloggers in the modest fashion field. Setting up Google Alerts, a daily digest of recent news and blog posts, using the above terms, led to many of the fora and blogs discussed in this chapter. While individual blogs and brands provided evidence of a growing participation and interest in 'modest fashion', which confirmed the hypothesis set forth by the *Modest Dressing* project, it was in the fora discussions and blog comments that debates on the concept of 'modesty' were more fully explored. The most prolific 'modest fashion' brands and blogs that appear when doing an online search mostly have very pronounced links to a particular religion. For that reason, if one is seeking a connection between modest dress and religion, it is not hard to find. Using links provided in fora and blogs and widening search terms to include 'religious modesty' and 'secular modesty' led to uncovering modest fashion discussions within a secular context, albeit much smaller in number.

The English-language blogs and forum discussion threads that I explore in this chapter come from both the US and UK. The religious fora along with the majority of the blogs were US-based, and the non-religious were both US- and UK-based. Due to the 'global' nature of the internet this did not preclude people from other parts of the world taking part and this would be apparent either because the discussant stated their location or from an icon displaying their national flag within the user profile accompanying their comments. I located the different discussion threads on the forum facilities of four different websites, two non-denominational Christian and two non-religious parenting sites. The fora on these four sites each contained a variety of discussion threads on modest dress that represented conversations and debates that were recurrent elsewhere online. The various discussion threads that I accessed varied in length, with some running for a matter of months and others for up to years. A thread on the *Mothering. com* site that started in November 2008 was still receiving posts at the time of writing.[2] While this *Mothering.com* thread had reached 575 comments, the same number of comments might well be found on a thread that only ran for three months.

All of the fora and blogs had a moderator, though it was not always clear who held this role, and they had the power to conclude a thread. Contributors to discussion threads and blogs had screen names so it was possible to identify recurrent posters within the same thread and across fora on the same website. It was not noted whether a poster was active across different websites, but deciphering this information would be problematic as it could not be presumed that it was the same person using the same screen name. The non-religious fora that contained the most discussion on modest dress were those aimed at mothers. Websites such as *Mumsnet* in the UK or *Mothering.com* in the US were also distinguished from the religious discussion fora for their marked levels of participation by both religious and non-religious women. This dialogue between religious and 'secular' participants was much less present or detectable on the religious sites, suggesting that the commonalities of the motherhood experience may explain why the parenting sites encouraged more religious–secular dialogue. On the Christian fora I observed, very few participants professed to having no religious affiliation. While there were many dissenting voices, these all tended to come from within the acknowledged boundaries of a wider Christian community. On the parenting sites it was not uncommon for a participant to declare their religious affiliation if they had one, as it put into context their perspective on what was being discussed.

VISIBLY CHRISTIAN?

On undertaking the Modest Dressing project it was obvious when doing the research that going out onto the street and identifying religiously motivated modest dressers would be a problem. While many women do meet a variety of religious modest dress guidelines (whether they know it or not), there is no way of knowing simply from observing appearance if that person is motivated to dress that way for religious reasons or if they would even describe themselves as modest dressers. Some visible signs of religiously motivated modest dress (hijab, sheital, etc.) can more commonly be decoded as forms of religious distinction. These distinctions only exist to the viewer if they are aware of or are familiar with particular visible markers or practices. Likewise, many garments send out visual codes that are wrongly read or interpreted. A woman may be wearing a headscarf tied in the style of a tichel but she herself may not be Jewish.

As Hamilton and Hawley point out in 'Sacred Dress, Public Worlds' (2000), there are forms of religiously motivated modest dress where intent and meaning are clear. For example, the Amish in their plain dress are visibly identifiable as being different and this serves the purpose of drawing a distinction between them and the outside world, from which they wish to remain separate. Conversely the casual observer today would be hard pushed to identify a Mormon by their attire, as their choice of clothing is based on a desire to conceal the Temple garment worn by many members of their Church because that garment is sacred and a personal reminder of the covenants made between the wearer and God. Whilst Mormon dress has in the past been designed in order to differentiate Mormons from the rest of society (or from other Mormon sects), what would identify a person today as Mormon is concealed, making it difficult to deduce intention from what the person is seen wearing (Fischer 2000). My focus here on the largely text-based discussion fora meant that I was identifying modest dressers by how they described themselves rather than only or primarily by how they looked (as in Cameron forthcoming 2013).

While the Modest Dressing project was an investigation across the three Abrahamic faiths, this chapter deals predominantly with the Christian material that emerged as well as that from fora, blogs and commercial sites with no overt religious association.[3] Those who are motivated to dress modestly because of their Christian beliefs are generally harder to identify by their appearance alone because of the lack of universally recognisable markers that would distinguish them as Christian (aside of course from the plain dress worn by many Amish and some Mennonite). Most of the clothes and styling that I saw on Christian modest fashion blogs were sourced from the high street or were thrift store finds. The Catholic US-based Pure Fashion has a website that details their modesty programme aimed at 14–18-year-old girls. They host fashion shows across America and use clothes from popular stores such as Gap, which are found in most malls. Images and film footage on their website of their catwalk shows illustrates that what the girls are modelling does not mark them out as being visibly Christian. Of course the whole point of many of the modest fashion blogs and programmes like Pure Fashion is to show people how they can wear mainstream fashion in a modest way. Comments online, however, state that for some Christians, dressing modestly is something that should be done in order to distinguish oneself from the rest of the world. The following quote comes from a survey of Christian men's views on women's dress, conducted by an organisation with links to the Fundamentalist Baptist Church: 'It says a lot about the character of a woman when she shuns the styles of this world and walks in such a way that she wants to let people know that she is different.'[4] Similar comments were found on blogs and fora but sometimes it was not clear to which version of the external world comments referred – whether digital ('in real life' or 'IRL') or majority (that is, non-Christian on- and offline). In one case it was made clear that 'IRL' was referring to 'offline', but this was qualified with the comment that most people in 'IRL' were non-Christians anyway. It was therefore the actual discussions online that articulated individuals' motivations to dress modestly, enabling me to explore the modest dress practices and discourses of Christian women as this was where it was visible to the observer.

MODEST MOTIVATIONS

Weight gain or loss, pregnancy and childbirth as well as general insecurities over the look of certain body parts play a significant role in deciding what to wear. Numerous studies into body self-perception and clothing practices have been undertaken which all highlight the use of clothing as camouflage (Chattaraman and Rudd 2006, Tiggemann and Lacey 2009). These findings were reflected in discussions on both religious and non-religious fora where many women discussed body dissatisfaction and frustration in not being able to find fashionable clothes on the high street that fit well and serve the purpose of concealing those areas of the body they dislike. Many commented on how changes in their bodies over time meant that what once would have been considered modest attire may now be skirting on the obscene. A post on a Christian forum reflected the frustration expressed by women right across the board over not being able to find what they considered modest and fashionable clothing.

> One of my problems is that I have [a] large bosom and because of the near steel like bras I have to wear ... it's bothersome ... It doesn't make a whole lot of difference if I wear a blouse buttoned up to my neck, having larger bosoms tend to draw unwanted attention ...[5]

A comment made by a Catholic woman on a modest dress discussion thread on a parenting site reiterates this, stating that with a 40H bust nothing she wore was deemed modest enough.[6] This of course has been a big topic of debate in the mainstream fashion media too. Women looking for plus-size clothes have also had the problem of finding clothing that covers but also keeps up to date with the current fashions. Some of the religious modest fashion brands profiled as part of the *Modest Dressing* project, such as the Muslim brand Shukr, were linked to by women on some fora as examples of companies with fashionable choices for the larger figure. Not only are a greater range of sizes available but the styles on offer are less form fitting and generally cover more of the body.

While many discussants in religious fora asserted their belief that modest dress was sanctioned by religion and cited scriptural references to support modest attire, issues relating to practicality were major influencing factors, sometimes superseding religious reasons for dressing modestly. 'Can we please stop with all the clothing/modest threads ... it's summer!'[7] The frustration vented in this quote was not uncommon and represents the feelings of a number of posters responding to the 'no pants' debate recurrent on predominantly Christian fora. With reference to biblical scriptures stating that women should not dress in apparel intended for men, the question of whether it is acceptable for women to wear pants (trousers) or be expected to wear skirts/dresses only was frequently found discussed on Christian fora. For many people it is something as simple as the weather that dictates what they wear each day. However, for those that are trying to adhere to a modest dress code it can be equally difficult to dress for hot or cold weather and still meet personal and community modesty requirements.

A blogger who describes herself as 'Hebrew Catholic' states: 'I live in NH [New Hampshire], where winter happens. Pants!'[8] Winter was one of a ten-point 'Pants Manifesto' she put together stating why she wore pants as opposed to skirts. This blog post invited over 300 comments. The first two comments alone represent the divergent responses to this particular topic. This blogger was advised to read *Dressing With Dignity* by Colleen Hammond, with the prospect that it might change her mind: 'Pants can be more "convenient," but I think we can all agree that we could use more penance in our life.'[9] The second comment in response to 'Hebrew Catholic' provided an alternative take: 'I also love wearing skirts … sometimes. I just don't think it's a moral issue. It's a practical one.'[10] The tone and manner in which some of these posts are made suggests not only frustration with the seemingly continuous debates regarding the 'dos and don'ts' of modest dress but with the way in which others taking part in the discussions, namely peers or members of the wider Christian community, appear to dictate and regulate what one should be wearing. Displays of competitive piety were observed through comments that positioned some posters as self-designated 'community regulators'.

Environmental factors were also cited by discussants on non-religious fora and blogs in relation to dressing modestly. An image that was picked up on by many of the modest fashion web contingent, as well as the wider media, was that of Nigella Lawson in Australia wearing the burqini. The designers and manufacturers of Nigella's suit stated that 15 per cent of their customers are women of no religion and put this down to the fact that many people were concerned about sun damage (Bunting 2011). This sentiment is supported by one Australian blogger posting about what she called 'secular modesty'. She was experimenting with tying hijabs not for religious reasons but because as a life guard she wanted a stylish way of protecting her head and covering her hair.[11]

The heightened awareness of and media attention aimed at such garments as the hijab is a relatively recent development, which begs the question whether someone experimenting with head coverings a few decades ago would have referred to them as hijab.

Work-related clothing issues were also cited as reasons for dressing modestly:

> With regards to clothing it is easy for me, and not because of church … I did a clinical program (at grad school) and we would literally be kicked OUT of the program or at least be made to CHANGE our clothes if we showed up to clinic dress[ed] immodestly (absolutely NO low cut clothing, no exposed skin in the back, wear pants NOT skirts, no heels, etc.)[12]

The above quote was posted on a Christian forum as part of a discussion on practising modesty. It appeared to be made partly in response to a discussion taking place on the problems some found in trying to maintain a modest dress code. This quote also alludes to the fact that for some women modest dress was not an 'issue' as they had been brought up in households that advocated modest dress from a young age so this was a normal experience for them. Other discussants spoke of their 'journey' towards dressing more modestly and the challenges associated with this.

Similarly in non-religious discussions regarding modest dress, dressing for the workplace dictated levels of modesty:

> I work in a blue-collar job and absolutely cannot be seen as a sex object by my male co-workers, so I wear loose fitting clothing (I'll wear short sleeved tops because I don't have tats on my arms – mine are all on my torso) all the time. I completely understand non-religious modesty.[13]

This second quote appeared in response to a Flickr photostream that discussed (and illustrated) modest dress from a non-religious perspective. This poster's remark about not being seen as a 'sex object' echoes exactly the reasons put forth by many religious women for dressing modestly. Not attracting attention, or the wrong kind of attention, from the opposite sex is not conceived to be a religious matter for this poster.

SACRED AND SECULAR SARTORIAL SOLUTIONS

These various sartorial dilemmas and frustrations with what (little) is on offer on the high street is exactly where modest fashion brands could find their non-religious markets. A common complaint coming from many women concerns the appearance of their arms and their desire to cover this area. The Jewish fashion brand Kosher Casual produces and markets Sleevies, a slip-on sleeve that allows a person to wear short sleeved clothing while keeping their arms covered.[14] For many Jewish women it is important that the arms are covered to below the elbow. Similarly there are a number of Christian women who desire a longer sleeve either through personal choice or as prescribed by their community or church. Wearing of the sleeves produces a layered effect without actually having layers covering the whole body. On their website, Kosher Casual state that their company, while having an obvious Jewish affiliation, still attracts a number of Christian customers.[15] No mention is made as to whether a non-religious or plus-size market also makes up a percentage of their customer base. A UK-based company, Fatphrocks, catering to the plus-sized market, has also produced and marketed a similar product called Wingz.[16] Fatphrocks were featured on the BBC reality TV entrepreneur programme *Dragon's Den* where they marketed the Wingz product to a niche market, specifically plus-sized women, rather than the 'modest' fashion market. Wingz serve the same purpose as Sleevies, allowing the wearer to conceal the arm area while wearing short sleeved garments but without the cumbersome extra layers underneath. Fatphrocks' target market is obviously larger women, but they do acknowledge on their website that there are any number of reasons for women wanting their arms covered, which include excess fat ('bingo wings'), scarring and religion.

It is evident from the above that some companies that are providing clothing solutions for the same problem, in this instance the desire to cover the arms, are targeting two different markets: the religious and secular. With regards to the actual garments, the difference between the styles and available sizes for Sleevies and Wingz mean that they are likely to appeal to one market more than another. Fatphrocks provides Wingz in three sizes that fit UK 6–28, while Kosher Casual's Sleevies come in small and extra small to fit younger girls and the 'average adult size'. In addition to the smaller sizes that the Sleevie is available in, the skin-tight styling of the garment is maybe not something that would appeal to the plus-size market. Likewise the sheerness of the fabrics used in some of the Wingz styles could be deemed too revealing for some orthodox religious customers. Kosher Casual use the term 'modest' frequently on their website, but highlight the fact that they are not catering solely for the Jewish market. Fatphrocks make no mention of the term 'modest' on their website but 'religion' is mentioned first in a list of reasons why women may want to cover their arms. The terminology that is being used to describe the problem and solution is noticeably different. Fatphrocks talk of 'coverage' and 'covering', emphasising how 'beautiful' a woman can be. Kosher Casual on the other hand frequently use the term 'modest' in reference to the desired effect created by clothing. This all supports the suggestion that while there is an awareness of clothing dilemmas affecting all women and that they are being solved the same way, the circles within which they are being discussed and resolved, along with the terminology used in this process, differ between the religious and secular.

SURFING THE SACRED–SECULAR DIVIDE

Much of the 'non-religious' discussion on modest dress was taking place on sites like Mumsnet and Mothering.com. Undertaking a discussion search for 'modest dress' on Mumsnet brings up threads within the site's forum topics of Style and Beauty ('Should you dress differently in your thirties?'; 'Tunic tops that are swingy not clingy?') and Feminism/Women's Rights ('Women's Clothing-revealing vs Men's Clothing-practical'; 'Women only wear short skirts to attract men?'), as well as responses to topical news features ('Well done Belgium, veil banned'). As mentioned previously, undertaking web searches using phrases such as 'secular modesty' did not yield nearly as many results as using 'religious modesty'. Modest dress discussions on non-religious sites were not promoted in terms of modesty. On delving into these discussions, the sartorial dilemmas raised echoed those found in many of the religious discussions on dress, the difference being the terminology used. As a comment posted on Mumsnet in response to the Christian Union's report on sexualised clothing for children (see below) suggests, the actual term 'modest' is not something that secular women are employing in discussions on their fashion choices: 'It was the repetition of the word "modest" that made me feel nauseous.'[17] During the course of the research it was only over the period of the Royal Wedding between Kate Middleton and Prince William that the term 'modest' in relation to fashion within a non-religious context appeared frequently through daily

Google alerts. Fashion commentators all trying to predict who would be designing Kate's dress spoke of expecting a 'modest' style. Kate has since been featured on numerous fashion blogs, both religious and non-religious, with her outfits and style being recreated using online style applications and clothes from the high street.

Spanning the religious–secular discussion, two key areas emerged over and above the perennial body image dilemmas and 'finding fashion that fits'. One is that modest attire can relate to what is perceived to be 'appropriate' for a particular place or occasion. A significant amount of comments on the Christian fora stemmed from questions relating to what was appropriate attire for women to wear in church. However, similar questions were posed on non-religious fora regarding 'appropriate dress' for a variety of occasions, including attending religious ceremonies such as church weddings or christenings but also job interviews and work-wear. The second key area is that for many people, dressing modestly is not an issue because they are meeting modest guidelines as part of their everyday existence. What were common on the religious fora, though, were discussants who took the stance of 'community regulator'. Meaning that if a person were to state that she would like to wear skirts more often but her job/lifestyle didn't allow it, advice, guidance and words of support would be provided by those who did wear 'skirts only'.

This demonstration of community regulation and competitive piety has been observed on Muslim and Jewish discussion sites too (see Tarlo in this volume and 2007) and further highlights the 'journey' that many women speak of in their quest for 'modesty'. This same 'nurturing' was not evident in the non-religious dialogue, where although advice and experiences were shared, displaying feelings of empathy, there was no evidence of the same hierarchical (or matriarchal) roles being asserted to the same degree. The different ways in which issues were discussed betrays the difference here between the religious and secular. An online etiquette appears to be adopted by those taking part, self-regulating what is appropriate to post. Some comments on the Christian fora suggest increasing frustration with the modesty debates, but hostility is restrained in comparison to what is permissible to post on the non-religious sites. This distinction between what is and what is not appropriate to say within a particular context was bluntly stated in the FAQ section of a Christian blogger's online fashion event:

> I also understand that there are non-Christians that are interested in dressing modestly and keeping fashion classy, and I invite them to have a

part in this event, just please refrain from using foul language in entries, etc.[18]

The similarities and differences between religious and non-religious discussions on modest dress were more pronounced when the subject turned to clothing for young girls. A significant concern in relation to modest dress was that of the rise in so-called 'raunch culture' and the commodified sexualisation of children. A feature of 'raunch culture' (Levy 2006) is that more and more women are dressed in scanty outfits and adopting the boorish behaviour of men that was once criticised. Likewise the selling of push-up bras for young girls in stores as diverse as Abercrombie and Fitch and ASDA, pole dancing kits for children in the toys aisle at Tesco, and T-shirts in Next emblazoned with logos such as 'So many boys, so little time'. These have all contributed to what media commentators term the sexualisation of children and are associated with the rise of raunch culture. On the Christian-related fora, which predominantly emanate from the United States, raunch culture was deemed a threat to family values and the Christian community as a whole. Following Iva Ellen Deutchman's argument in her paper 'Fundamentalist Christians, Raunch Culture, and Post-industrial Capitalism' (2008), the 'return to modesty' can be seen as part of a wider cultural battle being fought by the Christian right in America, whether manifested through movements like Pure Fashion, advice and style guides by speakers such as Shari Braendal,[19] or socio-cultural commentaries by authors such as Wendy Shalit.[20] While Shalit herself is not from a conservative Christian background, and 'beholden neither to conservatives ... nor to feminists',[21] the views expressed in her book A Return to Modesty are considered by some to convey and support a distinctly 'Christian worldview'. A reviewer of Shalit's book on a Christian blog, Fortifying the Family, recommends the book despite Shalit's 'Jewish background': 'The Christian community should be quick to acknowledge work done on the foundation of a Christian worldview, especially when done by a non-Christian.'[22] This comment is a good illustration of what could simultaneously be viewed as a sharing of values across faiths as well as an appropriation of views of others to support the interests of a separate group.

At the same time, raunch culture was deemed a major concern by many mothers, both religious and non-religious, conversing on Mumsnet. Steering children away from the seemingly increasing amount of immodest clothing aimed at pre-teens and teens is identified as a significant challenge to both religious and non-religious standards of modesty or good parenting. This has allowed for the development of a cohort of voices precisely because there is a universally perceived threat to the sanctity of childhood. The increasing amount of sexualised clothing aimed at girls has widely been acknowledged as a factor that could contribute to negative 'self-objectification' in pre-teen girls (Goodin et al. 2011). In the UK, a government report produced by the Mothers' Union, a Christian charity, put forth guidelines to prevent the sale of inappropriate clothing for children and pre-teens (Wintour 2011). Despite the fact that the *Mumsnet* forum had in 2010 launched its own campaign to stop retailers from selling products that sexualise children,[23] responses to this were mixed precisely because the government's choice of the Mothers' Union to do the research appeared to give religious organisations moral ownership over the issue. While discussants on the *Mumsnet* forum overall expressed support for such guidelines, the fact that the government report emanated from a religious organisation was less palatable for some. 'I take issue with yet again a Christian group being brought in to decide what is morally correct – plenty of non-Christians have sound morals (some of them are even <<whispers>> women!).'[24]

It was acknowledged that the concern remained the same for both religious and non-religious individuals and organisations ('Feminism and right-wing Christian conservatives overlap on this issue ...'[25]), though it would appear to be the ideology behind the motivation for pursuing modesty and modest dress that separates the two. Links to programmes like Pure Fashion and some modest fashion brands were found posted on different discussion threads on parenting sites but often they were mocked. Links to the church, perceived ideas of proselytising and the feeling that organisations such as the Mothers' Union were harking back to the Victorian age in their wider attitudes to women, clearly divided the religious and non-religious.

CONCLUSION: CONTESTING CONCEPTS

Research into body image, aesthetic preferences and ageing in relation to women's clothing choices has been undertaken by scholars but within a distinctly secular context (Chattaraman and Rudd 2006, Kwon 1992, Tiggemann and Lacey 2009, Twigg 2007, Clarke et al. 2009, Lynch et al. 2007). The influence of religion in the research subjects' clothing practices has either not been a feature or in one case was actually a factor that excluded the research data from inclusion in the final analysis. In Pilcher's (2010) study into children's fashion and 'revealing clothing' the interview data from two Muslim girls was omitted from the final paper. In a statement, Pilcher highlights that the girls had strongly disapproving views of revealing clothing, which was a product of their cultural upbringing. It was not noted specifically whether their religion was the only reason given by them for not liking revealing clothing. The interview data of another girl was included, which detailed her preference for clothing styles that she described as 'more covered' and her discussion of garments that would not be 'suitable' church attire. Clearly this research subject had a religious affiliation but as to how much this influenced her clothing practices was not discussed. Instead, the information provided by this girl was analysed alongside that of the others and used to highlight the practical concerns that all the girls had of wearing revealing clothing and their awareness of sexual modesty.

Scholarly debate on the clothing and appearance of girls is normatively secular and for this reason religious viewpoints are excluded as not being representative, which is where studies such as the *Modest Dressing* project bridge the gap. Clearly modesty, and concern with and disapproval of revealing clothing, is not just an issue for people who would describe themselves as religious. Discussion on modest fashion, online through blogs and brands, and scholarly research into women's clothing practices appear to be falling into one of two camps: the religious or secular.

Reading through the debates on the religious fora suggest that it is in the ideology behind the issue of modest dress that distinctions become apparent, not just between the religious and secular but also within different Christian communities. Therefore while many Christian women discussed their reasons for dressing modestly in relation to practical issues, such as the weather, work requirements or merely wanting to cover what they considered to be unsightly parts of their body, for others modesty in dress was an obligatory part of being Christian. In several of the religious fora that I observed, for many people, modest attire is sanctioned by religious scripture. It was the selection and interpretation of scriptural sources that constituted the terrain of discussion, and contributed to the lengthiness of some of the fora. The Apostle Paul's 'call for modesty' in the following passage from Timothy was frequently cited and debated: 'In like manner also, that women adorn themselves in modest apparel, with shamefacedness and sobriety; not with braided hair, or gold, or pearls, or costly array; But (which becometh women professing godliness) with good works' (1 Timothy 2.9-10, King James Version).

A male discussant on a *Christianity.com* forum asked women how often they actually thought about modesty and in what ways they practised this through their dress.[26] This garnered a significant amount of responses, both from women who wrote about how they dressed modestly but also from those who challenged this male poster's interpretation of the Scripture. The women who listed what they would or would not wear did so in reference to what parts and how much of their body should be covered. Some posted other reasons, supported by further quotes from the Bible, for themselves and other women to dress modestly – 'inappropriately dressed women are a stumbling block to men'. For many, this biblical reference was not asking women to cover up more, but was read as referring to women's preoccupation with their appearance rather than focusing on the 'heart issue', what is inside. Some discussants believed that it meant not wearing bold, expensive apparel that would draw attention to oneself. Indeed this last interpretation relates to many comments left by people critiquing the modest fashion blog phenomenon from across and outside traditions: 'I would think the entire idea of a "modesty fashion blog" goes against the rules of modesty. Isn't the POINT of modesty to not draw attention to yourself?'[27]

This is supported in a comment posted by *Oranges and Apples*,[28] a blogger who likes to 'do a bit of thinking around fashion, body image and related issues'. Initially she was not sure what 'modest' meant in relation to clothing: 'I would never have thought of myself as a modest dresser … I wear bright shouty clothes … like accessories and unusual cuts. I want people to notice my clothes. Surely that is the opposite of modest – attention seeking!' After some research of her own, she realised that modesty was being discussed in relation to being covered, something that for her was entirely practical, not spiritual: 'cold climate and lazy with the epilating!'. Non-religious discussion on 'modest fashion' is rarely overtly labelled as such, as indicated by this respondent to one of the *Oranges and Apples* posts:

> I find 'modesty' to be a very difficult concept, because the term is just so loaded. I don't feel comfortable wearing short skirts without tights, or strappy tops, or things that show a lot of cleavage, but I don't like to refer to this preference as 'modesty' (although I struggle to find another term to describe it!) because when I see other people talking about modesty it always does seem to relate to standards imposed on women from outside.[29]

The term 'modesty' comes with connotations and associations that a non-religious person may not actually identify with. Likewise, the term 'fashion' was seen as a conflicting concept to modesty by both religious and non-religious discussants. The rallying slogan 'modest is hottest', used by many Christian fashion bloggers and modesty movements, is now being questioned and critiqued by fellow Christians as contradictory and 'absurd'. Sharon Hode Miller, writing on the evangelical *Christianity Today* blog for women, *Her.meneutics*, states that while she advocates Christian modesty for both men and women, 'I hesitate to embrace the "modest is hottest" banner ... The Christian rhetoric of modesty, rather than offering believers an alternative to the sexual objectification of women, often continues the objectification, just in a different form.'[30] Contestation over terms is always likely to exist. No one definition of modesty is ever likely to serve the needs of all groups and the perceived subtext of the term means it can be outrightly rejected by some.

The initial post on modesty by *Oranges and Apples* was instigated by having been contacted by the Christian modesty blog, *Is This Modest?*,[31] which asked if she would mind them using her photograph on their site. *Is This Modest?* is an open forum run by both men and women on which outfits either sent in by readers or sourced by them are posted online for people to debate whether they are deemed modest or not. The site states that they believe there is no one definition of modesty and it exists to provide a space for discussion in an 'attempt to help young men and women look beyond the clothing to the heart attitude'. After researching their site, *Oranges and Apples* refused their request, objecting to their rationale for dressing modestly:

> ... women should dress modestly so as to not lead the men that see them into temptation (which seems to mean cause them to think about sex – it's about thinking as well as doing) ... I frankly didn't want to be judged by standards I hadn't signed up to, and didn't even understand.[32]

The sentiments expressed by *Oranges and Apples* reflect those of many women, both religious and non-religious. They have been heard frequently in the popular media in relation to the SlutWalks that took place after a Canadian policeman suggested that a woman's attire could increase her chances of being attacked (Topping 2011). Dressing modestly in order not to 'lead' men into temptation absolves men from any responsibility and this she believes is not far from saying that rape victims are to blame if they are wearing revealing clothes. On Christian fora, equal numbers of respondents would agree or disagree with *Oranges and Apples*: 'The stumbling block is a very much overused argument. It had a very real content in Paul's days and is far too widely assigned today.'[33]

Women's motivation is far more complex than would be allowed by narrow definitions of what modesty is. It is also clear that women's motivation for modest self-presentation cannot be contained within a binarised secular–religious dichotomy. To frame the discussion in this way would do an injustice to the complexity of women's decisions and understandings of their place in the world. The clothes that they choose to wear do not themselves as individual garments fall into modest–immodest or religious–secular categories. These distinctions are created and applied in relation to, and in the construction of, individual social worlds. It is obvious from reading about the assortment of sartorial dilemmas, issues of body management and practicality, that women, with or without religious reasons for dressing modestly, are faced with making a multitude of decisions on what to wear. Those areas that are perceived as being either religious or secular, and are divided by such perceptions, very quickly blur when faced with the question of what to put on in the morning.

ACKNOWLEDGEMENTS

Thanks go to Reina Lewis for her comments on earlier drafts of this chapter.

NOTES

1   The material contained within this chapter emerged from the AHRC/ESRC Religion and Society funded project, *Modest Dressing: Faith-based Fashion and Internet Retail*, which was led by Professor Reina Lewis of the London College of Fashion, with co-investigator Dr Emma Tarlo of Goldsmiths, London.
2   http://www.mothering.com/community/t/887265/modest-dressing-mommas/560. Accessed 12 January 2012.
3   See Tarlo in this volume for a detailed account of both Muslim and Jewish online discussions of modesty.
4   http://www.wayoflife.org/files/335de5e4421ca77981f29f0f58cb6654-78.html. Accessed 6 December 2011.
5   'Jaimestarcross' posting on 4 April 2010. http://forums.christianity.com/. Accessed 18 November 2010. Online access to forum no longer available.
6   'PatienceAndLove' posting on 7 March 2010. http://www.mothering.com/community/. Accessed 17 November 2010.

7   'Lea_3' posting on 5 August 2010. http://forums.christianity.com/. Accessed 18 November 2010. Online access to forum no longer available.

8   'Simcha Fischer' posting on 13 September 2010. http://simchafisher.wordpress. com/2010/09/13/pants-a-manifesto-2/. Accessed 25 October 2010.

9   'J.M.' posting on 13 September 2010. http://simchafisher.wordpress.com/2010/09/13/ pants-a-manifesto-2/. Accessed 25 October 2010.

10 'Elizabeth Butina' posting on 14 September 2010. http://simchafisher.wordpress. com/2010/09/13/pants-a-manifesto-2/. Accessed 25 October 2010.

11 No longer available online.

12 'dboe' posting on 17 February 2010. http://forums.christianity.com/. Accessed 18 November 2010. No longer available online.

13 'Peggy Archer' posting on 6 December 2008. http://www.flickr.com/photos/qathi/. Accessed 12 May 2011.

14 http://www.koshercasual.com/.

15 See Lewis in this volume for further discussion.

16 http://www.wingzfashion.com/.

17 'SpringchickenGoldBrass' posting on 9 June 2011. http://www.mumsnet.com/ Talk/in_the_news/1229354-Let-Children-be-Children/AllOnOnePage. Accessed 2 December 2011.

18 http://spacious-soul.livejournal.com/52031.html. Accessed 6 December 2011.

19 Shari Braendal (2010). *Good Girls Don't Have to Dress Bad: A Style Guide for Every Woman.* http://www.sharibraendel.com/. Accessed 5 January 2012.

20 Wendy Shalit (2000). *A Return to Modesty: Discovering the Lost Virtue,* New York: Simon and Schuster.

21 http://books.simonandschuster.com/Return-to-Modesty/Wendy-Shalit/ 9780684863177. Accessed 18 January 2012.

22 http://www.fortifyingthefamily.com/Modesty_Revisited.html. Accessed 9 January 2012.

23 http://www.mumsnet.com/campaigns/let-girls-be-girls. Accessed 29 October 2011.

24 http://www.mumsnet.com/Talk/mumsnet_live_events/1230688-Webchat-with-Reg-Bailey-author-of-the-government-report-on-sexualisation-of-children-Friday-10th-June-11am-to-12pm/. Accessed 29 October 2011.

25 http://www.mumsnet.com/Talk/womens_rights/1100422-Women-should-lead-and-direct-the-womens-movement/. 'Sakura' posting on 8 December 2010. Accessed 29 October 2011.

26 'Solomonsprayer' posting on 27 January 2010. http://forums.christianity.com/. Accessed 18 November 2010.

27 'AhHello' posting on 7 October 2011. http://getoffmyinternets.net/2011/10/07/so-modesty-fashion-blogging-is-a-thing/. Accessed 10 October 2011.

28 http://www.oranges-and-apples.com/. Accessed 13 June 2011.

29 'RavelledSleeve' posting on 20 October 2010. http://www.oranges-and-apples.com/ 2010/10/modesty-again-i-just-dont-get-it.html#disqus_thread. Accessed 13 June 2011.

30 http://blog.christianitytoday.com/women/2011/12/why_we_can_dump_modest_ is_hott.html. Accessed 6 January 2012.

31 http://isthismodest.com/.

32 http://www.oranges-and-apples.com/2010/01/modest-dressing.html. Accessed 13 June 2011.

33 'Johnnz' posting on 13 June 2011. http://www.christianforums.com/t7462216/. Accessed 19 December 2011.

REFERENCES

Bunting, Madeleine (2011). 'Nigela Lawson and the Great Burkini Cover-up'. *Guardian*, 23 April. http://www.guardian.co.uk/lifeandstyle/2011/apr/23/nigella-lawson-burkini-bikini-swimming. Accessed 25 October 2011.

Cameron, Jane (2013). 'Sartorially Sacred or Fashion Faux Pas: Visual Interpretations of Modesty Online', in Abby Day, Giselle Vincett and Christopher R. Cotter (eds), *Social Identities Between the Sacred and the Secular*. Farnham: Ashgate.

Chattaraman, Veena and Rudd, Nancy Ann (2006). 'Preferences for Aesthetic Attributes in Clothing as a Function of Body Image, Body Cathexis and Body Size'. *Clothing and Textiles Research Journal*, 24: 46–61.

Clarke, Laura Hurd, Griffin, Meredith and Maliha, Katherine (2009). 'Bat Wings, Bunions, and Turkey Wattles: Body Transgressions and Older Women's Strategic Clothing Choices'. *Ageing and Society*, 29: 709–26.

Deutchman, Iva Ellen (2008). 'Fundamentalist Christians, Raunch Culture, and Post-industrial Capitalism'. *Journal of Religion and Popular Culture*, Summer, Vol. 19. http://www.usask.ca/relst/jrpc/art19-raunchsex.html. Accessed 24 May 2011.

Fischer, Gayle Veronica (2000). 'The Obedient and Disobedient Daughters of the Church: Strangite Mormons Dress as a Mode of Control', in Linda B. Arthur (ed), *Religion, Dress and the Body*, Oxford and New York: Berg, pp. 73–94.

Garcia, Angela Cora, Standlee, Alecea I., Bechkoff, Jennifer and Cui, Yan (2009). 'Ethnographic Approaches to the Internet and Computer-Mediated Communication'. *Journal of Contemporary Ethnography*, 38:1: 52–84.

Goodin, Samantha M., Van Denburg, Alyssa, Murnen, Sarah K. and Smolak, Linda (2011). '"Putting on" Sexiness: A Content Analysis of the Presence of Sexualising Characteristics in Girls Clothing'. *Sex Roles*, 65: 1–12.

Hamilton, Jean A. and Hawley, Jana (2000). 'Sacred Dress, Public Worlds: Amish and Mormon Experiences and Commitment', in Linda B. Arthur (ed.), *Religion, Dress and the Body*. Oxford and New York: Berg, pp. 31–52.

Hine, Christine (2000). *Virtual Ethnography*. London: Sage.

Kwon, Yoon-Hee (1992). 'Body Consciousness, Self-Consciousness, and Women's Attitudes toward Clothing Practices'. *Social Behavior and Personality*, 20:4: 295–307.

Levy, Ariel (2006). *Female Chauvinist Pigs: Women and the Rise of Raunch Culture*. London: Pocket Books.

Lynch, Annette, Radina, M. Elise and Stalp, Marybeth C. (2007). 'Growing Old and Dressing (Dis)gracefully', in D. C. Johnson and H. B. Foster (eds), *Dress Sense: Emotional and Sensory Experiences of the Body and Clothes*. Oxford and New York: Berg.

Miller, Daniel and Slater, Don (2001). *The Internet: An Ethnographic Approach*. Oxford and New York: Berg.

Pilcher, Jane (2010). 'What not to Wear? Girls, Clothing and "Showing" the Body'. *Children and Society*, 24: 461–70.

Shalit, Wendy (2000). *A Return to Modesty: Discovering the Lost Virtue*. London: Pocket Books.

Tarlo, Emma (2007). 'Hijab in London: Metamorphosis, Resonance and Effects'. *Journal of Material Culture*, 12: 131–56.

Tiggemann, Marika and Lacey, Catherine (2009). 'Shopping for Clothes: Body Satisfaction, Appearance Investment, and Functions of Clothing among Female Shoppers'. *Body Image*, 6: 285–91.

Topping, Alexandra (2011) 'SlutWalking Phenomenon comes to UK with Demonstrations in Four Cities'. *Guardian*, 9 May. http://www.guardian.co.uk/world/2011/may/09/slutwalking-phenomenon-comes-to-uk. Accessed 22 November 2011.

Twigg, Julia (2007). 'Clothing, Age and the Body: a Critical Review'. *Ageing and Society*, 27: 285–305.

Wintour, Patrick (2011). 'Cameron-backed Report to Protect Children from Commercialisation'. *Guardian*, 3 June. http://www.guardian.co.uk/politics/2011/jun/03/cameron-backed-report-commercialisation-childhood?CMP=twt_gu. Accessed 18 October 2011.

FORA

http://www.christianforums.com
http://forums.christianity.com/ (Forum access no longer available online.)
http://www.mothering.com/community/f/
http://www.mumsnet.com/Talk

BLOGS

http://blog.christianitytoday.com/women/
http://www.flickr.com/photos/qathi/
http://www.fortifyingthefamily.com/
http://getoffmyinternets.net/
http://www.oranges-and-apples.com/
http://simchafisher.wordpress.com/

WEBSITES

http://isthismodest.com/
http://www.koshercasual.com/
http://www.sharibraendel.com/
http://www.wayoflife.org/
http://www.wingzfashion.com/

7

'CAN WE DISCUSS THIS?'

Elizabeth Wilson

This chapter attempts to explore some of the obstacles that make discussion of modest dress so difficult. Modest dress for women (and indeed for men) is enjoined by the orthodox of all three Abrahamic religions, but it is the Muslim veil, niqab, hijab, *chador* or burqa that has acted in recent decades as a flashpoint for, or a symbol of, a number of different issues, many remote from dress and indeed arguably both from one another and from religion. The 'veil' condenses the following concerns voiced by different interest groups: the role of women in society and whether the veil oppresses or empowers them; the role and relationships of men and women, sexually and in the family and whether men and women should occupy different spaces or should mingle freely; the place of immigrant groups in Western societies (and for that matter whether they have a place at all); the public role of religion, particularly in Western societies, in the context of the secular state; and the status of various freedoms such as free speech and freedom of the expression of personal and group identity. Deeply held, incompatible and therefore hotly contested beliefs home in on what has sometimes been dismissed as 'just a piece of cloth'.

Pnina Werbner has written a wide-ranging overview of the significance of covered dress in contemporary Britain and France, starting from 'the paradox that sexual intimacy is neither intimate nor private' and citing Michel Foucault, who argued that individual actors are always subject to 'normalising discourses and discursive practices' enunciated by 'experts' (Werbner 2007: 161). Beliefs about sexuality and appropriate sexual behaviour are central to ideological struggles over the veil, as are beliefs in many societies about women as bearers of the shame and honour of families and groups. Foucault is correct, moreover, in noting how in all societies clothing is more generally regulated, by state, church, government or employer. In the pre-industrial West, for example, sumptuary laws attempted (with mixed success) to restrict the wearing of lavish dress to the upper classes.

The regulation of dress may actually be more successful in contemporary societies than when the Tudors tried to prevent merchant upstarts from wearing cloth of gold. British banks and supermarkets are examples of institutions that reinforce their brands by insisting on colour-coded outfits for their basic grade employees. In Britain, the supermarket Sainsbury's dresses its counter hands in burgundy tracksuits piped with orange; the sales personnel at upmarket Waitrose are clothed in grey aprons, grey and white striped shirts and lime green ties, slightly reminiscent of early twentieth-century servants' or shop assistants' wear. Managers of both sexes in these stores, by contrast, wear business suits, emphasising the hierarchy of employment.

Uniforms constitute an important dimension of the regulation of dress; in the armed forces and in some countries in schools, uniforms are considered essential to the maintenance of discipline and are held to promote loyalty, pride in the organisation and a sense of group identity. This belief has been tested by research and found wanting (Barkham 2011), but it has mystical status, at least in the UK, where a blazer and a tie (for girls as well as boys) are bizarrely held to provide the moral stamina and ambition to succeed that would otherwise be lacking. Yet blazers, the last remnant of the British Empire, are no longer worn by adults at all, other than in sports-related situations – old toffs at Lords cricket ground or lines persons at Wimbledon. It is true that jackets termed blazers appear from time to time on the catwalk, but these are draped and usually slightly fitted jackets merely suggesting a 'sporty look' and far removed from the genuine blazer, which is box shaped, made from hard, felt-like material and has a crest on the breast pocket; and while some urban lesbians may wear ties, that is very different from forcing adolescent girls to appear in men's neckwear. The purpose of these school uniforms is, as well as somehow promoting loyalty and discipline, to prevent boys from wearing subcultural or gang-related items and to quench girls' sexual appeal. Uniforms are also clearly related to modesty insofar as they attempt to suppress sexuality – even if they sometimes unintentionally enhance it (old style officers' dress uniforms, for example, or indeed, for some individuals, nuns' habits). It could even be argued that the more enveloping forms of covered dress by concealing womanhood makes the woman more alluring and so defeats its own purpose. So while forms of modest dressing are not exactly a uniform, they play a similar role. All assert an authority other than the wearer's.

The fashion cycle might be seen as the opposite of a uniform, since uniforms are perceived as unchanging (although they do change) and outside fashion. In fact the contemporary 'discourse' of fashion seems to be in opposition to any strictures or restrictions on dress – even, paradoxically, fashion 'rules'; the idea that women, especially, 'dress as we please' has become a cliché of fashion journalism since the 1970s, along with the idea that there are no more fashions, only styles. This has been one expression of the ideology of individualism to which Western societies adhere, while actually being in some ways as rule-bound as ever, not least in the matter of dress. Certain rules, such as the wearing of mourning or prohibitions from wearing trousers for women, have hugely relaxed or disappeared altogether. New 'rules' and customs, however, even if not statutorily enforced, have arisen, yet the lack of clear rules can also cause discomfort and uncertainty. Nor does it prevent certain items of clothing from causing offence, hostility and outright fear, for example hooded anoraks worn by youths. Such items of clothing become overburdened with meaning, symbolically weighted, none more so than Muslim covered dress – which I shall refer to, generically, as 'the veil', while aware that it takes different forms and that there are differences within Muslim communities as to what the correct form of covered dress is (or if it is required at all).

That the significance of the veil is more difficult to discuss than other matters related to dress arises above all from its religious nature. However, the veil also condenses a number of arguments around competing views on a variety of other issues.

One source of dislike of covered dress is that in Western societies it is associated with immigrant communities, although many practitioners will have been born in the 'host' country. The fear is that the indigenous culture will be diluted or, in the notorious words of British Prime Minister Margaret Thatcher in 1979, 'swamped' by the incomers. Individuals who express such views often deny vehemently that they are racists, but at the very least it must be seen as a form of prejudice that constructs an alien 'Other'. This Other is perceived as not a proper part of the body politic, as essentially an intrusion that should be expelled. As with 'hoodies', hostility also arises from fear: fear of the unfamiliar, which is interpreted as threatening. This was true of public reaction to punks in the 1970s and even to hippies before that, long haired men and patchouli-scented women feared as the outliers of drugs and decadence. But the dislike is particularly virulent in the case of veiled women. In 2006 the then Labour Home Secretary, Jack Straw, requested that women visiting his surgery in his north of England constituency, Blackburn, home to a large Asian community, not wear a niqab, because it 'signified difference and separation' and damaged community relations. He rejected accusations that his remarks were racist, but they certainly did not help community cohesion and appeared to express his own inability to cope with difference rather than accommodate it.

Further, to object to the wearing of garments that signify a particular ethnic or national identity is hard to reconcile with ideas of freedom of expression and the right to self-definition. If there is a right to express one's identity as a Rastafarian or an existentialist or a punk, why not as a Muslim? Yet it seems that forms of the veil symbolise difference in a manner that arouses (unwarranted) hostility, as other forms of distinctive dress do not. The Scottish kilt might be the subject of mirth, but is perfectly acceptable (although after the Jacobite Rebellion of 1745 it was forbidden, since at that time it signified resistance to domination by England). Hasidim of both sexes wear distinctive dress and individual Jews from this community may encounter hostility, but their clothing is not the subject of intense and ongoing largely negative comment in the mass media. So, given that Muslims, both individually and as communities, have been subject to considerable and sustained hostility in Britain and other Western countries, it is hardly surprising that one use of the veil (and, although less frequently, 'traditional' Islamic male dress) has been to express a Muslim identity in the face of rejection. This is the veil as essentially a political statement and is a new, urban form of covered dress.

As mentioned earlier, supporters of Islamic dress sometimes make use of the defence: 'What is all the fuss about? It's just a piece of cloth.' But this is a form of denial, for no garment is ever 'just a piece of cloth'. All garments represent ideas and ideologies, and the veil – in the early twenty-first century the most contested of all items of clothing – is a powerful symbol of a world view. Leila Ahmed, indeed, has argued that Islamist organisations, notably the Muslim Brotherhood, have regarded the veil as 'strategically important' for these groups and a visible sign of the Muslim's resistance to the West and Western civilisation (Ahmed 2011: passim).

In the early and mid-twentieth century, the Turkish leader, Kemal Ataturk, took it as read that the emancipation of women must include unveiling. Ahmed's detailed account, which concentrates on Egypt, demonstrates how complex the issue is, relating it to the whole history of war and imperialism in the region. She writes:

> In much of the Arab world, the process [of unveiling] ... happened gradually and without enforcement. Women in the region (with the exception of the Arabian peninsula) unveiled throughout the first half of the C20 for a plethora of reasons, among them an expression of their longing for the goods, opportunities, and amenities of modernity ... But it is noteworthy that the process of unveiling occurred initially because the Western meaning of the veil – as a sign of the inferiority of Islam as a religion, culture and civilisation – triumphed and came to profoundly overlay the veil's prior indigenous meanings (common to all three monotheistic religions in the region) of God-given gender hierarchy and separation. (Ahmed 2011: 44)

Only a more critical assessment in the Middle East and elsewhere of Western culture since the 1970s led to a re-evaluation of the veil as a mark not only of female dignity, but also, again, of a new, more Islamist nationalism. The new veiling arose in Egypt in the post-Nasser period in spite of government attempts to prevent it, as part of a movement dissatisfied with the oppressive and corrupt regime supported by the United States.

The revival of Islam and the development of new and stricter forms of the religion have meant that covered dress has once again become the norm in many communities. Many not only cover their heads, but wear all-enveloping covered dress, including the burqa and the niqab. In the case of Egypt, a key player in this change, women began to readopt the veil after the humiliating defeat at the hands of Israel in 1967. The growing influence of the Muslim Brotherhood was important in its call for a transformation of Egyptian society. The veil would be a central symbol of a new religious awakening, which, among other things, promoted gender segregation and egalitarian principles of social justice. Ahmed argues that Muslims became disillusioned with the unfulfilled promises of a Westernised modernity and began to seek a different path, rejecting the internalised Western imperialism that had once seemed the path to progress. This involved a change in self-identification. Whereas formerly, immigrants at least to the West had identified themselves as Pakistani, Bangladeshi, Somali and so on, they increasingly adopted the transnational religious identity of Muslim.

The Muslim Brotherhood has been influential far beyond Egypt. Ahmed argues that many Brothers fled to Saudi Arabia from persecution under post-

Nasser governments. There they not only had access to the support of Saudi wealth, but provided a coherent Islamic philosophy that they and the Saudis were able to export, for example to Bosnia and the Indian subcontinent.

One result of the new, politicised use of the veil is the common sight today of small girls wearing a hijab. It is a statement of an identity that is religious but also political. Pnina Werbner (2007) discusses in some detail the French refusal to allow schoolgirls to attend schools wearing a scarf (and Nicholas Sarkozy instigated a total ban on the niqab in 2010). Britain has taken a sensible and more pragmatic position, as she points out, and has thereby largely (although not completely) avoided conflict. Nevertheless, there is an argument against the wearing by small children of a scarf (which was never part of Islamic practice in past times), because it sexualises them prematurely as surely as do the 'pre-teen' bras and cosmetic sets marketed to pre-pubertal girls.

The most disturbing recent example of the religiously motivated oversexualisation of small girls is the ongoing conflict in Jerusalem and other Israeli communities, such as Bet Shemesh. There, as reported by Harriet Sherwood (Sherwood 2011: 5), some members of a religious nationalist sect, who are both orthodox and committed Zionists, have mounted a campaign to force women and girls to dress modestly. In Bet Shemesh these ultra-orthodox Jews have sought to enforce strict orthodox observation, for example of the Sabbath, but have also demanded the separation of men and women in public places, even to the extent of separate checkout queues in supermarkets. And just as Afro Americans were required to sit in the back of the bus in the American South, so women are pressured to sit in the back of the bus in Bet Shemesh. Asked why they focused so strongly on the way small girls dress (mounting vituperative demonstrations outside schools and 'screaming "whore" and "slut"' at primary school children), one protester explained that 'even an eight-year-old draws my eyes'. In other words, even at that age and younger, girls should cover their flesh, lest they tempt grown men, as though all men were paedophiles.

This is an extreme position, but it relates to the whole inflammatory issue of women's role in Islam, a further aspect of the political dimension of the veil, or what it represents. At the outbreak of the war in Afghanistan, Western feminists suddenly found their inboxes cluttered with emails from new 'friends' that they had never known they knew. Cherie Blair and Laura Bush wrote to describe the awful injustices endured by Afghan women and implored their new best feminist friends to support a war that would emancipate these oppressed women. The veil and the oppression of women were collapsed together in the interests of American neo-colonial aggression and the women of the Middle East were to be rescued by Western armed intervention.

The assumption that Muslim women were straightforwardly oppressed in the 'backward' societies in which they lived was, suggests Leila Ahmed, part of the imperialism she describes. How relative this view is may be illustrated by the experience of Lady Mary Wortley Montagu, an intrepid eighteenth-century British traveller. Visiting the Ottoman Empire in 1717, she was piqued by the reaction of women at the Sofia hot baths to her outfit. Not only did her riding habit appear 'very extraordinary' to them, but they were shocked when she showed them 'my stays, which satisfied 'em very well, for I saw they believ'd I was so locked up in that machine that it was not in my own power to open it, which contrivance they attributed to my husband' (1997: 149). What the Englishwoman wore as fashionable and, presumably, modern, to the Turkish women seemed as oppressive as their veils and seclusion did to her. She was also impressed by Turkish women's rights in areas such as property ownership, where British women had none.

The rift in understanding and bafflement on both sides is no less marked today. Muslim women, some but not all of whom describe themselves as Muslim feminists, have argued that to dress modestly restores women's dignity and that it enables the woman to be seen and related to as a person rather than as a sexualised body. They have also consistently pointed to women's rights within Islam, the right to work or to own property, for example, as if these rights negated any argument that could be made against the veil. But the one does not cancel out the other and against this, Nira Yuval-Davis claims 'that all fundamentalist [i.e. political] religious movements, whether Christian, Jewish, Hindu or Muslim, use the control of women's bodies symbolically to assert a wider agenda of authoritarian political and cultural social control' (quoted in Werbner 2007: 162).

A common liberal position is to take refuge in the concept of 'choice'. It would be wrong for a woman to be forced to cover up, but it is perfectly acceptable if it is her 'choice'. 'Choice' is the default position of consumer culture, but in The Paradox of Choice: Why More is Less, Barry Schwartz describes some of the shortcomings of the notion of choice as the measure of all things. First, and most obviously, market choices are dependent on the ability to pay, so there is massive inequality in the world of consumer choice. Even if incomes were equal, however, choice could not solve all our problems. In the first place, we have too many choices about things that are essentially the same. We stress over which car, for example, to buy within a certain price bracket when the differences are infinitesimal. We spend hours shaving off the cost of a utility bill, but have actually lost money in doing so, since our time also has a price (Schwartz 2004). Different styles of jeans do make a difference, but only a marginal one; the proliferation of choice of coffees can result simply in increased dissatisfaction if the cappuccino is too milky, the macchiato not milky enough and the white Americano insufficiently strong.

In any case, to talk of Muslim covered dress in terms of choice does not address the issue. Muslim women wear the veil for many different reasons. For some, covered dress may be not a choice, but seen as a requirement of their religion. Some wear it as a badge of identity. Others might simply feel uncomfortable if they did not cover their heads – for them it is the normal thing to do. Others may, indeed, be forced by their families or may come under pressure from the community to dress in this way. Whatever the reason, nonetheless, to adopt modest dress is not a 'lifestyle choice' similar to choosing bootcut as opposed to skinny jeans or apricot jam instead of strawberry. The decision to adopt modest dress may, and probably will, lead to further decisions that do come within the range of a consumer choice, such as the colour of a hijab. However, the initial decision is surely more serious than a consumer whim.

Moreover, to wear modest dress conveys a strong idea of how it is appropriate for a woman to be and it is here that secularists and Muslims may find themselves with no common ground. The idea that if a woman reveals her hair, arms, legs and even her face, she acts in an immoral way and is a temptation to men, seems, to a secularist, insulting to men as well as to women. Rape and sexual violence are endemic throughout the world, as are domestic violence and rape within marriage (a concept not universally recognised). Yet these crimes are not confined to those communities in which women go uncovered. The idea that a man cannot function and should not be expected to control himself if he has caught sight of part of a woman's anatomy institutionalises a very low view of men's self-control, while at the same time relieving them of responsibility for their own behaviour. It lays the blame for male misbehaviour – and crimes – on the shoulders of women, a classic case of blaming the victim. It also expresses the belief that men are more sexual than women in an unequal gendered partnership of desire.

Men as well as women are enjoined in Islam to dress modestly. Yet in the streets of Western capitals young Muslim men are quite often seen with

gelled hair and tight trousers walking alongside sisters or girlfriends who
are swathed in dark material. As Timothy Garton Ash expressed it:

> When, on a hot day in London, I see a woman wrapped in a black sack
> tagging along beside a guy in light t-shirt, jeans and sneakers, my first
> reaction is: 'How bloody unfair!' John Stuart Mill, who enunciated
> the liberal's classic harm principle, was himself passionate against 'the
> almost despotic power of husbands over wives'. But before we leap to
> this conclusion, shouldn't we ask the women themselves? Or do we
> paternalistically ... assume they don't know what is good for them, and
> must be forced to be free? (Garton Ash 2011: 33)

Nevertheless, it is hard not to feel that the double standard so prevalent
everywhere in relations between the sexes operates here as well. This is
no more unjust, perhaps, than unequal pay for women and may be less
important, nevertheless it does institutionalise a form of public inequality.
Observant Muslim men and women do not appear in public on equal terms.
The woman must render herself close to invisible, while men seem to strut
about as they please.

Yet as Garton Ash concedes, modest dress is not necessarily a sign of
submission and oppression, and the claim by Muslim women that the
veil is a sign of liberation and agency often embraces a strong critique of
Western fashions and Western stereotypes of femininity. Muslim women,
like Western feminists, have attacked the fashion and beauty industries for
proposing and even enforcing narrow and stereotyped ideals of female
beauty (particularly slenderness), which oversexualise women. It is less
perhaps the fashion industry as such than the totality of Hollywood (or
what used to be thought of as Hollywood – that is, global mass culture)
and celebrity culture that present women as sexual beings and nothing else.
Madonna, Britney Spears and the soft porn imagery of MTV rather than
Dior or Prada influence the parade of styles that mass fashion offers. Narrow
norms of what constitutes female beauty diminish the self-confidence of
young women rather than enhancing it, to grow old is to be air brushed
out of existence, while the proliferation of actual pornography appears to
have influenced male expectations both of sexual behaviour (for example,
expecting oral sex even when the woman is unwilling) and of how the
naked female body should look (with shaved pubic hair, for example).

Here, Western feminists can make common cause with Muslim women,
who have used arguments that are close to or directly deploy those used

by secular feminists to critique fashionable contemporary dress styles and the restrictive norms of beauty, and more generally, the sexism still so widely prevailing in secular societies. In a discussion about the 'slut walk' demonstration in 2011, when women marched to protest against the belief that a woman who dresses like a 'slut' is inviting rape, the comedian Shaista Aziz, who wears hijab, said:

> I don't cover up to please men, I do this for myself. I don't think that a woman should cover up and then get respect, I think women should be respected. But maybe there's an issue with women respecting themselves ... [but] I'm quite shocked by some of the things on sale ... [for example] a make-up range for kids ... I find these things very disturbing, but sexual abuse, rape is about power, it's nothing to do with what a woman wears. (McVeigh 2011: 24)

Leila Ahmed (2011) has suggested, nevertheless, that the renewal of Islam, primarily influenced by Saudi Wahabism, incorporates an essentialist ideology: biology is woman's destiny in that her main role in life is her duty to her family, her husband and children. This implies a view of gendered human behaviour as innate. This is not exclusively an Islamic view. It has, on the contrary, been very widely held in Western societies. Indeed, both the first and second 'waves' of Western feminism struggled against the view that men and women were essentially different – the idea vulgarly reprised today in concepts such as 'Men are from Mars, women are from Venus'. In the Victorian period the marital ideal was of 'separate spheres'. This envisaged that:

> Nature had endowed all civilised men with an active, initiating procreative sex drive, which demanded its healthy outlet in regular but not excessive sexual intercourse, while women's reciprocal sex instincts were supposedly more moderate and focused more on the joys of emotional nurturing of the young. This polarisation of supposed sexual natures was not necessarily scientifically endorsed by many medical experts, but was insidiously and consistently implied. (Szreter and Fisher 2010: 34)

So dominant were these views in the late nineteenth century that some feminists embraced them, arguing that women's innately different qualities should be valued for their unique contribution, for example as lovers of peace, or because their inborn maternal instinct should be deployed as a force for good.

It is partly because women in Western societies have struggled for so long against such views that their reassertion within resurgent Islamism can be hard to accept. The view of men and women as innately different led historically to gender apartheid, that is, the view that men and women should be physically segregated, although this was never so ruthlessly imposed in Western societies as in Islam. In the nineteenth and twentieth centuries, Western feminists struggled hard for the many rights they were denied: the vote, ownership of property, equal pay and others. Until after the Second World War, girls and boys were almost always educated separately, while women (and for that matter men) covered their heads. So many Western women feel that their rights have been hard won and that these rights are still fragile. Muslim women who defend their own religious practices and views can be understood (or misunderstood) as attacking these rights and as undermining the secular conviction that no institution, state or church, has the right to dictate capriciously how women should live and behave.

A recent oral history of the sexual lives of English couples during the period between the wars and until 1963 found that in the first half of the twentieth century husbands and wives were highly reticent in discussing sex, even within marriage. In Western societies it was psychoanalysis and the growing popularity of the 'talking therapies' that changed this, so that today discussion of sexual matters is – *pace* Foucault – freer and more widespread (yet not necessarily more 'liberated') than previously. In this pre-war climate where sexual discussion was largely taboo, young women felt it very important to retain their innocence, not just ignorance, as central to their 'attractiveness and respectability'. Innocence and modesty were to be prized and preserved. The researchers note that sexual historians such as Jeffrey Weeks have advanced the view that it has been all progress since that period, a 'Whig' view of sexual history as one of continual enlightenment and improvement, from a dark ages of ignorance to a modernity of happier sexual lives, especially for women (Szreter and Fisher, 2010: passim).

Certainly practical improvements in contraception, say, as well as changed attitudes have improved the sex lives of many couples. However, it is surely more contradictory than that and it is useful to bear in mind that – notwithstanding the very different histories and traditions of different religions and societies – there are many women who would still today prefer to see themselves in a less hectically sexual way. 'Modesty' has, on the whole, not done well for women, having, as it does, inescapable overtones of submission and self-effacement, but it does provide a counterbalance to the belief that women should at all times be sexually eager and sexually experienced. The idea that women are 'up for it', 'gagging for it' is as offensive and exaggerated as the belief it displaced, the idea that most women are 'frigid'.

Where Western women have at times embraced the idea of covered dress, this has seemed to be less from a sense that it will enhance their dignity as individuals, than from shame at their own imperfections. When in 2011, icon of domestic femininity Nigella Lawson wore a burqini swimming outfit in Australia it caused a furore of comment. Many women defended her choice on the grounds that such an outfit protected the privacy of her body as well as protecting her from dangerous levels of the sun's rays. The *Guardian* newspaper ran a piece on companies that sell large quantities of modest swimwear, to non-Muslim as well as Muslim women. Yet the non-religious reasons that women have adopted these swimsuits appear depressingly negative. Women spoke of the effort of displaying your body on holiday, depilation, a tan and a perfect figure being minimal requirements, so that it seems as if a burqini was a way of covering the shame of being fat, pasty or just imperfect, rather than a positive gesture. *Guardian* columnist Madeleine Bunting found the burqini 'brilliantly subversive' and 'iconic', but a contributor to the letters column, Dr Annette Magnussen, expressed a different view. The burqini was only 'revolutionary' in the sense that it:

> … means a woman's – more or less – only choice to beat prying eyes is to [cover] herself … even on a beach, instead of facing up to her critics and enjoying herself no matter what. True I am no celebrity and no one cares about my bulging belly. Still, I would never sacrifice either the amenities of a secular state or the pleasure of feeling the sun, wind and water on my skin (as men so naturally do). If people do not like my body they can look the other way. Would Nigella Lawson have worn a burkhini if she were skinny? Lawson has carefully crafted her image as a voluptuous food goddess and, let's face it, her cooking is not for the calorie conscious … What a statement it would have been to live up to the consequences in real life!' (*Guardian* letters, Thursday, 28 April 2011)

To suggest that the answer to the pornified society is for women simply to hide, to retreat from public view, is to acknowledge defeat.

So the significance of the veil stretches far beyond religion. Yet for the secularist it is the religious aspect of the veil that may be the most unwelcome. The paradox of the conflict between religion and secular society is that only in a secular society can the right of all religious believers of whatever faith to practise their belief be assured.

A secularist, therefore, may not find the appearance on the streets of clothing that testifies to religious belief entirely welcome; but cannot reasonably object, since a cornerstone of secularism is respect for differing beliefs. If an individual's religion involves the requirement to dress in a certain way, then it is oppressive to forbid this. What may be queried in secular society is less the behaviour of individuals than the intrusion of religion into the public sphere in an organised, institutional way. So a different legal system (whether Sharia law or the different legal practices of the indigenous peoples in Australia) is difficult to reconcile with a universal system of law that treats all individuals equally. The secularist is equally within his or her rights to object to the existence of religious schools as a form of indoctrination unchosen by pupils. A secularist or atheist should not endorse political bans on the niqab, or indeed any other form of dress, but neither should s/he support the power of a religious institution to force women to conform to specific dress codes.

While, however, there is no inhibition in arguing the toss about school uniforms, even if these arouse strong disagreement, to dispute religious dress (or any aspect of religious practice) is quite another matter. Yet dress practices ordained by any religion must be problematic for the non-religious observer. The attempt to advance arguments against 'modest dress' involves a questioning of the principles upon which such arguments are based, and such questioning is vulnerable to interpretation as an attack on an individual's faith. This is partly because religion as a subject has been placed beyond the pale of polite discourse. This difficulty in discussing religion has been reinforced by the view of some Muslims that because they feel 'offended' if others criticise their religion, no criticisms should be made. It has on the other hand paradoxically led to more forthright attacks on religion from atheists such as Richard Dawkins and the late Christopher Hitchens.

Sigmund Freud once explained the relationship of the Conscious and Unconscious by means of the following metaphor. They can never meet, he said. Just as the polar bear and the whale do not meet because one is in the water and the other on the ice (that the polar bear is often no longer on the ice due to global warming does not invalidate the metaphor), so these separate regions of mental functioning are cut off from one another.

The metaphor translates well to the confrontation of the believer and the non-believer. For in order for two individuals to have a useful argument, it is necessary for there to be some basis of common ground. A member of the Conservative party can have a meaningful discussion with a Labour party supporter because both believe in the parliamentary system and universal suffrage. Even the Tory and a revolutionary communist can have a debate, since both at least believe in the meaningful nature of political action. Such is not necessarily the case when the faithful and the non-believer come face to face. An Islamist might argue that everything comes from God and that therefore political activity is meaningless and voting wrong, ruling out debate with Conservative or socialist alike.

More difficult is the fact that the believer's beliefs are a matter of faith, not reason. Consequently an attempt to question religious beliefs and precepts on reasonable grounds simply does not work and can quite easily arouse defensiveness and anger at what is interpreted as a personal attack. On the other side, atheists may feel if not offended, at least deeply frustrated when a believer dismisses their arguments with comments such as, 'Not to be religious is like being tone deaf' or more brusquely, 'You'll go to hell'.

Over the centuries both Christianity and Islam have been very successful in stifling debate and in punishing those who have dared to question religious dogma. This constitutes worldly rather than spiritual power, but the success of religion has been in collapsing the two, so that to question the validity of religious belief is denounced, not as a challenge to this worldly power, but as an attack on the faith of the legions of believers.

In demanding the right to special treatment for their beliefs, the religious place their views beyond the reach of debate. Hence the title of this chapter: is it possible even to discuss arguments for and against the wearing of the veil from a secular point of view? Is it even possible for the secular and the religious individual to talk about it at all? There may be discussions within the Muslim communities, but does anyone outside Islam have the right, or indeed the possibility, of putting a point of view? The option of simply reducing the veil to a question of 'choice' is the easier – in a way, the politer – option.

Yet choice does not address the task. Secular feminists have a responsibility to fight their corner. This presents them with the difficult necessity of arguing against two opposite problems and of insisting that two wrongs do not make a right. On the one hand the struggle against the pornification of culture is extremely important, but on the other, a puritanical covering up is not the solution. It is important to reassert that the human body, clothed or unclothed, is a cause for celebration. A rediscovery of the body at the end of the nineteenth century was led by artists, such as those who surrounded

Diaghilev in the Ballets Russes. Works such as *L'Après-Midi d'un Faune* and *The Rite of Spring* celebrated eroticism and the human body in a revolt against the oppressive attitudes of the Victorians. The German *'erotische Rebellion'* before the First World War led to a new seeking after the natural in the youth and nudity movements of the 1920s. It is true that these movements to some extent fed into the Fascist Aryan ideal of human beauty, but the intention at least was a freer and less voyeuristic culture. Today the lightly clad sporting body can perform miracles of skill, while in modern ballet men and women dance together – in forms that are often close to gymnastics – in minimal clothing, yet without being sexually titillating or even erotic, some modern dance achieving an almost abstract quality.

It is quite hard to attack vulgar sexual objectification and puritanism simultaneously. Yet that is what is necessary if there is not to be a descent into a toxic mix of 1960s 'permissive' sexism and puritanical religiosity.

REFERENCES

Ahmed, Leila (2011). *A Quiet Revolution: The Veil's Resurgence, from the Middle East to America*. New Haven, CT: Yale University Press.

Barkham, Patrick (2011). 'Uniform Wars'. *Guardian*, G2, 24 August: 8.

Garton Ash, Timothy (2011). 'Believe in Equality, Liberty, Fraternity? This Time, Don't Follow the French'. *Guardian*, 11 April: 33.

Guardian letters, quoting Dr Annette Magnussen, Thursday, 28 April 2011.

McVeigh, Tracy (2011). 'Slut Walk – the Big Debate'. *Observer*, 15 May: 24–25.

Montagu, Lady Mary Wortley (1997). *Selected Letters*. Isobel Grundy (ed.). Harmondsworth: Penguin.

Schwartz, Barry (2004). *The Paradox of Choice: Why More is Less*. New York: Ecco Press.

Sherwood, Harriet (2011). 'The Battle of Bet Shemesh'. *Guardian*, G2, 1 November: 5.

Szreter, Simon and Fisher, Kate (2010). *Sex Before the Sexual Revolution: Intimate Life in England, 1918–1963*. Cambridge: Cambridge University Press.

Werbner, Pnina (2007). 'Veiled Interventions in Pure Space: Shame and Embodied Struggles among Muslims in Britain and France'. *Theory Culture and Society*, special issue, 'Authority and Islam', 24 (2): 161–86.

Part 3

Manufacturing and Mediating Modesty: The Industry and the Press

8

MODESTY REGULATORS
Punishing and Rewarding Women's Appearances in Mainstream Media

Liz Hoggard

Long before I am near enough to talk to you on the street, in a meeting, or at a party, you announce your sex, age and class to me through what you are wearing – and very possibly give me important information (or misinformation) as to your occupation, origin, personality, opinions, tastes, sexual desires, and current mood. I may not be able to put what I observe into words, but I register the information unconsciously; and you simultaneously do the same for me. By the time we meet and converse we have already spoken to each other in an older and more universal tongue. (Lurie 1992: 3)

As a consumer journalist, I am asked why newspapers and magazines rarely write about 'modest dress' (in a cross-faith context) as a fashion story in its own right. Certainly UK newspapers are full of stories about the burqa and the niqab; about high-profile British converts to Islam, such as writers Lauren Booth or Yvonne Ridley, wearing a head covering; or headlines about Belgium and France being the first European countries to outlaw the burqa.

When Baroness Warsi, the first Muslim to sit as a full member of the British Cabinet, wore pink salwar kameez ('traditional dress') to a meeting with British Prime Minister David Cameron, the photograph went round the world. Her colourful outfit stood out against a sea of male suits. But almost without fail these stories are treated in media terms as 'News' or 'Comment' and not as 'Fashion' or even as 'Lifestyle'. There is, it seems, a nervousness about treating women who dress modestly (in a way that satisfies their spiritual and stylistic requirements for reasons of faith, religion or personal preference) as fashion.

So how do you move a story on from the news pages to the Fashion or Lifestyle sections? In this chapter I will primarily be discussing print media in Britain (from broadsheet newspapers to mid-market titles such as the *Daily Mail* and tabloid newspapers). The key difference between daily newspapers and glossy magazines (which cover fashion, lifestyle, women's interest) is lead time and currency. With a daily newspaper you can respond to a story immediately (either in the next day's paper or on the website). With glossy magazines, the lead time can be anything from six weeks to three months, so stories are chosen that are not especially time sensitive, or are seasonally-driven (for example, summer beach fashions, winter Christmas decorating tips, and so on).

In contrast, the contents of a daily newspaper are chosen at a morning conference where the overall editor and key section editors (news, features, sport, fashion, business, etc.) debate the key topics of the day – and what the paper's response to them will be. This response will inevitably be 'guided' by the newspaper's politics (is it left or right wing?), its own readership (age, sex, social demographic) and its desire to be ahead of the pack in terms of exclusives and breaking stories.

Although every newspaper now has a fashion and style section (partly because it offers a change of editorial pace with glamorous/colourful/ whimsical images and photographs), stories will inevitably have to fight for space with the key news and politics stories of the day.

At the daily conference the fashion journalist pitching the story has to convince the editor that it deserves a longer, more in-depth treatment than usual – maybe it is a key catwalk or street trend that is breaking; a celebrity or the wife of a head of state who has worn an unusual garment or designer, and so on. The journalist will argue that the idea is not just a flash-in-the-pan stunt, but deserves to be written about as a feature, first-person column, popular culture analysis, or even illustrated by a glossy colour photo-shoot.

To convince the editor, the journalist must prove the story has longevity – will it still be as gripping the next day, or even in a week's time when you actually run the shoot? The story needs to be fresh, inventive, look great on the page – and push the boundaries. As well as convincing editors that it has intrinsic interest and value, there are also the advertisers to be kept happy, of course (who need to see their brands represented in the pages of the feature). It also needs to appeal to an increasingly youthful 17–25 demographic, who all advertisers are keen to reach.

Arguably faith-based fashion ticks all these boxes. And yet it seems that most mainstream fashion journalists are still uneasy about representing modest dress as a bone fide fashion story. It is often regarded as worthy, moralistic, off-putting for a secular readership.

This rule can occasionally be broken when it is a 'famous' woman who experiments with faith-based fashion – such as rapper/hip hop star M.I.A., who turned up in a multi-coloured burqa, black high-heeled sandals and long black velvet gloves to the 2010 Spike TV Scream Awards in Los Angeles. M.I.A., who has a track record in political activism, wore a burqa festooned in large hearts and flowers, with the words 'I love you' emblazoned across the bottom. Arguably because it was a red-carpet appearance (rather than a visit to a traditional place of worship), fashion critics felt comfortable deconstructing it as a defiant style gesture.

Similarly when American idol Lady Gaga sports a lace face veil, everyone enjoys the sense of frisson. Once again such a gesture can be safely filed under 'pop star with crazy fashion sense' without any fear of it being a symbol of political or religious affiliation. Even when Gaga turned up at the airport in Los Angeles with sunglasses and black netting on her face, it was viewed indulgently by the mainstream newspapers – rather than as a threat to national security by a potential terrorist.

Arguably the other way to smuggle stories about modest apparel into the mainstream press is to focus on women who combine wearing 'traditional dress' with Western luxury fashion brands. Journalists are currently fascinated by women such as Pakistan's stylish young Foreign Minister Hina Rabbani Khar, who teams oversized Robert Cavalli sunglasses, a Hermès Birkin handbag and classic pearl jewellery with a modest covered head-dressing. Again she is regarded as a 'safe' fashion icon because she is wearing symbols of First-World consumer capitalism.

When the Queen greeted Hayrünnisa Gül, wife of Turkey's president, as she and her husband arrived for lunch at Buckingham Palace, in November 2011, newspapers were fascinated by the image of the First Lady of Turkey tottering gingerly on the red carpet in six-inch platform shoes. It was, in fact, a fabulous collision of two different traditions of 'modest dressing', with Hayrünnisa Gül in hijab and long, loose dress (apart from the very Western platform ankle boots) and the Queen in knee-length coat and hat (and sensible court shoes). Interestingly, Hayrünnisa Gül's choice of shoes helped to demystify her choice of modest dress for the style press. It amused them ('here is a woman like other women, liable to wear unsuitable shoes'), and stopped them regarding her as inaccessible or 'other'.

And in 2011, *Vanity Fair* even voted style icon Sheikha Mozah Bint Nasser al-Missned of Qatar to its International Best-Dressed List, highlighting a woman whose haute couturier is Jean Paul Gaultier while embracing modest standards of dress in Islam (always wearing the hijab, long sleeves, pants, or ankle-length skirts). Her official wardrobe during a state visit to the UK in October 2010 prompted the British designer Julien Macdonald to declare her a style icon. '"[She is] glamorous and sophisticated, the very epitome of a royal," said the designer. "Not since Jackie O has any first lady had such global resonance in terms of fashion. I would love to dress her. Her personal style is rich with power and confidence, yet retains a real femininity that many women aspire to," he added' (Fox 2010).

Clearly *Vanity Fair* should be applauded for its fashion diversity in choosing Sheikha Mozah of Qatar alongside fellow winners such as the Duchess of Cambridge and actresses Carey Mulligan and Tilda Swinton. But let's not forget that this makes good market sense for advertisers. After all, in a global recession, the luxury market increasingly caters to the growing Middle Eastern and emerging couture markets.

ETHNIC FASHION

It is certainly true that newspapers and glossy magazines will write about 'traditional' or 'ethnic' fashion when the international catwalks showcase a new trend for boho chic, tribal knits, crocheted skirts, kaftans, beading and embroidery. In this case it is presented as exotic 'fantasy wear' from faraway places, which has been appropriated and given a contemporary spin by Western couturiers. A bit like going on a guided safari tour. Back in 2004, actress Sienna Miller was the poster girl for vintage 'boho' chic; while models Lily Cole and Kate Moss have both promoted the 'ethnic' kaftan look (Moss's collection for Topshop High Summer 2009 was based around the tribal trend, with ethnic influences, feathers and animal prints).

What we rarely see in the papers, however, is normal, everyday coverage of UK faith-based fashion brands – the stories behind the designers and entrepreneurs, the customers at whom they are aimed (who may include nurses, teachers, mothers of teenage girls, alongside fashion-conscious Jewish, Christian and Muslim women). And very rarely do we get a proper critique of modest clothing designs themselves – are they stylish/ practical/aesthetic/elitist/expensive/affordable? Could you wear them to work? Will there be a new market for 'modest' bridal wear, maternity wear or plus-size clothing? What's the best way to layer, if you're a funky hijab-wearing medical student?

This seems puzzling when fashion does co-opt many of the symbols of modest dress when it needs an influx of creativity or playfulness. Many items of modest dress have already been adopted by the high street – usually as a fun, guerrilla fashion – such as turbans and scarves; wigs and hairpieces; hoods, high collars and snoods. We have even seen harem pants becoming a popular teenage street fashion trend.

The maxi dresses and skirts offered by a cool British online retailer such as Maysaa (www.maysaa.com) were totally on-trend for Spring/Summer 2011 and Autumn/Winter 2012. Polo necks are a big trend for Autumn/ Winter 2012; while half of the sales of urban sportswear brand Elenany (www.elenany.co.uk) now go to non-Muslims, according to the label's designer, Sarah Elenany. So it was heartening to see The Independent newspaper running a feature about the designer behind the Maysaa label, Hana Tajima-Simpson, exploring how she is pioneering a new group of 'Hijabistas' – up-and-coming Muslim fashion designers who are doing their bit to forge an indigenous British Islamic identity. The Guardian newspaper has also been good at running pieces by young Muslim fashion designers and fans (such as articles on the best stores to buy hijab-friendly summer fashion).

But on the whole, the mainstream media insist on treating modest clothing as a 'uniform' of religious observance rather than as fashion – even though modest dressers are clearly a distinct consumer group who need representing. No wonder they are increasingly turning to fashion blogs and YouTube because conventional fashion magazines don't speak to them.

THE MODESTY DOUBLE STANDARD

For liberal feminists and right-wing columnists alike, modest dressing seems to cause anxiety in the mainstream press. It is often presented as suspect, other, reactionary – an infringement of our basic dress codes. But interestingly there are many people who are actually 'rewarded' for dressing modestly in our culture. These include:

1) Older women who obey the rules by avoiding showing too much flesh. The fashion police are the first to haul us over the coals if we expose flabby upper arms, crepey cleavage or problem knees. The newspapers love age-appropriate dressers such as Paul McCartney's second wife,

Nancy Shevell, Carole Middleton (mother of Prince William's wife, Kate Middleton) and even Madonna when she keeps elegantly covered-up. But they are on constant alert to catch out serial offenders against modesty such as fifty-something 'mutton dressed as lamb' celebrities Nancy Dell'Olio, Carole Vorderman and Ivana Trump.

2) Royal brides (Kate Middleton, Zara Phillips) are also held up as an emblem of modest dressing. In April 2011, fashion writers swooned over the Duchess of Cambridge's full-skirted, Grace Kelly-inspired wedding dress. It was almost like turning back the clock to 1956, as they itemised the intricate chantilly lace appliquéd bodice and long sleeves, the piety of the neckline, the dramatic train, 'modest' veil and diamond tiara. Kate Middleton was applauded for her 'demure' and 'discreet' sense of style; her restraint, her upright, formal posture. Interestingly just before the wedding itself, many newspapers worked themselves up into a frenzy about whether she would wear a veil at all. Royal etiquette was deemed to be at stake when the *Daily Mail* revealed she wanted to wear a simple garland of flowers in her hair, which would scream 'informal' and 'middle class', much to the horror of the English aristocracy (already appalled that William had chosen to wear an unmanly engagement ring). In the event, Kate's modest choices kept everybody happy. In fact in December of that year, *The Times* newspaper identified 2011 as the year of ladylike dressing – thanks to fashion's obsession with pretty, demure dresses, nude tights and beige court shoes. Poster girls for 'appropriate' (that is, modest) dress included the wife of the Prime Minister, Samantha Cameron, and Kate Middleton herself.

3) First Ladies (Carla Sarkozy, Michelle Obama, Crown Princess Letizia of Spain, HSH Princess Charlene of Monaco et al.) are required to be modest dressers, who do not outshine their husbands. The key is to be smart, conservative, rather than sexy. Carla Bruni, a former model with a reputation for posing nude, completely reinvented her image when she married the French President, Nicolas Sarkozy – you could write pages about the semiotics of her new 'demure' wardrobe. From pale pink to royal purple, it's always the same pared-down, nun-like shift for Carla. Cap sleeves. Pin-tuck neckline. Narrow belt. Working with arch fashion collaborator John Galliano, Dior's English-born designer, Carla brought the new modesty to the international spotlight during the Sarkozys' state visit to meet the British Royal Family in 2008. Instead of a show-stopping outfit, she opted for an extremely demure – and French – look, wearing an elegant Christian Dior grey coat cinched in

at the waist by a thin, black belt. The ensemble, reminiscent of Jackie Kennedy's look for a visit to London in 1962, was topped off with a grey structured beret. Fashion critics swooned that she had reinvented herself as an appropriately modest consort through dress alone.

4) Public sector workers (nurses, teachers and probation officers) are also expected to be exemplars of modesty, never revealing unseemly flesh. In June 2011 it was revealed that the East and North Hertfordshire NHS Trust had even ordered a cover-up of nurses wearing too-revealing clothes. Employees now face disciplinary action if they are caught showing too much décolletage or midriff. Miniskirts are banned – and tight-fitting leggings also outlawed. Ironically, newspapers ran the story accompanied by saucy images of Barbara Windsor from the film *Carry on Doctor*.

5) Men are expected to observe modest dressing. Long trousers, jackets, ties, high-necked jumpers are the traditional school uniform in winter. Shorts, polo shirts and sandals are only permitted in summer; woe betide the man who reveals flesh in winter. Fashion designer Tom Ford even said that men shouldn't wear shorts at all. It's fascinating how male modesty is discreetly protected, when in contrast, the female body is open season – everything from our bra size to our love of control pants is eagerly discussed. One of the more delicious stories of 2010 was when an ex-employee stole confidential information (including 'intimate measurements') from Savile Row tailor Ede & Ravenscroft who have made clothes for Prince Charles, David Cameron and Boris Johnson and even the uniform for members of Oxford's Bullingdon Club, the notorious dining club where Cameron and Johnson were student members.

CLASS MODESTY

Of course modest dressing is as much about class as it is about sexuality and ethnicity. And it has increasingly become a media sport to punish and reward 'lower-class' women who overdress, or reveal too much on feast days and festivals (Royal Ascot, pop concerts, film premieres). In June 2011, the *Daily Mail* lambasted middle-aged female fans at a Take That pop concert in Cardiff for their immodest drinking and partying.

Royal Ascot is a key part of the English Season – that social marathon of balls, dinner parties, regattas and racing that runs from April to August. So it is a particularly sensitive arena for keen society watchers. Seeing the lower classes disporting themselves in pseudo-aristocratic clothing (hats, tiaras, ballgowns, fur, white tie) makes these commentators shudder about 'Royal Chavscot'. In fact the Royal Enclosure at Ascot has a 'modest' dress code all of its own, which runs as follows. Only formal day dress with a hat or substantial fascinator will be acceptable. Off the shoulder, halter-necks, spaghetti straps, dresses with a strap of less than one inch and miniskirts are considered unsuitable. Midriffs must be covered and trouser suits must be full-length and of matching material and colour.[1] Meanwhile gentlemen are required to wear either black or grey morning dress, including a waistcoat, with a top hat. If you don't comply, bowler-hatted stewards will ask you to leave the enclosure.

Modesty and understatement is presented as the truest sign of superior social status. Less is more. Because the rules are so arcane, few of us will ever grasp the essentials to the fine art of underdressing, of course. The truly rich pare everything back so the rest of us look vulgar, nouveau riche, with our bling and our constant accessorising. We're back to Coco Chanel's dictum to her wealthy clients to dress 'as plainly as their maids' (though as the critic Fred Davis (1989) neatly points out in his famous essay, 'Of Maids' Uniforms and Blue Jeans: The Drama of Status Ambivalences in Clothing and Fashion', you need to have a maid in the first place to do that, and it costs far more to look 'truly poor' than just ordinarily so).

SLUTWALK PROTESTS

The mainstream media has fairly strict rules when it comes to proper or 'appropriate' female dress – revolving around notions of female modesty, submissiveness and propriety. It is claimed that these rules are to 'protect' women and young girls from oversexualisation and loss of innocence in a culture where women are celebrated for their looks and 'hotness'; a world where porn-chic is all about cosmetic add-ons – false eyelashes, stripper nails, wigs and hair pieces – rather than the natural 'body beautiful'.

Comment features in newspapers about 'appropriate versus transgressive' female dress are often written by female journalists, but largely it's a male editor's view of the world. The *Daily Mail* never runs photographs of women in trousers (trousers are considered too masculine) although it doesn't mind printing images of half-naked models in underwear to illustrate health and beauty features. *The Daily Telegraph* prefers a good-looking woman in a hat, especially during the Season.

Interestingly these strict paternalistic boundaries about modesty/ immodesty were challenged during coverage of the SlutWalk protests – demonstrations triggered by a Canadian policeman who said that women were more at risk of sexual assault if they dressed like sluts. As the protests spread like wildfire through Canada and America to British cities, commentators became confused. Was it a call to arms or a glorified 'vicars and tarts street party', offering men yet another titillating display of flesh? As Eleanor Mills and Francesca Angelina asked in the *Sunday Times*:

> Is this a flowering of feminism in a generation that has been somewhat apathetic about women's rights? Or is the exercise a naive belief that the world should be as you want it to be, rather than seeing it for how it really is?

Janice Turner in *The Times* wondered if these marching militants would simply join the male fantasy lexicon of naughty nurses and sexy schoolgirls. After all, as she argued, 'Slut advertising dominates, flogging us perfume or handbags. Slut behaviour is expected of young girls: that they be sexually available, hot-to-trot 24/7, performing sexual services mostly without expecting any reciprocal pleasure, just like the stars of the porn films that the boys their own age watch on home PCs.'

For Natasha Walter, feminist author of the book *Living Dolls* (which analyses the sexualisation of girlhood), images of young women taking to the streets in corsets and glittery basques were muddled and self-defeating because 'it is still defining women in terms of their sexuality – this idea that what we're saying is that we're proud to be sluts'.

Interestingly Anastasia Richardson, the 17-year-old who co-ordinated the SlutWalk protest in London, disagreed, arguing that the march was a celebration of equal clothing rights. 'Women are very welcome to come on the walks in hot pants and bras, but they are fighting for the same things as the women who come in burkas [sic]; the right not to be sexually assaulted no matter what way you choose to express yourself,' she said at the march.

And indeed at the SlutWalk protest in London, the *Independent on Sunday* reported that a speaker in a hijab spoke of rape atrocities in Iraq and stressed that her mode of dress – like short skirts – was irrelevant.

Arguably what the protests did was allow a generation of women to debate the thorny issue of modesty/immodesty on their own terms. For Asiya Islam in the *Guardian* it was actually a protest against the scrutiny that tries to control all women:

The main issues that have arisen in the debate is SlutWalk's use of and attempt to redefine the word 'slut' and its alleged white supremacist and classist nature, which fails to be representative either of women of colour or of 'real' sluts or sex workers ... For me, however, SlutWalk is a movement aimed against the discourse rather than the literal language of slut-shaming – discourse that categorises and attempts to cage in women, discourse that manifests itself in myriad forms including the varying use of words like sexy, hot, bitch, slut etc.

SlutWalk also highlighted a real double standard at work around representations of nudity or semi-nudity in the mass media – when Spanish fashion chain Desigual offered the first 100 shoppers to their London store on Regent Street two free items of clothing if they arrived at their shop in their underwear in June 2011 (the same month as the London SlutWalk), newspapers gleefully ran the pictures of shoppers queuing in their underwear, without any fuss or moralising.

MODEST COVER-UPS AS THE NEW FASHION TREND

What is interesting is that as debate rages around modest apparel – and the apparently loaded symbol of the veil – cover-ups of some sort are becoming the hot new fashion trend for women in the UK (a recent survey found that 75 per cent of women hated their upper arms more than any other part of their body).

Responding to this, retailers are busy launching stylish cover-ups, shrugs, shawls, stoles and capes, gilets, wraps and lightweight pashminas that you throw on and layer up for day to evening.

British shopping guru Mary Portas's new Armery designs have revolutionised the newly commodified 'arm market' with rocketing sales figures. Having made a reputation in retail consultancy and brand management when Portas started her own shop as part of a British TV series, she aimed directly at those areas perceived to be a 'problem' to the discerning 40-plus woman. Working with her partner, *Grazia* magazine fashion journalist Melanie Rickey, Portas has come up with tights for the arms – a stretchy high-denier hosiery tube in various colours and weaves, allowing you to slip your arms inside so you can discreetly conceal problem areas.

At the same time as Portas launched Armery in 2011, supermarket ASDA announced a new T-shirt promising to banish bingo wings. The 'body sculpt control top' claims to decrease the circumference of upper arms through a mesh of elasticated nylon and Lycra. Marks & Spencer also launched a 'Personalised Fit' service which allows customers to choose the sleeve length of their Little Black Dress online, after conducting in-depth research through customer panels and finding that women wanted more length options in their dresses.

Meanwhile fashion brand Yummy Tummy makes bodice tops, tanks, high-waisted shorts, leggings inspired by Fifties foundation garments – that allegedly hide your problem areas and takes you from overheated offices to a freezing wait outside a club.

And yet it's still very hard for 'modest apparel' brands, such as ModBod and sister brand Blend, to get mainstream coverage in newspapers because they were set up by designers of a particular faith group (in this case Mormon). In contrast, fashion cover-ups are seen as practical and fit-for-purpose rather than a moral or religious statement.

But boundaries are blurring. In 2011, the UK mainstream fashion site *SoSensational* (www.sosensational.co.uk) launched a new section designed specifically for women who require modest clothing for religious or cultural reasons – billed as the first general fashion website in the UK to have added a section specifically for women who require modest dress. The site was set up by fashion journalist Jan Shure and image consultant Cyndy Lessing to help grown-up women find stylish on-trend clothing. There are longer-length dresses, skirts and coats, tops, blouses and jackets, plus scarves for extra cover and T-shirts and camisoles to go under dresses and tops to avoid necklines being too revealing. What's so interesting is that they have chosen 'modest' clothing from designer and premium brands including Browns, Matches, Harrods, Selfridges, Jaeger and All Saints. This is on-trend fashion that simply happens to be modest.

Similarly companies selling 'modest swimwear' are increasingly appealing to non-Muslims. When UK chef Nigella Lawson wore a burqini cover-up to the beach in Australia in 2011 (see Figure 20), newspapers were full of articles debating if the full head-to-toe black suit, complete with hood, was a practical clothing gesture or a subversive political statement (she wore it only a week after France's ban on women wearing the burqa and niqab came into force).

As Madeleine Bunting observed in the *Guardian*: were we witnessing an icon of sexy English femininity turning to a Muslim sportswear website for help in combating the ageing, carcinogenic ravages of the Australian sun – or was it to conceal the curves from the prying eyes of a global audience?

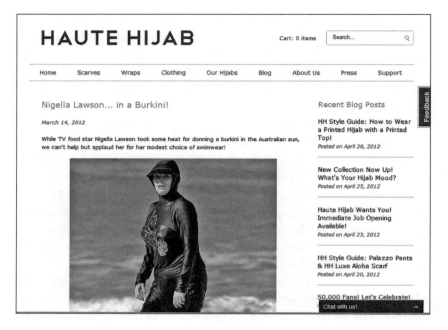

20 Nigella Lawson in burqini goes viral in the modest blogosphere. *Haute Hijab* blog post, 14 March 2012, screenshot. Accessed 17 April 2012.

Kausar Sacranie, 36, who designed the all-encompassing black swimsuit-and-hood combination Lawson wore for her Bondi Beach trip, says she wasn't surprised when Lawson placed an order with her company, Modestly Active. According to Sacranie, around 15 per cent of her customers are non-Muslims. Sacranie started the company in 2007 with her husband Ismail, after struggling to swim in T-shirts and leggings – something many Muslim women do to avoid stripping off. She has since sold thousands of burqinis, mostly through word-of-mouth recommendations. Now Sacranie is preparing to launch a range of swimwear without hoods, for non-Muslims and anyone who prefers to leave their head uncovered. As she points out, the outfit frees women from the pressure of living up to the 'perfect bikini body'.

Umran Ashman has run the website *Modestkini* (www.modestkini.com/en) since 2005, and alongside her 'full cover' burqini-style swimsuits, she offers semi-covered styles, from short-sleeved tunics with three-quarter-length leggings to sleeveless dress styles with cycling shorts. The site sells thousands of the swimsuits every year to women in the UK and abroad, and Ashman says many of her customers are non-Muslim.

Or how about the ResportOn, a tight-fitting hoodie covering the hair, acclaimed as the new sports hijab? Made from a white antiperspirant sports fabric, the hoodie is attached to a turtle-neck T-shirt, with a special opening at the back allowing easy access for wearers to readjust their hair. When the *Guardian* featured it in their pages, female commentators vowed to track it down to help with bad hair days.

SURVEILLANCE CULTURE

I would argue that what emerges from studying coverage of 'modest fashion' in the mainstream media is how much secular and religious feminists have in common – especially an understanding of how the female body is constantly under surveillance. Arguably the panic about modest dress is just the other side of the coin in terms of what happens to all women. Clothing is visual and tangible. It is also political and social.

The media reaction to Lawson's decision to wear a burqini reveals an obsession with women's bodies and how they should or shouldn't be displayed – and the fierce patrolling of different social conventions governing them. On a beach, a woman is expected to expose her body, and it is that refusal which captured attention. And of course famous women's bodies are scrutinised for extra bulges, cellulite and telltale signs of ageing. Few women can fail to understand Lawson's urge to wrap up. By wearing a cover-up, Lawson is defying our social conventions, as well as protecting herself – her privacy and her skin.

Women live daily with their imperfections (too fat, too thin, too womanly), while the male body is venerated and protected. Women endure the indignity of mixed changing rooms in many high-street stores; men have separate cubicles to protect their modesty. Surely the whole point of fashion is that it's about expressing our identity – our tribal allegiances and our rebellion – through what we buy and what we wear? We all choose to cover our bodies and dress in a way that satisfies our own code of conduct and stylistic requirements.

What is heartening is the way that both feminism and the pro-modesty movement can share common goals – among them, the insistence that women should be free from sexual objectification. After all, both feminists and modesty campaigners have applauded the young women who organised a 'girlcott' of Abercrombie & Fitch's 'Who Needs Brains When You Have These?' T-shirts.

Of course the moral panic in the mainstream media about showing too much flesh – or even hiding the body under too many layers of fabric – is only part of the story. Because whether you are considered overdressed or underdressed, discreet or brazen, depends entirely on who is actually making the rules in the first place.

NOTE

1   http://www.ascot.co.uk/?page=Dress_Code. Accessed 5 December 2011.

REFERENCES

Adewunmi, Bim (2011). 'Faith-based Fashion Takes Off Online: Clothes Designed for Women who Want to Dress Modestly are a Growing Phenomenon'. *Guardian*, 16 June.

Bergin, Olivia (2011). 'Nigella's Burkini Fails to Get the Fashion "Seal" of Approval: What Was the Motivation Behind Nigella Lawson's Latest Swimwear Statement?'. *Daily Telegraph*, 19 April.

Boden, Nicola (2008). 'Sarkozy's Circus has Landed: Carla Covers up for the Queen as Husband Calls for UK–French Fraternity'. *Daily Mail*, 26 March.

Boyle, Katherine (2010). 'Fashion Week: Is Modesty Back?'. *Washington Post*, 10 September.

Bunting, Madeleine (2011). 'Nigella Lawson and The Great Burkini Cover-Up: Was Nigella Lawson's Beach Burkini a Defence Against the Australian Sun, or a Subversive Political Statement?'. *Guardian*, 23 April.

Connell, Claudia (2011). 'Nancy's Dell'usional Dress Sense!'. *Daily Mail*, 17 June.

Davies, Natalie (2010). 'MIA Wears Customised Burka to LA Awards. Singer Protests at Recent Burka Bans in Full Face Veil and High Heels'. *The Week*, 19 October.

Davis, Fred (December 1989). 'Of Maids' Uniforms and Blue Jeans: The Drama of Status Ambivalences in Clothing and Fashion'. *Qualitative Sociology*; 12:4: 337–55.

Fox, Imogen (2010). 'Sheikha Mozah Hailed as New Queen of Fashion by Julien Macdonald. British Designer Claims That Emir of Qatar's Wife has More Global Fashion Resonance than any First Lady since Jackie O'. *Guardian*, 29 October.

Hoggard, Liz (2008). 'The Politics of Dressing like a First Lady. Forget the Big Issues, it's What you Wear to the Party Conference that Matters'. *Evening Standard*, 30 September.

——— (2009). 'Carla Sarkozy and her Perfect Little Dress'. *Evening Standard*, 9 June.

——— (2010). 'Clothes Maketh the Man: Men are Notoriously Private about the Content of their Trousers, the Notch they Fasten their Belt'. *The Independent*, 26 April.

——— (2010). 'Core-drobe Craze'. *Evening Standard*, 15 November.

———— (2010). 'The Thursday Essay: Royal Ascot is a Real Class Act. Ladies' Day at Royal Ascot Means Hats, Tailcoats and Demure Hemlines. It's all for Fun – but Decode the Dress, and Social Divisions are Laid Bare'. *The Independent*, 17 June.

———— (2011). 'Right to Wear Arms: Armoury, the Hot New Fashion Trend, Mary Portas has Proved that Hosiery Works Just as Well on the Arms as on the Legs'. *Evening Standard*, 7 November.

Islam, Asiya (2011). 'Why I'll be Joining the London SlutWalk'. *Guardian*, 11 June.

Levy, Andrew (2011). 'Nurses Told to Stop Showing Off Their Bodies'. *Daily Mail*, 16 June.

Littlejohn, Georgina (2010). 'Lady Gaga Subjected to Private Body Search at Airport After Refusing to Remove her Veil'. *Daily Mail*, 11 March.

Lurie, Alison (1992). *The Language of Clothes*. London: Bloomsbury Publishing.

McCorkell, Andrew and Pickford, Mary Ann (2011). 'Thousands March to Change Outdated Attitudes on Sexuality. SlutWalk was Formed After a Canadian Policeman Made Ill-Considered Remarks about Rape and Women's Appearance'. *Independent on Sunday*, 12 June.

Mills, Eleanor and Angelina, Francesca (2011). 'Who Are You Calling A Slut?'. *Sunday Times*, 12 June.

Mower, Sarah (2011). '"Carole Middleton is My New Style Crush": Thanks to the Royal Wedding, Age-Appropriate, Frump-Free Dressing is Having a Moment, with Mother Middleton as its Poster Girl'. *Daily Telegraph*, 18 May.

Nathan, Sara (2011). 'The Take That Effect: How Middle-aged Fans Go Mad When the Ageing Boy Band Comes to Town'. *Daily Mail*, 17 June.

Ostler, Catherine (2011). 'Tiaras at Dawn: How Kate Wants to Wear Flowers in her Hair, but Camilla Backs a More Traditional Look at the Royal Wedding'. *Daily Mail*, 7 April.

Paxman, Lauren and English, Rebecca (2011). 'You Might Find the Stairs Tricky, My Dear: Queen's Astonishment as Turkish President's Wife Turns up at the Palace in a Pair of Killer Heels'. *Daily Mail*, 23 November.

Qureshi, Huma (2011). 'The Next Sporty Must-Have is Not Just for Muslim women. The ResportOn, A Tight-Fitting Hoodie Covering the Hair, is the New Sports Hijab – but it's Attracting Orders from Non-Muslim Women and Men'. *Guardian*, 6 June.

Rose, Hilary (2011). 'The Year of Ladylike Dressing: As 2011 Draws to a Close, the Backlash Against Fake Tans and Micro-Minis is Complete'. *The Times*, 10 December.

Tarrant, Shira (2009). 'The Great Cover-Up: Can High Necklines Cure Low Morals?'. *Bitch*, May.

Taylor, Jerome (2010). 'Beautiful and Islamic: the New Look on the Catwalk'. *The Independent*, 2 July.

Turner, Janice (2011). 'Slut Walks Are Treading on Dangerous Ground'. *The Times*, 14 May.

Unknown (2010). 'Britain's First Female Muslim Cabinet Minister Baroness Warsi Brightens up Downing Street'. *Daily Telegraph*, 14 May.

Unknown (2011). 'Update: Designers, Critics Praise Middleton's "Elegant," "Discreet" Dress'. *US Weekly*, 29 April.

9

INSIDER VOICES, CHANGING PRACTICES
Press and Industry Professionals Speak

Reina Lewis (editor and contributor)

This is an edited transcript of two industry panel discussions held at the London College of Fashion in June 2011 as part of the research project *Modest Dressing: Faith-based Fashion and Internet Retail*.

Panellists:

Liz Hoggard (LH), journalist and author

Jana Kossaibati (JK), blogger, hijabstyle.co.uk

Reina Lewis (RL), Principal Investigator of *Modest Dressing* research project

Shellie Slade (SS), founder of ModBod, Utah, USA.

Hana Tajima-Simpson (HTS), designer and founder, Maysaa, and blogger, *stylecovered.co.uk*

Linda Woodhead (LW), Director of Religion and Society Programme

LW   Welcome everybody, I am Linda Woodhead and I'm Professor of Sociology of Religion at Lancaster University and director of the Religion and Society Programme. This is a £12 million research programme with money that comes from the British government, fed through two research councils; the Arts and the Humanities, and the Economic and Social Research Council (AHRC and ESRC). It's a programme that runs for six years and the reason that such a large sum of money was given to this topic of religion was because there was perceived to be a need to increase the amount of research and knowledge about religion in this country and elsewhere.

21 E-retail web pages from (clockwise from top left) Funky Frum, Losve, Shabby Apple, Jen Clothing, screenshots. Accessed 20 April 2012.

Let me hand over to Professor Reina Lewis from the London College of Fashion, who is the principal investigator on the *Modest Dressing* project (with Dr Emma Tarlo from Goldsmiths as her co-investigator and Jane Cameron as the project researcher).

RL   The research project, *Modest Dressing: Faith-based Fashion and Internet Retail*, set out to examine how e-commerce and forms of fashion mediation online were meeting the needs of women who are motivated to dress modestly for reasons of religious belief. Although we used both the terms 'dress' and 'fashion' in our title, it was really crucial to me that we had the word 'fashion' in the name of the project.

Using the term 'fashion' is essential because more and more, predominantly but not exclusively, young women are creating pious dress that is overtly fashionable and that relies on garments from within the mainstream fashion system, rather than on items of so-called traditional or ethnic clothing. A younger generation has grown up with consumer culture and expect to express all aspects of their identity through participation in consumption and display. For this international cohort it is possible to dress modestly and modishly (see Figure 21). In the UK it has been Muslim designers and entrepreneurs who've led the way in the development of the niche market in modest clothing. In the United States and Canada other faith groups that have dress requirements show similar developments in the commercial production and distribution of apparel. We found this most notably, but not exclusively, among orthodox and ultra-orthodox Jews and among some Christian groups including the Mormon Church of Jesus Christ of Latter-day Saints (LDS).

Why online? It was our hypothesis that the economic advantages of e-retail were making it possible for companies and brands to meet the needs of this niche market and I had a hunch that women seeking modest apparel online were more likely to shop from companies outside of their faith, because shopping online is de-territorialised and de-materialised. Nobody sees what you look like or what you buy.

I didn't design this project to focus on internet retail simply because this was the arena where niche products were being marketed; it was also because commercial websites, all of whom so far originate from within a faith community, can themselves be regarded as part of a new internet-based fashion discussion about modesty especially now that most commercial websites engage with customers through blogs and social media. It was also our contention that the internet was bringing women from different faiths and from secular backgrounds into discussions with each other. We found young women, on the internet in blogs, on YouTube and in discussion fora, dispensing advice on how to achieve their varying interpretations of fashionable modesty (see Figure 22).

What were our conclusions? Our research did indeed demonstrate that there is a thriving online market for modest clothing: a market that is growing, segmenting and diversifying. It is also a market that is being fuelled by women from a variety of faiths with consumers increasingly shopping from brands originating in faith groups other than their own. We found that brands are often prepared to adapt their offering and their web presence to welcome cross-faith consumers (see Figure 23), and I know Shellie Slade has some examples to offer about this later. We identified that the internet is facilitating discussions about modest dressing and behaviour in commercial and non-profit online modes. These discussions involve women in forms of intra- and interfaith dialogue that they might not enter into offline, with bloggers like

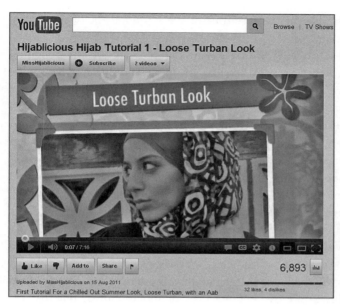

22 'Hijablicious Hijab Tutorial 1' on YouTube, screenshot. Accessed 31 May 2012.

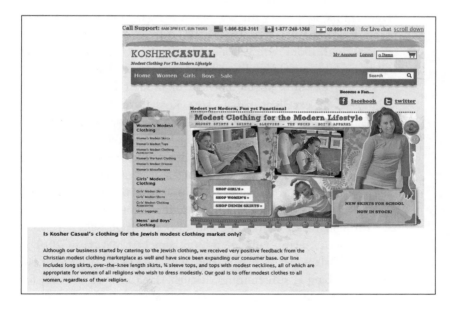

23 Kosher Casual e-retail homepage and FAQ, composite screenshots. Accessed 24 April 2012.

Jana Kossaibati at the forefront of the development of thoughtful new 'netiquettes'.

Modest dressing is not solely the preserve of the religious. We discovered a vocal cohort of modest dressers who define themselves as non-religious or secular as well as religious women who don't say that faith is the key motivator for their modest self-presentation. For some women, 'modest' is a useful term, whilst others might simply say that they dress in ways appropriate to their age, occupation or location – as Liz Hoggard will be discussing. As well as including secular dressers, one of the key contributions of this research, in the European context especially, is to widen understandings of Muslim modest dress to include Muslim women who are committed to modest self-presentation but who do not interpret this to include a headscarf, a hijab, let alone a face veil or niqab or burqa.

We have concluded that the internet is not simply selling products that facilitate pre-existent practices of modest dress, but that the internet is, through the combination of commerce and commentary, helping to grow and legitimise modest practices. We are able already to distinguish a second generation of modest dress designers, like Hana Tajima-Simpson with her brand Maysaa, and the New York brand Eva Khurshid (see Figure 24), who are able to combine modesty with more radical fashion-forward aesthetics in ways that would have been unlikely for the first generation of companies.

To help us think about the field of modest fashion, we have assembled an excellent panel. Jana Kossaibati started her blog – hijabstyle.co.uk – aged 18 in 2007 and the blog is now firmly established as one of the UK's leading Muslim style blogs. A busy full-time medical student, Jana has also found time to report for *Vogue.com* and the *Guardian* and has been featured on the BBC and LBC radio. Shellie Slade is founder of ModBod in 2004 and sister brand Blend. Based in Springville, Utah, ModBod not only sells online and through direct marketing, but also retails in selected stores across America. Hana Tajima-Simpson launched Maysaa in 2010. A convert to Islam, Hana first started with her blog, *Style Covered*, in 2008. This blog is still running, though Hana now also writes for her company's Maysaa blog and their virtual magazine. Liz Hoggard is an arts journalist, appearing regularly in publications such as the *Evening Standard*, *The Observer*, *The Independent*, *Selvedge* and *Marie Claire*.

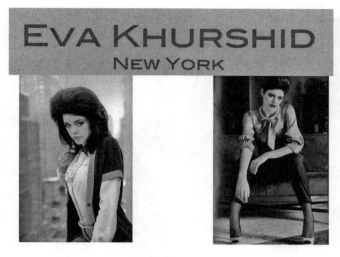

24 Eva Khurshid
New York, Fall
2009, Look Book.

Liz has a new book out with Clare Conville and Sarah-Jane Lovett called *Dangerous Women: The Guide to Modern Life*.

[applause]

JK   My name is Jana and I'm the editor of a blog called *Hijab Style*, which was the UK's first style guide for Muslim women. It's dedicated to all things to do with style and fashion but with a particular focus on the needs of Muslim women who wear the hijab or headscarf. I started this back in September 2007, mainly out of a general interest in blogging, wanting to do something that I enjoyed. But I also found that there was pretty much nothing out there in terms of a dedicated resource for Muslim women's fashion and for modest dressing. There was no central hub that you could go to in order to find out about what was happening; everything was quite scattered, a couple of things here and there. So over time with *Hijab Style* I tried to develop it into such a website where it brings all these elements together. As you can see (see Figure 25), it encompasses everything from showcasing Muslim fashion designers to putting together ideas for items from the high street into an outfit, or ideas from the

Outfit Ideas

Muslim
Fashion
Designers

Readers'
Style

Runway
Fashion

25 Range of contents covered
by *Hijab Style* blog, composite
screenshots.

mainstream runways and even getting readers to send in their
own photos.

So you might be wondering why there is even a need for a
Muslim fashion website in the first place, and I think the answer
is twofold. Firstly, from the practical side of things it can actually
be pretty hard for Muslim women to find clothes which are
appropriate to them; they need to be loose fitting, long-sleeved,
full length and so on. And it's quite a challenge to put something
together which fulfils those needs but at the same time is still
quite true to your personal sense of style, and this is a dilemma
that I've found with pretty much every single Muslim woman
I've spoken to. And the second thing I think it's pretty obvious,
but the hijab in the media has been quite politicised. I subscribe
to Google alerts with my keyword as hijab and every single day
there's five new stories about hijab being banned here, hijab being

forced there, you know, Muslim women are being oppressed by hijab and what have you. And that's quite an intense focus and so really I felt that there was a need for something, where Muslim women can talk about hijab for themselves rather than being spoken for, and also just in the context of the reality of wearing the hijab. For most women it's just a part of what you just wear every day, it's not like you're going out there to make a political statement or anything. So I think naturally, just like anything else, blogs provided a way for women to talk about modest dressing on their own terms.

And speaking in general, the internet I think was pretty key in paving the way for an international modest style scene, as you could call it. There are loads and loads of fashion blogs out there written by Muslim women today. There's loads of new online stores coming up, loads of new designers who just promote themselves through Facebook and Twitter. And you begin to see a much greater interest and awareness of the concept that there can be fashion and style which is dedicated to modesty, but which is not just limited to traditional or cultural clothing. Pakistanis don't just have to wear a salwar kameez, Moroccans don't just have to wear kaftans. And so the internet was a way for Muslim women around the world to exchange ideas, look at what each other are wearing, you know, new ways of styling your headscarf, and so on.

In terms of retail, there has been in the past two or three years a huge burst of new companies and new designers who seek to cater to Muslim women or women who dress modestly. And actually a lot of these brands are emerging from the UK and from the USA, although countries such as Malaysia or the Emirates or Turkey have kind of already had some established designers. And in the UK, interestingly, it's mostly actually been very young women, say in their late teens or their early twenties who've initiated these new companies and they've found a chance to turn their talents and interests into real businesses and they've realised that there's a market out there for these types of clothes. This slide shows just a few of the brands which currently cater to Muslim women or modestly dressed women in the UK (see Figure 26). Some of them focus on clothing, but others just sell scarves and accessories. In saying that, however, I think it's really important to note that the market is very much in its infancy. There's still a lot of room out there to expand

26 Muslim and modest fashion brand logos, composite screenshots. Accessed 10 June 2011.

and to diversify and to cater to a lot more styles. For example, you've got nothing out there which really caters for bridal wear or for maternity wear or plus-size clothing, and what have you. So I think slowly we're going to see that this market will be expanding and more and more brands will be sort of appearing in the near future. Thank you.

[applause]

SS　　I'm Shellie Slade and I come to you from the United States to explain a little bit about the Christian market that I'm involved in. I am a member of the Church of Jesus Christ of Latter-day Saints, otherwise known as Mormons.

　　　I'm in the state of Utah, just outside of Salt Lake City, Utah, where our company is based. ModBod was a name picked by

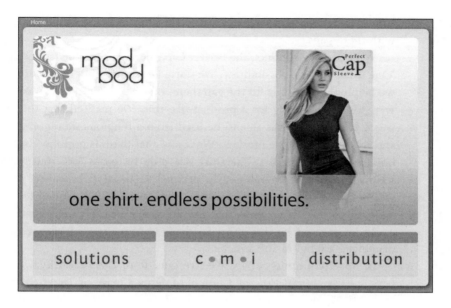

one shirt. endless possibilities.

solutions   c • m • i   distribution

27 ModBod,
'One shirt, endless
possibilities'.

my husband; it means Modern/Modest Body which we thought encompassed not only the religious aspect of modest, but also the fashion side with modern. The name meant we weren't a strictly religious branded company although that's why we did start the company.

This T-shirt is the first product we came out with in 2004 (see Figure 27). We call it the perfect cap sleeve. With the religion that I'm a part of we believe in keeping the shoulders covered, the cleavage area covered, the mid-section and back covered. So what I was finding was, as I had four darling beautiful daughters, in the market there were not a lot of products that were available for my pre-teen daughters, that's the ages 8 to 12. And when I would go to the stores, what I would find is products that were just miniatures of the teens or the women's items. And as I looked at some of these fashions on the body I realised they left gaps and a lot of them were gaps in the cleavage area, the shoulder area, the stomach area, the back area. So I went to work to formulate a product that would deal with these gaps.

With our first product, the Perfect Cap Sleeve, we use the tagline, 'One shirt, endless possibilities'. We started to see that not only were we helping young girls fill the gap there, but the moms and women were also clamouring for a product like this. We realised that this was a product that was able to be used from a religious standpoint, and that it was a niche product. We found that there is nothing else out there in the market. The shirt is a little bit more form fitting so that might not be religiously deemed as modest; however, it was designed to be an under-piece. It was specifically designed for layering so that those areas that the fashion world left uncovered could be covered by this shirt. So that's how we started: just my daughters, a religion and a niche.

In our community where we live outside of Salt Lake City we have a large population of Church of Jesus Christ of Latter-day Saints [LDS] people and so it was very easy to spread the word that we had started this product. We started with direct marketing: friends of friends told friends, and everybody has a friend that lives outside of their state or outside of their country and pretty soon we were spreading across the whole country via this direct marketing sales situation. When we went outside of our LDS community we found that there were many like-minded Christian women and girls, and fathers who did not want their daughters dressing like what they saw in the fashion magazines. So that helped to even further launch our company. After the first six months of being in business we had over $1 million in sales, which was absolutely fascinating and mind-boggling, not only to me but my husband who by then I had convinced to quit his job so that he could help me, so that I could get more than three hours of sleep!

Demand started to go beyond just the girls to the moms. They saw the product and went, 'I would love something like that, I don't like bending over and showing my cleavage area or having it exposed with the shirts that I can buy at the mass market places.' We also were finding that family values groups were coming along, wanting to get the product. And so this actually kind of presented a problem of how and where we could sell it.

We began to get requests for more products than just our Perfect Cap Sleeve. These are some of the products that came out

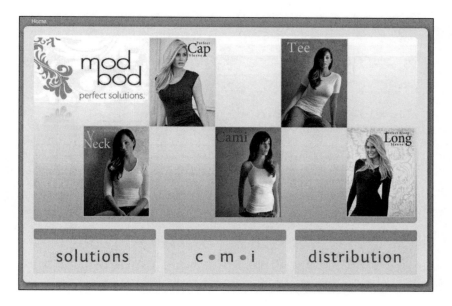

28 ModBod,
product range.

in the first year (see Figure 28), to provide a way to get more
fashion pieces on women's bodies that they normally couldn't
wear because of the immodesty of the fashion pieces. The Perfect
Cami [camisole] was our next piece. Although it's deemed very
immodest by a lot of religious groups, including the LDS religion,
because it does show the shoulder, this was a perfect under-piece
for anything that had a shoulder to it but was low cleavage and
didn't have the long length to it especially when the fashion was
for cropped tops. Also it wasn't as hot to wear under clothes,
especially important for customers in areas such as the south of
the United States. We have kept these products since our launch;
we just change the colours.

After our first six months or so where we got outside of our
community, we started having requests for different types of shirts.
And so we came up with long sleeves, three-quarter sleeves, different
necklines. We were seeing that all these different products started

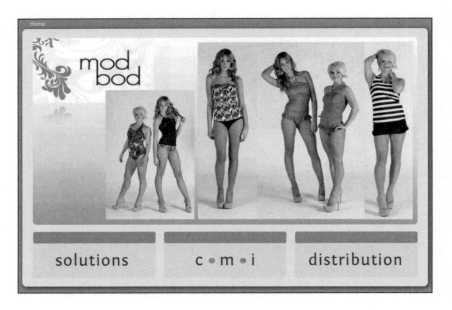

29 ModBod swimwear.

to appeal to different religions and different religious-minded or value-minded women.

We market our product in a number of ways: we have our own stores and our outlet store and our website. We use our website to show how our products can provide modest solutions to wardrobe problems, to make things less revealing. Women or mothers of teens often find our website through Googling modest fashions, or from other consumers who tell their friends.

In our second year in business, Walmart had us exclusively design a range for them (see Figure 29). Corporate Walmart did not want to invest in that risk of offering a modest, or more modest, swimsuit to their consumers, so they asked us to do that, which we gladly did and this is our fourth season with them. We are now in about 140 stores and are one of only five swim lines that Walmart carries outside their corporate swim line.

We also sell in 'big boxes' like Costco, where we are toted or presented as their modest clothing. We also do a private label range for Nordstroms and then we have boutiques across the country and in Canada that sell our product. Boutiques from several different types of religions carry our product; and secular boutiques as well, because it's a wonderful layering piece for women who just are concerned about not sharing what they have with others.

Facebook and Twitter are other ways that we kind of get the word out there. And we also use bloggers. We have our own blog and we use bloggers like Hana or Jana would be and just different types of religious bloggers will pick us up as well.

[applause]

HTS   My name is Hana Tajima; I'm the designer and co-founder of Maysaa.com. My motivation was never something as practical or sensible as seeing a gap in a vast and valuable market or knowing the power and reach of the internet, although those are both excellent reasons. It was more an inability for me to stop designing. I grew up the daughter of artists so it seemed perfectly normal to spend ridiculous amounts of time with a pencil in hand; that and a fascination with the mechanics of a Singer sewing machine kind of led to a need to make things out of cloth. Which is why it was very important that I had a business partner, someone who saw the potential and could put in the numbers in a way that made for a viable company, which we did two years ago and launched this time last year.

Maysaa is essentially a website so our online presence is the most valuable asset that we have. The look and the feel of it for me was really key. It needed to look like an established company that people could really trust, but at the same time be individual and fresh enough not to fade into the vastness of the internet. This I learned from the various blogs that I have and, most importantly, the first one, *Style Covered* (see Figure 30). This was the initial reach into the potential customer base. It took a lot of initial networking to get visitors but after underestimating the power of YouTube and through hijab tutorials and things like that, and just blogging in general, I managed to get a strong readership.

And it was only really at that point that I understood the importance of Maysaa as a label that catered to but didn't speak down

30 *Style Covered*
blog pages,
screenshots.

to or directly at Muslim women (see Figure 31). I didn't want people
to buy just because I was a Muslim designer or to take for granted
that they would. What I understood was that our direct competition
wasn't other modest labels in particular, it was more high street
names, and what made us different were the designs themselves. As
a new convert I was looking at these from more of a design, in a sort
of naïve wonderment about the possibilities. I had no real idea other
than religious boundaries about where I could take the designs.

31 Maysaa.com home
page, screenshot.
Accessed 10 June 2011.

You're talking about a market that has such a diverse cultural and
ethnic background that it's impossible to cater to everybody, so I just
thought I wouldn't bother trying to cater to them; I would kind of
keep to a very specific and personal design aesthetic, because I think
the connection that you're able to have with people if you keep to
such a personal perspective is much more intense.

Our best-sellers, and they were sold out within a few months,
were the scarves, which you can see here (see Figure 32). I think
because they were completely unique, when I designed them I had
no frame of reference for what they might end up being; like in
the same way that I might approach a dress, there's already sort of
a formula of a way that you can create a silhouette and things like
that, so it was a completely new area of design for me and I think
that echoed the wish of girls everywhere to experiment and dress

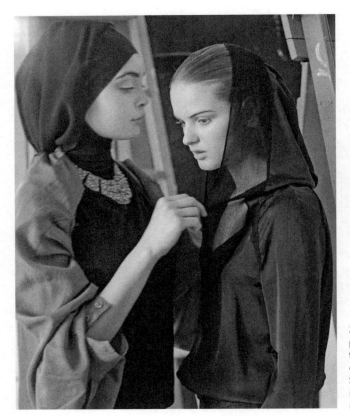

32 Maysaa scarves
photographed
for Maysaa
digital magazine,
September 2010,
issue 2, www.
maysaa.com.

in a way that was relevant but also practical to them. We didn't go down the route of appearing niche because I personally hate the idea of being pigeonholed. I wanted this ambiguity and subtlety in both the designs and the way that we presented them (see Figure 33). Nobody is just one aspect and I think it's important that women are able to discover a specific part of themselves in a design, rather than having me say, 'Oh you cover up, so isn't this perfect for you'. I think commercially as well it's easy to overlook the emotional connection that you have to have with a customer. But in saying that, there was a risk in not being so direct in our marketing and in our image as coming across as an Islamic label, but thankfully the risks have paid off. That's about it from me, thank you for listening.

33 Maysaa digital magazine, September 2010, issue 2, www.maysaa.com. Accessed 30 March 2012.

[applause]

LH   I got quite excited thinking about how the press handles modest fashion, and I just thought why don't I actually write this as a feature? Why not, when we write about fashion and culture and popular culture all the time and there are these really groovy young women in the East End running modest labels? So I went back and told my paper and they were underwhelmed, to put it mildly, because they just didn't understand the story, and my friends, who are secular feminists, were a bit concerned whether this was what we should be following.

But, you know, we've been debating it. And actually what's interesting is that I realised that I'd been writing about modest dress in the mainstream for the last year or two because it's been a big fashion story. So I thought, well who is it that's rewarded for wearing modest dress and why are we getting this discrepant thinking that sees it as non-fashion when in fact some of us, that is, women over 40, are expected to dress modestly.

I've made a list of people that I thought were probably rewarded for modest dress and/or encouraged towards it. I suppose we first started writing about it when the cult of the first ladies happened, so when Carla Sarkozy came over and played a blinder by being an ex-nude model who came to meet the Queen and Gordon Brown and had a wardrobe of extraordinary, demure, you know, brilliant sort of Jackie O type dressing, so everyone sat up and took notice. And then of course we had the Michelle Obama story and again, what a fantastic, interesting woman to look at, very different aesthetic; modest but athletic; naked arms rather than cleavage or a great deal of leg, so again we were writing about that all the time.

I began to see how that was feeding through in terms of representations of women over 30 in papers. With the Royal Wedding of Kate Middleton and Prince William, everyone absolutely loved the fact that it was an Alexander McQueen dress – and that Sarah Burton had worked out that in order for a woman to move that much around the Abbey would need an appropriate aesthetic that wasn't too fashion forward. It was womanly, referenced Grace Kelly, pretty much covered without much flesh on show. And I loved that Mrs Middleton, who'd had a lot of aggro in the press for dressing too young, for looking like her daughters, had worked out a brilliant outfit.

It seemed to me that the people who were applauded at that whole fantastic adult pantomime were the people who'd understood the power of modest dressing, particularly in images that are going to go round the world. If anything goes wrong, I mean those poor girls, Beatrice and Eugenie in the wrong hats, you do get punished for it.

The other set of people who are encouraged to dress appropriately are women of my age group; there's definitely an idea of what you should and shouldn't be wearing when you are over 40. Looking at the presentation of Nancy Dell'Olio in the papers this week, I quite like the fact that she doesn't stick to any of these rules, but there's great discussion about how dare she look ridiculous when she should be covering up. There's definitely a feeling when you get to a certain age that you should dress more modestly and I think you do find yourself thinking, 'Oh, this is a bit short …' It's like a form of self-censoring.

The other people who get rewarded for modest dress of course are men. I was reading Jana's piece when it was first in the *Guardian* about how you decide what to wear in the morning and I was a bit troubled by it in some ways, as a form of self-censorship for women. But then I thought if you change the first person pronoun and made it a man discussing clothing for their various roles that day, then it would be completely normal. I want trousers to cover my legs, I want to have loose clothing I can move in, should I wear shorts, oh maybe that would be a bit awkward at work. We see it as completely normal that there isn't anxiety about male dressing in the same way there is about female dressing.

I found some of the imagery about the recent SlutWalks troubling. In lots of ways I think it's fantastic: these radicalised young women who are looking at sexual politics. I'm just not terribly thrilled about them walking out in the street in their underwear. They are absolutely connecting that what I wear doesn't tell you anything about me, doesn't give you any right to make assumptions. There have been some Muslim girls that have gone on the walks as well. But Janice Turner, a very good journalist in *The Times* on Saturday, wrote a piece about the danger of this – it may alienate people who agree with the radical sexual message but feel alienated because they prefer to dress modestly, or younger women or older women who feel that they can't connect to this debate; and that would be a pity because it's actually a really good rallying cry.

There is this constant pressure about dressing appropriately and modestly and yet, on the other hand, if people do it and make it a point then it becomes a thing that society gets anxious about. You know, show flesh, don't show flesh. I spend a lot of time apologising on behalf of my newspaper! [laughs]

[applause]

RL   Shellie could you say a bit more about marketing through some of the big retailers?

34 ModBod, 'Long sleeves and layering'.

SS   Right. Costco started because one of our local Costcos there in our community became interested in putting the product into their store. Costco is very big where we're from and basically across the western United States it's huge. And so they saw a need of course that they could not fill and weren't willing to spend the money themselves to fill that need. When the local Costco noticed our product, they took the product and presented it to the national buyers and the national buyers picked up on that – and we actually do basically a roadshow programme with Costco. So we go to a Costco for ten days, and then we move on to another roadshow. We do about 10 to 15 of those a week, you know, at the same time. And what we noticed is that when we looked at the Costco roadshow scheduling we were toted [presented] as a modest shirt company. So anybody looking for modest clothing would automatically come, but if you didn't read the magazine and know that we were toted as a modest shirt company, you wouldn't have known that's what we were from our display at the store (see Figure 34). You would look at the pictures and then the rep would explain what the products do. And getting kind of to the secular women or to other religious groups, there's a couple of Costcos in the Los Angeles area that if we don't take long sleeves during the summer, the Jewish community there kind of revolts against our reps, and so we get calls from the rep, 'You must send a tower or two of shirts in the long sleeves.'

RL   Because in Utah you don't need sleeves in your very hot summers?

SS   Well in California as well, summer is very warm and so that's not a product we carry during the summer months, but it was requested at these Costcos to accommodate the Jewish consumers. So we'll see various things like that pop up where different products are requested for different religions or even just if there's a high population of medical groups in a certain area. The nursing community is very interested in our product because it's designed to fit closely to the body so that you can layer it or wear it underneath any type of fashion; so the scrubs, when you're bending over and moving around a patient, you're oftentimes exposing and showing things, so that kind of kept them covered and also provided a little bit more of warmth.

RL   There are a number of other modest brands, especially originating within Utah, within the LDS community. Do you see them as competitors? Is the market big enough at the moment for all of you?

SS   You know, I think the market is big enough for all of us right now. When we started we were one company; we started and then there were about 20 companies that came into being with the almost exact same products. Like I said, it was a niche and as soon as people saw that that niche was growing, they thought they could jump on and help and profit from that niche. But we're back down to two and it's us and another company.

LW   And Shellie, talk about the way that your turnover has grown. Has it
      grown very fast? Did it grow steadily, slowly and then fast? Is it still
      growing and what is it now?

SS   Well, for the first six months after we started, we used direct market-
      ing, home selling, like Mary Kay cosmetics or Tupperware.

RL   Through the community.

SS   Right, through the community, and we had about 120 women
      that sold the product. A lot of them were in the community but
      as soon as that person found out, this person started selling it. Of
      course their friend in Ohio or Florida was sure she could sell it
      as well because there wasn't anything like that available in those
      areas. So it spread very quickly and then as we started to do that
      the boutiques picked it up, and then several of the boutique buyers
      ended up being buyers for Walmart or someone at Costco – that's
      how the local Costco buyer picked that up. She came to a boutique,
      saw it, thought it was a fantastic product, took it back to her store,
      'Can we please get these in', so we move to corporate sales. It's
      just sort of branched out from that. In the first six months we
      had a million dollars in sales and we had sort of thought that
      after the first eight months we would be done – we gave it about
      eight months. My husband and I started it, and we said that eight
      months and we're done if it doesn't go – and that was seven and
      a half years ago.

RL   Hana, I was very struck that your competitors aren't the other modest
      brands, even though there's a lot more coming. Can you say a little
      bit more, because do you think there's a sense also of support with
      some of these new start-ups or are you sort of wary about how it's
      going to happen?

HTS   I think definitely, especially among the younger designers, there's a
      lot of support. There's not very many of them so you kind of know
      each other from different events and things like that. So there is
      a group of us that are very supportive of each other. I think the
      element of competition doesn't necessarily come from other faiths,
      but it's more like the old guard and the new guard. So you'll have

the more established companies that may be a little wary of the direction that the new designers are taking modest dressing or Islamic dressing in. So it's more of a contention in that regard rather than ...

RL   It's a generational ...

HTS   Yeah, exactly.

RL   And we're talking about something that's grown quite quickly in the last five, eight, ten years. This is a really rapidly changing story, which is why even in the five, six years that I've been working on this, I can now talk about a second generation who are breaking the mould. It was the same with the Muslim lifestyle media here. When they started it was one magazine fits all, one brand fits all; and for a community, whether it's the gay community with the start of the gay lifestyle press 15 years ago, when there's very little around that meets the needs of that community, everybody in that community requires the media, the brand, the television programme to represent them. But now you could say that people who are more fashion forward are going to come to this brand, somebody who wants something more conventional can choose that brand ... Even if the product is similar, it's also about the way you're presenting it and marketing it, which can be very different. Jana, do you want to say anything about that sort of generational change?

JK   Yeah. Because I'm a university student my social circle might be a little bit biased, but in terms of myself, my friends, the people I surround myself with, they still very much focus their efforts on the high street – that is actually where they buy most of their clothes. I think they have an impression that modest clothing or Islamic clothing brands are quite frumpy, quite old-fashioned, still quite ethnically based. I think that's very much true of some of the brands which have been around for about eight, ten years. They are still very much conservative, not in terms of coverage but in terms of the styles, the colours of the prints. But now you've obviously got designers like Hana. I'm wearing, for example, a top by another friend of ours called Sarah Elenany (see

35 'Brotherhood T-Shirt hoody', Elenany e-retail webpage, screenshot. Accessed 20 April 2012.

Figure 35), with a blazer from the high street. Sarah is another designer who is starting to push the boundaries in terms of the kind of styles they offer and that's really just now starting to pick up. And a lot of girls still aren't really aware of these brands, but it is definitely picking up. Although saying that, even though it's still the young who are a little bit disillusioned with these traditional brands, my mum is a 50-year-old lady and she's a professional, she doesn't like the traditional brands either; she still finds they're not quite as smart and as elegant as she wants them to be; they don't quite cater to her needs as someone who's in the workplace. So although there is this generational gap, I think a lot of it is to do with culture and lifestyle as well.

LW   Can I ask you both a question about the global market? Do you think that as British designers in this area you are offering something that other parts of the world will find attractive and if so, what? What's the advantage that you might have in your designs and why have you gone to Malaysia and say a bit more about that.

HTS   Well I think especially for my brand, you'll find among like South-East Asian countries there is something very appealing about British design and coming over as someone who's British is an advantage.

LW   What? Why?

HTS   I don't know. I think it is just like the cool factor or whatever, having that international base is something they really like. Malaysia and South-East Asia in particular have really picked up on Maysaa and that's our biggest customer base. We're seen as a London label, even though probably more of our customers are in Malaysia. So it's definitely good to have that kind of Britishness about and also the design aesthetic. You are moving into an area where people are more like a global nation, where there's much more blurring of boundaries between ethnic dress and things like that. People are looking at things that are outside their comfort zone or outside their traditions. I mean, because I'm half Japanese, half English, my aesthetic is always really blurred anyway. So it's good for people looking for things that do kind of work on the edges of boundary and tradition.

RL   And I think Britain is quite often recognised as leading the way, especially in Muslim design. There was an article in the European press two weeks ago with some Dutch and German designers saying we have to start doing this because everybody's going to England to do their shopping. And this is where the internet allows the transmission of ideas and also discussion, although actually selling products internationally gets difficult because of the way the prices go up with shipping and with import duties.

LW   I want to ask you, Liz, what would it take to change the story? Often young women say to me, 'Why can't we have a whole issue of a fashion magazine about modest dressing?'

LH   Yeah, it's interesting — there's obviously a lot of concern around it from left and right. But as I listened to Shellie talking about ModBod, I realised I'd done a story on 'shapewear', this sort of layered stuff with a triple-ply, three-weave, designed to be worn in layers to hold your stomach in. Women often want to cover up because we feel embarrassed about that bit of our body or, as you say, for flexibility of movement. So I realise we have covered something similar as a fashion story, but we probably wouldn't have included your company because that would be seen as a faith-based decision, and that would probably make people nervous around fashion, which is silly really. I don't know why we don't seem to be able to look in a grown-up way at fashion and modest dress; it still seems to ring lots of warning bells everywhere.

RL   I think it does and I think people get very anxious. One of the things I say when people ask me about the research project is that we're not here to promote or to oppose modest dressing, however defined, because there are many different versions and definitions of how to do it. We are seeing that there's this growing phenomena and what we want to do is document and analyse it, but it's almost as if the minute you bring it up it raises anxieties, as if somehow you're going to be contaminated.

BA   My name's Bim Adewunmi. I'm a journalist and I was interested in the parallels between the growth of modest fashion online and the online community views on natural hair. I recently cut off all my hair which I used to chemically relax and now I'm growing it out natural. I discovered the importance of the internet in helping me through my 'journey' with natural hair. There are really established people who've been on the internet pretty much from the beginning and perhaps weren't so popular but have really grown super popular. Then there is a second set of younger people who have newer ideas on products and on styles and so on.
       There's a whole natural hair community online now. Most of the blogs I look at are American. So it's interesting that the British seem to be leading the way for modest dressing, but for black natural hair we're still looking to America. I suppose you have quite a unique position at the moment of being British and people looking to you. I find it really interesting that this is something that is growing so fast and the hub seems to be Britain.

HTS   Yeah, I think as well that the really good thing about being on the internet is that we've been able to be really fluid in our movement. Before we started out we had no idea that it was really going to pick up in South-East Asia, but within a few weeks of us deciding that we wanted to be there, we could just up and set up distribution, because there's no physical store holding us down – we don't have to worry about leaving behind our core customers here. So it's a really good way of being able to react to our consumers, to find new markets and things like that.

LW And I have to say that when Hana is in Malaysia she's actually mobbed on the streets; she can't go out in public. She's seriously that much of a celebrity ... from your blogs, isn't it?

HTJ Yeah, initially from the blog. It was really surprising for me going out there. I had no idea that it was going to be that kind of response, but for some reason Malaysians in particular had really picked up on the blog and on the label and, yeah, it's quite bizarre.

RL Digital media is really huge in Malaysia, with very high internet use among young people, plus mobile phones and apps and Facebook and Twitter. I was very struck by Bim's comparison that when relaxed hair or natural hair was so big in the 1960s and 1970s, there were some print publications but like any specialist media at the time, they had a smaller circulation; it simply wasn't possible to go global with the same reach and speed as today. The way to transmit ideas and build communities changes as the media changes. The internet is fascinating precisely because it has both the ability to market and move products and to exchange and move ideas. And sometimes they're coming from the same source.

JK I think personally, even though my blog is supposed to be for the UK, in fact my UK readers only form 25 per cent of the people that visit the website. About another 25 per cent may be from America and Europe and the rest of them are actually South-East Asians. It's phenomenal how techie the Malaysian, Indonesian and Singaporean people are and it's been quite interesting that although I started very much with a UK focus, it did expand into talking about what was happening in other countries as well. I think that perhaps as a faith group, Muslims, because they are such a diverse group, really appreciate looking at what's happening in other countries and they're really willing to adopt the kind of trends which are happening in other countries and specifically the UK. We are definitely seen as the 'cool' bunch, you know, when it comes to fashion. You know,

I have people explicitly say, 'Oh God, I wish I lived in the UK, you have so many amazing brands, so many amazing companies', and that's really good.

RL   The UK is seen as leading in terms of modest style coming from Muslim brands and Muslim communities and that's one of the reasons why when we designed the research project we knew we'd have to look into North America to find similar activity among Christian and Jewish groups. But some religious groups have concerns about digital communications media. For example, some of the ultra-orthodox Jewish groups that we looked at were part of communities in which access to the internet is quite highly regulated and controlled. So this brings an additional challenge. It is not simply that everyone in a brand's territories is wired all the time; there's the other challenge of how do you find websites that are sufficiently regulated or that pass certain community or parental filters in order to sell your product and in order to have those conversations. The internet is experienced and encountered in very different ways, and of course you can't have the internet if you don't have electricity and enough money and technology, and so on.

ST   Sean Tonkin, University of the Arts, London. Shellie, I run a sports club and we are often discussing the problem of finding suitable clothing for sports — not exclusively, but mostly for women. Do you think there is a market for more modest-based and faith-based dressing for sports other than swimming?

SS   Yes, there is. What's interesting is the breadth of women that buy our product. We have a local gym in town, plus different spas and resorts that carry the product … and we get demands for more. As Reina alluded to, we have grown so quickly and basically just put back in every ounce of money that we make to keep growing, so you have to pick and choose what you expand to, but that is definitely a market that is being looked at and is being actually sought after. You know, a lot of it's a little bit more revealing than women want to be; you're bending over, you're lifting weights, you're stretching, you're moving and, especially if you're a middle-aged woman and you're trying to lose that weight, you might feel uncomfortable about that. If you're a younger woman you don't want to be stalked at a place like that, so that's some of the concerns and needs that we have been asked to respond to and that's why we're considering this market.

INDEX

Italic indicates an illustration of, or relating to, the entry in question.